Twentieth-Century
German Literature

KU-529-887

Harry T. Moore

Twentieth-Century
German Literature

HEINEMANN · LONDON

Heinemann Educational Books Ltd
LONDON   MELBOURNE   TORONTO
JOHANNESBURG   AUCKLAND
IBADAN   HONG KONG
SINGAPORE   NAIROBI   NEW DELHI

ISBN 0 435 38590 9 (hard-cover edition)
     0 435 38591 5 (paperback edition)

Published in Great Britain by
Heinemann Educational Books Ltd,
48 Charles Street, London, W.1 X 4AH
Printed and bound in Great Britain by
C. Tinling & Co Ltd, London and Prescot

CONTENTS

AUTHOR'S NOTE

In this survey of recent German fiction, poetry, and drama, I have consistently applied the word "Germanic" to the material because the book deals not only with the two Germanys of the present but also with Austria and the German-speaking parts of Switzerland.

The title of each work discussed appears first in German, with its date—that of the first publication of a book and, when discoverable, of the first performance of a play. A literal translation of the title follows. If this differs from the title of a known translation, that is also given, as in: "Robert Musil's *Die Verwirrungen des Zoglings Torless* (1906; *The Aberrations of Young Torless*, translated as *Young Torless*)."

This book obviously cannot deal with all the Germanic novels, poems, and plays from the beginning of our century to the middle 1960's. Inevitably, someone's favorite book or author has been omitted, as in all such works as the present one. But I have tried to make this survey as comprehensive as possible.

The translations from the German are my own and have no pretensions beyond what has been called "free rendering."

I wish to thank the Guggenheim Foundation for granting me a Fellowship during a time when parts of this book were written.

GERMANIC LITERATURE, 1900-1914

The Nervous Prewar Waltz

In the latter part of the nineteenth century, Germanic literature was dominated by naturalism, that extension of realism with an addition of scientific determinism. The Germanic novels, plays, and poems of the time reflected the successful war of 1870–1871, the spreading new empire, and the theories of Darwin, Marx, and the naturalistic French novelist Émile Zola.

Gerhart Hauptmann, who competes with Bertolt Brecht for the honor of being the greatest modern German playwright, began as a naturalist, and in this vein he wrote the finest of his early dramas, *Die Weber* (1892; *The Weavers*), a sympathetic story of the Silesian workers' revolt against the introduction of machinery; this play, without a central hero, is regarded as a masterpiece of naturalism for its portraits of the weavers and for its picture of the machine as the mechanizing agent of fate. But before the nineties were over, Hauptmann had, without altogether abandoning naturalism, become a romantic writer, notably in *Die versunkene Glocke* (1897; *The Sunken Bell*), the story of the bell-founder Heinrich, split apart by the conflict of his love for two women, his wife Magda and the pagan, elfin mountain-girl Rautendelein.

It was also in the nineties that the neo-romantic poets came along—

Rainer Maria Rilke and Stefan George—as well as the poet-dramatist Hugo von Hofmannsthal. Friedrich Nietzsche, essentially a philosophical poet, had become a dominant force in the intellectual circles of Germany, even though his theories were not completely understood there (or elsewhere). It was ironic that Nietzsche's Superman, a figure projected to leap over the petty manifestations of the new burgher Germany, became the ideal of the strutting militarist.

In the First World War, the Germans resented the name their enemies gave them—Huns. Early in the war, Kipling wrote a poem with the refrain "The Hun is at the gate," and in both world conflicts Winston Churchill applied this label to the Germans. But it had been first used by Kaiser Wilhelm II, who early in the century told his troops that he wanted them to be as ferocious as the Huns of old.

D. H. Lawrence, in love with a German woman and living in and out of Germany in the years just before the First World War, wrote of the bristling military spirit of that nation in his story "The Prussian Officer." The country itself was certainly aware of this element, for there were often emphatic reactions against it, as in the "Zabern Affair." In Alsace, before the war, a lieutenant in the town of Zabern who cut down a lame cobbler with his saber was released from custody on grounds of "supposed self-defense." This judgment so infuriated the Reichstag that it censured the government. Nevertheless the country kept training recruits and making cannon, and the soldiers kept parading everywhere, stiffly in unison in the famous goose step.

Austria-Hungary was more relaxed. If there was a large army, it seemed to exist for the sole purpose of supporting the young officers whom Arthur Schnitzler and others wrote about in their Viennese comedies of waltzes and roses. The Dual Monarchy (the Austrian emperor had capitals in both Vienna and Budapest) was top-heavy with bureaucrats, as one of them—Franz Kafka—showed in his novels. The Dual Monarchy was not really warlike except in its tendency to suppress the Balkan countries. That tendency, however, led to the most extensive war that history had so far known, the "Great War" of 1914.

There were several crises between 1900 and 1914—Germany's confrontation with France over Morocco, the Turkish revolt, Italy against Tripoli, the war among the Balkan states—but these crises did not seriously disturb the daily lives of Germans and Austrians. If Berlin's pavements rattled with spurs, the manufacturing towns were filled with the smoke which signifies the economic health of such places; Vienna was gay, and the countryside of the Dual Monarchy was a checkerboard of prosperous farmlands. But many of the men and women dancing in the ballrooms of the capitals were tense and wary.

Major Poets: Survivors and Victims

Of the three outstanding Germanic poets of the early twentieth century, Stefan George was born first, in 1868; then Hugo von Hofmannsthal, in 1874; and lastly Rainer Maria Rilke, in 1875. George, a Rhinelander, traveled widely in his youth and met many of the leading literary men of other countries. In his later years he did not leave Germany, except to take vacations in the Swiss Alps. He had few friends and a small but ardent band of disciples. The magazine he founded in 1892, *Blätter für die Kunst* (*Pages on Art*), lasted until 1919.

George's early work was a reaction against German naturalism. His poems were symbolistic in the French manner and indeed were informed by French and Latin elements rather than German traditions, such as folk songs or the verses of Heinrich Heine. In *Der siebente Ring* (1907; *The Seventh Ring*), George finds a classic symbol in the youth whom he calls Maximin, who died at the age of fifteen. George again writes of Maximin in *Der Stern des Bundes* (1914; *The Star of the Covenant*), which shows the new life made possible by the influence of this youth's radiance and beauty. By 1928, when George brought out *Das neue Reich* (*The Kingdom Come*), he was widely recognized in Germany as a poetic prophet. Because of his Nietzschean views, celebrating the heroic man rather than the mass man, the Nazis admired George's work, and after they came into power they tried to draw him into their circle. He ignored their advances and went to Switzerland, where he died in 1933; his friends refused to let the Nazi government remove his body to Germany, and he was buried in a Swiss grave decorated by a wreath which Goebbels had sent.

George had included a wreath in one of his verses, "Der Ringer" ("The Wrestler"), a typical poem in its celebration of the strong young male:

> His arm—astonishing and admired—rests
> On his right hip, and the sun plays
> On his stalwart limbs and on the laurel wreath
> Upon his brow, as the cheers rise slowly
> From the crowds of people as he comes
> Along the green-strewn street.
> The women hold their children high—

Teaching them to cry his name out joyously
And hold out to him palm-leaves of homage.
He goes strong-footed as a lion,
And solemn, after many obscure years,
Now honored by the nation, and he does not see
The ecstatic throng or,
In the midst of it, his rejoicing parents.

Here we have maleness celebrated but wrapped in its own isolation, perhaps a projection of the lost but continuously eulogized Maximin of the George cult, in a poem whose dramatic strength survives even a literal and unadorned translation. Much of George is in this verse: a neo-Hellenic vision of physical splendor presented from an essentially romantic point of view.

Hofmannsthal, a Viennese Jew, was also a romantic, but he was a very different poet than George, largely because of his more widely ranging humanism. He began, however, as a semi-disciple of George, and some of his early poems were published in George's magazine, *Pages on Art*. Hofmannsthal must be classified as a poet, along with George and Rilke, although after 1900 he devoted his energies largely to the drama; we will consider his work further under that category.

Of all modern Germanic poets, Rilke has the widest reputation. Born in Prague, then the capital of Bohemia in the Austro-Hungarian Empire, he was brought up as a Catholic. His father, frustrated in his desire to become an army officer, hoped that his son would be one; but his mother, who had hoped for a daughter, dressed the child in girl's clothes. After his parents separated, the boy was sent away from home. Years of unhappiness in a military academy followed before he returned to Prague and attended the German University there, but he did not take a degree. At nineteen Rilke went to Munich, there beginning the wanderings that characterized the rest of his unsettled life, during which he lived in Italy, Russia, France, Switzerland, Scandinavia, North Africa, and Spain. He was residing in Paris when the First World War broke out.

By this time Rilke was a well-known poet, although not a popular one. His first notable verses appeared in *Das Buch der Bilder* (*The Book of Pictures*), originally published in 1902, when he was twenty-seven; they were reissued in an enlarged edition in 1906. In 1905 he had brought out *Das Stundenbuch* (*The Book of Hours*) and in 1907 and 1908 *Neue Gedichte* (*New Poems*). His early work, in the 1890's, had been sentimental and vaguely impressionistic; early in the twentieth century, after his association as friend and secretary to the sculptor Auguste Rodin, Rilke's verses became more substantial; his new familiarity with the plastic and the problems of creation in the medium of sculpture had given the poet an awareness of forms, and some of his poems were even concerned with statuary. Consider, for example, one of the items from the second part of *New Poems*—"Archaïscher Torso Apollos"—inspired by a statue in a museum, and beginning: "We did not know his fabulous head, in which ripened the apples of his eyes." Nevertheless, his torso gleams, as if a candelabrum set within it glows upon the breast and loins, the stone all kindling with light, no part of it failing to see you. Then Rilke suddenly flashes out his last phrase: "Du musst dein Leben ändern"—"You must change your life."

This dramatic abruptness at the close was characteristic of many of the *New Poems*, such as "Letzter Abend" ("The Last Evening")—from the first part, 1907—in which an officer is with a girl in a house on an estate; they hear the noise of a passing army that the soldier apparently will soon join, but now he calmly plays the clavichord. As he finishes, and the dawn breeze comes up, the girl stands by the window, her heart beating violently; then, like a moving-picture camera, the focus shifts to the console and onto "der schwarze Tschako mit dem Totenkopf": "the black shako with its death's head." Similarly, in another of Rilke's *New Poems*, "Der Panther" ("The Panther"), there is a recording consciousness that watches the animal gracefully pacing his cage in the Jardin des Plantes in Paris, and sometimes in the animal's eye the pupil's curtain silently opens: "Dann geht ein Bild hinein, / geht durch der Glieder angespannte Stille—/ und hört im Herzen auf zu sein" ("Then one image enters / and goes through the tensioned stillness of the limbs—/ and in the heart it ceases and is quiet"). In such poems, Rilke displays an important growth beyond the aesthete's preciousness of his earliest work: he demonstrates that he knows how to build a verse and then bring it to conclusion with dramatic intensity.

In addition to his poems, Rilke wrote some prose volumes in the years preceding the First World War, including *Die Aufzeichnungen des Malte Laurids Brigge* (1910; *The Notebooks of Malte Laurids Brigge*, also translated as *The Journal of My Other Self*). This novel-like volume chronicles the loneliness of a young Dane haunted by his past and living in Paris, in part a reflection of Rilke's own experiences during those years. *Malte* influenced Jean-Paul Sartre in his own first novel, *La Nausée* (1938; *Nausea*), and Rilke's book is now regarded as a pre-existential classic; as the critic Walter Kaufmann says: *Malte* sounds "many existentialist motifs," particularly "the quest for authentic existence."

Rilke's own existence (to use the word in another sense) was along the margin of modern society. He married the sculptress Clara Westhoff but soon left her (with a daughter), although their relationship remained cordial. Rilke was a homeless wanderer, living for the most part in castles borrowed from titled ladies who admired his work. He had no money and, during the war, found military clerical duties crushing. But he could never be called a parasite because he was continually producing some of the greatest poetry of the modern world, often at the cost of great agony.

Rilke had one popular success in his lifetime, with the prose poem *Die Weise von Liebe und Tod des Cornets Christoph Rilke* (*The Tale of the Love and Death of Cornet Christopher Rilke*). Written in 1899, first published as a book in 1906, this little volume surprisingly began to sell widely in 1912, when German militarism was starting to flourish. Based on a fragment of family history, the poem tells the story of a young officer's experiences in the Turkish wars.

Rilke's greatest works, *Die Sonette an Orpheus* (1923; *Sonnets to Orpheus*) and *Duineser Elegien* (1922; *The Duino Elegies*, also translated as *Duinese Elegies*) belong to the period after the First World War, although the *Elegies* were begun as early as 1912, when Rilke was on a visit to the castle of Duino in what was then Austria. He finished the first two "Elegies" at that time, but his inspiration returned only intermittently; he wrote parts of the "Elegies" in Spain in 1913, and completed the third (begun at Duino) in Paris in that same year. Then the war came, and until it was over he did not recapture his urge to go on with the sequence (there were ten poems when it was completed in 1922). The *Duino* and *Orpheus* poems will be treated further in a later section.

Some Additional Poets

Other poets of the period include Georg Trakl, Georg Heym, Rudolf Alexander Schröder, Rudolf Borchardt, and Ernst Stadler; Schröder was born in 1878, three years after Rilke, Borchardt the year before him, Stadler in 1883, and Trakl and Heym in 1887.

Georg Trakl, an Austrian, was a heavy drinker and a drug addict who apparently took his own life while serving as an ambulance-corps officer in Poland in 1914. Trakl was a morbid poet, some of whose work was technically a forerunner of expressionism. His first collected volume of verse, *Gedichte* (1913; *Poems*), was influenced by Villon, Baudelaire, Verlaine, Rimbaud, Stefan George, and Hofmannsthal, as well as by Dostoevsky and Nietzsche—which does not mean that Trakl was without an individual vision. If he made use of French and earlier German influences, he did so in a highly independent manner: he brought a new kind of ecstatic symbolism into German poetry, and if his writings at times drew upon such emphatically metrical poets as Villon, they also took much from the newer verse-librists, for he wrote in a long-lined, highly colored style.

Trakl also manifested the influence of Friedrich Hölderlin, with his concept of Heilignüchtern, or holy calm. This was most evident in his later poems, as found in his posthumous collection, *Sebastian im Traum* (1915; *Sebastian Dreaming*), an autobiographical sequence reflecting many of the experiences of Trakl's early years. His last poem, "Grodek," was named for a Polish battle which was fought shortly before his death; in this work he hears the autumnal forests at evening resound with the clamor of deathly weapons, over the blue lakes and golden meadows; the woods of night greet, under their golden branches, the spirits of the heroic dead. At the end of the poem Trakl mentions their as yet "unborn grandsons," but whether he is being ironic in suggesting that they will inherit a world of chaos, or whether he is sounding a note of hope for the future, is impossible to tell—and Trakl's own death, coming so soon after the poem, sheds little illumination on its meaning.

Georg Heym was killed in 1912. He drowned after the ice on a lake broke while he was skating. But even though he was spared Trakl's 1914 world, his works were prophetic of it. Heym was a Silesian who, like Trakl, was influenced by Villon and Baudelaire and Rimbaud; his two volumes of verse, *Der ewige Tag* (1911; *The Everlasting Day*) and *Umbra Vitae* (1912; *Shadow of Life*), reflect the horrors of modern existence, particularly in the large industrial cities. Again like Trakl, Heym was in the verve of his utterance a forerunner of expressionism. On the other hand, their contemporary Rudolf Alexander Schröder inclined more to the classical and the formal; he translated Homer, Virgil, Horace, and Racine. His volumes include *Lieder und Elegien* (1911; *Songs and Elegies*), *Deutsche Oden* (1913; *German Odes*), which are stately and balanced; his earlier *Hama* (1908) is wittily smooth; his comparatively late *Mitte des Lebens* (1930; *In the Midst of Life*) has an importance as religious poetry.

The slightly older Rudolf Borchardt, who lived on until 1945, was from a Jewish family that had been Protestant in East Prussia. A formal poet who translated the classics, including Pindar, Borchardt excelled in his German versions of Dante and Provençal poets. He wrote several volumes of original verse, including *Jugendgedichte* (1913; *Youthful Poems*) and *Vermischte Gedichte* (1924; *Miscellaneous Poems*), collected with his prose in *Ausgewählte Werke 1900–1918* (1925; *Selected Works*).

We get away from such types of writing with the somewhat younger Ernst Stadler, an Alsatian killed fighting in the German army in 1914; Stadler, like Trakl, was a trail-blazer of expressionism. His most important work appears in the posthumously published *Der Aufbruch* (1915; *The Beginning*), a glorification of the historical consciousness of that variegated land, Alsace. The title piece projects a vision of the war to come; but as Stadler's editor, Karl Ludwig Schneider, pointed out in 1954, this poem does not justify or celebrate war, as some readers have assumed. Stadler is an exciting poet, writing in vibrant long lines in which image grows out of image; his death in the First World War was as great a loss to German poetry as Wilfrid Owen's was to British.

A poet who died in 1914, though not in the war, was Christian Morgenstern (born in 1871), who is now best remembered for his nonsense verses and vaudeville-like popular ballads, such as his *Galgenlieder* (1905; *Songs of the Gallows*) and *Palmström* (1910), rather than for his mystical-anthroposophical writings. But the man who was perhaps the most widely discussed German poet of the years before 1914 (he lived until 1920) was Richard Dehmel, who wrote of the forests of his native Brandenburg as well as of the streets of Berlin. Dehmel brought out several volumes of lyrics in the nineties, following these in 1903 with a novel in verse, *Zwei Menschen* (*Two People*). *Verwandlung der Venus* (1907; *Transformation of Venus*, subtitled *Erotic Rhapsody*) and the verses in *Schöne wilde Welt* (1913; *Beautiful Wild World*) revealed Dehmel at his most sensual and pagan; he tried always to synthesize the physical and spiritual elements of love but was not successful at all times in crossing the boundary between the rhapsodic and the absurd. Dehmel, who served in the army during the war, brought out his *Kriegstagebuch* (*War Diary*) in 1919. His military experiences were again dealt with in the posthumous "cosmopolitical" comedy *Die Götterfamilie* (1921; *The Family of the Gods*). One of the reasons for Dehmel's eclipse may be that he was the poet of a transitional period, caught between the fading out of realism and the flare-up of expressionism; such a period can be survived only by such stubborn and essentially sturdy, self-motivated geniuses as Rilke and Stefan George.

A Germanic Poet of Switzerland

An important poet of this time was the Swiss writer, Carl Spitteler, who died in 1924, in his eightieth year. Much of his significant work belongs to nineteenth-century Germanic literature, but some of it appeared in the twentieth; indeed, when he won the Nobel Prize in 1919, the committee particularly mentioned *Der olympische Frühling* (*Olympian Spring*), first published 1900–1905; revised in 1910. The psychologist Carl Jung drew some important examples from Spitteler's epic prose poem of 1881, *Prometheus und Epimetheus*, in the resolution of which Jung found the ideal balance between those inward-directed and outward-directed human types which he called introvert and extrovert.

A schoolteacher and journalist in his youth, Spitteler at twenty-nine inherited enough money to permit him to devote all his time to writing. He turned out several novels and tales, including the autobiographical *Imago* (1906), and in 1924 he issued a later version of his earlier epic (for the first time under his own name rather than under the pseudonym Felix Tandem), *Prometheus der Dulder* (*Prometheus the Sufferer*). But it is *Olympian Spring* which remains his masterwork, a poem in five parts, with thirty-three cantos, written in iambic rhyming couplets. This is a series of stories of the Greek gods, believably humanized as characters who are often comically and satirically presented. Hermes, Dionysos, Aphrodite, Zeus, Apollo, and others undergo revealing adventures— Aphrodite's takes place on earth, where in a spicily amusing sequence she and her naked nymphs lead mankind in a merry dance. Later, when Zeus wants to destroy all human beings because they lack any justification for existence, Aphrodite intercedes, arguing that she is no different herself. Zeus finally determines that mankind may be redeemed by justice, and as a test he sends Herakles down to earth as a harbinger of what man can be.

For all its brilliance, *Olympian Spring* has linguistic handicaps, even for those in the German-speaking world, for Spitteler often revels in Swiss-German locutions, and this limits the response to the poem outside parts of Switzerland; in any case, it is a work of exuberant poetic creativity that virtually defies translation. It nonetheless has a place in modern literature because of its philosophical depth. In the first version, Spitteler was pessimistic almost to the point of nihilism, but in the final revision published in 1910, he ends on a note of hope when, in the last canto, he projects Herakles' noble vision of his task of regenerating mankind.

The Theater: Vision, Wit, Spectacle

Germany in the early twentieth century competed with Russia for the honor of possessing the most exciting theater in Europe. In both countries, drama was stimulated by the productions of a remarkable director: Konstantin Stanislavsky in Russia, Max Reinhardt in Germany (and in Austria). Both men at one time or another were influenced by Edward Gordon Craig, son of the radiant English actress Ellen Terry. Craig, whose doctrines were not taken seriously in his own country, had written:

The art of the theater is neither acting nor the play, it is not scene nor dance, but it consists of all the elements of which these things are composed: action, which is the very spirit of acting; words, which are the body of the play; line and color, which are the very heart of the scene; rhythm, which is the very essence of dance. . . . One is no more important than the other, no more than one color is more important to a painter than another, or one note more important than another to a musician.

Craig also said: "Now, then, it is impossible for a work of art ever to be produced when more than one brain is permitted to direct; and if works of art are not seen in the theater this one reason is a sufficient one, though there are plenty more." Craig's dream was not fully realized because there was no single genius who was at once playwright, designer, and musical composer; but such men as Stanislavsky and Reinhardt went a long way toward fulfilling the ideal.

Reinhardt not only revived the classics—Greek and English, as well as German—but he also encouraged new playwrights. His elaborate productions of *Oedipus Rex, Faust,* and *Hamlet* were balanced by those of the works of Hofmannsthal, who became a poetic playwright of great power. He also flourished as a translator who provided the spirited text of *Elektra,* which Richard Strauss set to music. One of Hofmannsthal's greatest successes was *Jedermann* (1911), an adaptation of the English morality play *Everyman.*

Early in the century, Hofmannsthal was involved with the anti-naturalist literary group, Jungwien (Young Vienna), which also included Hermann Bahr, Richard Beer-Hofmann, and Arthur Schnitzler. These men engaged in various forms of literary activity, but their influence was greatest in the theater. Bahr, a noted critic, eventually the explicator of expressionism, wrote a sophisticated Viennese comedy, *Das Konzert* (1909; *The Concert*), which was an international success; it related the story of two married couples whose lives became entwined and later unentwined.

Beer-Hofmann, who wrote verse and fiction as well as drama, met his greatest success with his first play, *Der Graf von Charolais* (1904; *The Count of Charolais*), which concerns a young count who accepts a debtor's servitude in order to obtain his father's dead body from a usurer; this drama, while revealing the general uncertainty of human affairs, accents the strength of family ties. In *Jaâkobs Traum* (1918; *Jacob's Dream*) and *Der junge David* (1933; *The Young David*), Beer-Hofmann, who was of Jewish origin, dealt prophetically with Old Testament figures and situations.

A very different type of member of the Jungwien movement was the dramatist Arthur Schnitzler; he perhaps had more in common with a Hungarian contemporary, Ferenc Molnár, whose plays, such as *Liliom* (1909), *A testőr* (1910; *The Guardsman*), and *A hattyú* (1920; *The Swan*), reached beyond Budapest to become international successes. Similarly, Schnitzler's comedies went from Vienna to other European capitals and to New York. During the last two decades of his life (he died in 1931) Schnitzler specialized in novels and short stories, but he remains best known for his plays, beginning with the series of dialogues titled *Anatol* (1893), regarded as the extreme of Viennese sophistication and continually revived across the years; they helped sound the death knell of Germanic naturalism. *Liebelei* (1895; *Flirtation,* also translated as *The Reckoning*) is a drama about a girl who commits suicide upon learning that her lover has been killed—what motivated her suicide, however, was not his death but the knowledge that it came about in a duel over another woman. *Der grüne Kakadu* (1899; *The Green Cockatoo*) is a play set in eighteenth-century Paris, in a cabaret where aristocrats disport themselves in the days—rather, nights—before the Revolution. *Reigen* (*Hands Around*), a series of erotic sketches written in 1900, was forbidden production under the Dual Monarchy and did not appear on the Viennese stage until 1920.

Schnitzler, a Jew who had begun his career as a physician, wrote one of the outstanding Zeitstücke, or topical plays, in *Professor Bernhardi* (1912), which satirizes clericalism and anti-Semitism but does not spare Zionism. In the drama a Jewish doctor clashes with a priest at the bedside of a dying man; the conflict spreads to the world outside and creates an uproar there.

Most of Schnitzler's work deals with romantic-erotic matters—he wrote some lively stories about Casanova—and his comedies of Viennese society are sophisticated wit equaled in the modern world only by Molnár and some of the French writers of boulevard plays. But Schnitzler often had more originality and usually greater depth than his rivals; as a playwright he was ahead of O'Neill and the expressionists in experimenting with such devices as the soliloquy and the interior monologue.

Schnitzler's career as a novelist will be considered in a later section, with the fiction of Hermann Sudermann, Ricarda Huch, and others. But let us now consider a theatrical contemporary of Schnitzler, Gerhart Hauptmann, who is a far more important dramatist than either Schnitzler or his young Viennese associates. As noted earlier, Hauptmann broke away from the naturalism of the nineties, particularly in *Die versunkene Glocke* (1897; *The Sunken Bell*), and then he wrote some of the most notable verse dramas of the modern world, including his historical play *Der arme Heinrich* (1902; *Henry of Auë*). In *Kaiser Karls Geisel* (1908; *Charlemagne's Hostage*), he dealt with the subject of nymphomania.

In a return to naturalism in *Rose Bernd* (1903), Hauptmann wrote a melodramatic tragedy. This is the story of a servant girl who is loved by the mayor of a village; their relations are discovered by a scoundrel, who attempts blackmail. As a witness in the ensuing slander case, Rose perjures herself and later she gives birth to a child in a field and then strangles it. She is arrested and charged with murder. The play ends with the young man to whom she had been betrothed saying: "Das Mädel—was muss die gelitten han!" ("The girl—how she must have suffered!").

Hauptmann's own favorite play was *Und Pippa tanzt* (1906; *And Pippa Dances*). It has a strong, realistic first act, set in a tavern in a factory district, but the rest of the action is elusively symbolic. *And Pippa Dances* is perhaps most significant today as one of the forerunners of the expressionist movement that was so important in the German theater of the 1920's.

The true beginnings of expressionism, however, go back to Frank Wedekind's *Frühlings Erwachen* (1891; *The Awakening of Spring*), the work of an actor with a flair for writing of the erotic. *Die Büchse der Pandora* (1903; *Pandora's Box*) was a sequel to *Der Erdgeist* (1895; *Earth Spirit*), a series of plays about a woman named Lulu who goes through a number of love affairs until Jack the Ripper puts an end to her. *Schloss Wetterstein* (1910; *The Castle of Wetterstein*) virtually repeats this story. In *Franziska* (1912) the main character is another woman who has had a number of love affairs, but this heroine surprisingly finds happiness in marriage.

Wedekind, a figure of somewhat diabolic appearance, slightly lame, usually acted in his own plays, several of which were produced by Reinhardt. The critic Arthur Eloesser has said that Wedekind's works at first made people want to cross themselves because the playwright seemed a tangible manifestation of Satan, but that the future would perhaps accept him as a priest who had listened to the shameful and disturbing confessions of humanity; his work, Eloesser further stated, had its own confessions of faith bound in a purpose opposed to nature in such a way as to have made Wedekind the true ancestor of expressionism.

By the time Wedekind died in 1918 the first play that was definitely expressionist had been written by Reinhard Johannes Sorge—*Der Bettler* (1911; *The Beggar*). Sorge was subsequently converted to Catholicism and wrote religious mystery dramas; one of the many writers to become a victim of the war, he was killed in action in 1916. The rest of the history of expressionism belongs to the period after the armistice.

Thomas Mann: Bürger into Artist

Thomas Mann, whose career began exactly as this century opened, is the greatest German novelist of the period. But his elder brother Heinrich, whose first novel, *Im Schlaraffenland* (*In the Land of Cockaigne*), appeared in 1901, also stands high in this category. He was an unflinching realist, whose best-known novel internationally is *Professor Unrat* (1904; translated as *The Blue Angel*, or *Small-Town Tyrant*), which was made famous in the film (*The Blue Angel*) starring Emil Jannings and Marlene Dietrich. Heinrich Mann, early drawn to social themes, in 1907 brought out *Zwischen den Rassen* (*Among the Races*), a dramatization of the conflict between moral and ethical values. In *Die kleine Stadt* (1909; *The Little Town*), the "little town," which is in Italy, is set into an uproar by the visit of a theatrical touring company that has in it the seeds of a number of small comedies and tragedies. Heinrich Mann's *Das Kaiserreich* trilogy, a satiric treatment of the empire, was delayed in publication, the separate volumes appearing as *Der Untertan* (1918; *The Patrioteer*), *Die Armen* (1917; *The Poor*), and *Der Kopf* (1925; *The Chief*); they depicted the time of Wilhelm II as one of greed and corruption and of devouring bureaucracy. This trilogy made Heinrich Mann one of the most popular German authors in the

Weimar Republic after the war, and his earlier books were widely re-printed.

The other important German novelists of this period wrote their finest books in the 1920's and will be considered later, except for the earlier work of Heinrich Mann's younger brother who proved to be the outstand-ing German novelist of the age. He also ranks among the most important writers of the modern world.

Thomas Mann, who late in his life characterized his books as "desperately German," was born in 1875 in the old Hanseatic town of Lübeck, near Hamburg. His locally prominent family had disintegrated by the time he became a young man; the famous old house where they had lived as leading citizens was destined to become the local library. The father of Thomas and Heinrich Mann was a grain merchant who died when Thomas was fifteen, and the family fortune withered away. The mother of the future novelists was partly German and partly Portu-guese and West Indian Creole; she moved to Munich after her husband's death, and there Thomas Mann joined her when he had finished his schooling.

He began writing and before he was twenty had published stories and poems. During a year spent in Italy with his brother Heinrich, Thomas Mann began work on his first novel, *Buddenbrooks*. It was accepted for publication just after its author was invalided out of his term of com-pulsory military service.

That huge novel was published in two volumes in 1900 (dated 1901), when its author was only twenty-five. It is a family-chronicle story, sweeping across several generations in the style of various Scandinavian authors of the nineteenth century. It represents Mann-family history and some autobiography, but rather than mere record it is characterized by the inventiveness of significant imaginative writing. In the story there is a wide range of effects, of comedy and disaster, until at last the family produces the delicate and artistic Hanno, who at fifteen dies of typhoid fever—dies because, as the author shows, in that moment of the crisis of the fever when life calls, "if he shudders when he hears life's voice, if the memory of that vanished scene and the sound of that lusty summons make him shake his head, make him put out his hand to ward it off as he flies forward in the way of escape that has opened to him—then it is clear that the patient will die."

In addition to his skill at the long novel and the short story, Mann showed his ability to deal with that genre which, in the last part of the nineteenth century, Paul Heyse and others had made virtually a German property—

the novella. In 1903 Mann published *Tristan*, a volume that in addition to the title story contained another short novel, "Tonio Kröger." "Tristan" itself is an ironic comedy set in a tuberculosis sanitarium: the plump little man who falls hopelessly in love with one of his fellow patients, a beautiful young Hausfrau, is a grotesque parody of the romantic. And "Tonio Kröger," an intensely autobiographical story, presents another ironic view of the romantic.

Like Mann himself, Tonio is the scion of a famous old Hanseatic family, and like Mann he has a foreign mother. As a boy he loves his violin and his poetry and his friend Hans, the blond little athlete of the schoolyard, who tolerates Tonio without understanding him. Later Tonio shyly loves Ingeborg, the mayor's blonde daughter, but she is unaware of him except as a clumsy boy in the dancing class she attends.

The story switches to the time when Tonio is thirty and a successful writer in Munich. He goes north again and visits the family mansion, now the town library. When he is questioned by the police as a suspicious character, he realizes that he can get out of this difficulty at once by telling the police that he is a member of the once-great Kröger family. Instead, he takes some proofsheets out of his pocket, which prove that he is an author, a shameful enough thing in the eyes of the Bürgerschaft, though not sufficiently illegal to justify imprisonment, and so Tonio is turned loose. Something of the kind happened to Mann when he re-visited Lübeck years after leaving it—he was detained for a while on suspicion of being a swindler wanted by the police.

In the story, Tonio moves on to a Danish coastal resort after his escapade with the authorities; there at a party he sees Hans Hansen and Ingeborg Holm—or a reincarnation of them in the flush of youth. They dance gaily and are of course completely unaware of the dark and sensitive Tonio. Stung by his persistent loneliness, yet also exalted, he writes to a woman friend in Munich, saying that he exists between two worlds and is at home in neither of them; his friend has called him a bourgeois, and the bourgeois try to arrest him. Tonio feels that he is "a bourgeois who strayed off into art," and his conscience troubles him because of it, for there is something vagabond and bohemian and anti-bourgeois in the artist, and this, Tonio feels, is criminal. He longs for the healthy, the normal, the blue-eyed. He sees into an unborn and formless world that needs ordering, a world in which both tragic and comic human figures, as well as some that are tragic and comic at once, beckon to him to redeem them—"and to these I am drawn." But as for his love for the blond and fair, the happy and commonplace, this should not be chided:

"It is good and fruitful. There is longing in it, and a gentle envy; a touch of contempt and no little innocent bliss."

These ideas have been imitated so often since 1903 that they have lost some of their force; but as time passes and the pale copies fade, the words of Tonio Kröger again take on freshness. They are not only important for an understanding of all Mann's work, but they are also a credo for the artist who still has to struggle with himself and others in a world of merchants, among people who cannot understand him—people for whom he has feelings touched by some contempt and a large amount of innocent bliss.

Between the publication of "Tonio Kröger" and the outbreak of war in 1914, Mann brought out three more books, a novel, a novella, and a volume of tales. The novel was *Königliche Hoheit* (1909; *Royal Highness*), a tenderly comic story of a prince in a fairy-tale kingdom who marries an American heiress. The tales, including the title story, "Das Wunderkind" (1914; "The Infant Prodigy"), have all been translated into English; they are slight but good. But the novella, *Der Tod in Venedig* (*Death in Venice*), which appeared in 1913, is one of Mann's masterpieces.

It tells the story of a distinguished middle-aged author, Gustav von Aschenbach, who goes to the Venice Lido for a holiday. En route from Germany he has seen a hideously painted old man—a ghastly prophetic symbol—frolicking with some youths. On the Lido, Aschenbach is abruptly and violently attracted to an adolescent Polish boy, whom he hears called Tadzio. Under the golden spell of Tadzio, the rigid disciplinarian Aschenbach begins to remember the Platonic dialogues. The boy seems to be coyly aware of him and to be shyly flirting with him. Then, in a moment of intensified climax, Mann breaks off the story with a sudden jab of fatality and irony. It is a powerful tale, not merely about the feelings of an artist but about art itself and its relation to life. In *Death in Venice*, Mann importantly makes use of symbolism within a framework of reality, with the lyric and the ironic blending wonderfully.

Just before the war, Mann's wife (he had married Katja Pringsheim in 1905) was sent to a Swiss tuberculosis sanitarium for a few weeks' treatment, and he accompanied her to this place reminiscent of the setting of his story "Tristan." Later he felt that he would like to write a short comedy about the sanitarium. This grew into the long novel *Der Zauberberg* (*The Magic Mountain*) which, partly because of wartime delays and distractions, took him twelve years to write; it came out in 1924. While working on it, he published, in the last year of the war,

Betrachtungen eines Unpolitischen (*Reflections of a Nonpolitical Man*), which, happily for his reputation throughout the world, has never been translated into English. It was as if in 1918 Mann looked up from his study table, realized that his country was at war, and decided to support it. But the Hohenzollern and Prussian cause was insupportable, particularly at that time when so much of the nation was backing away from it. Fortunately, within four years Thomas Mann repudiated his early "nonpolitical" views in an address later published as "Von deutscher Republik" (1923; "The German Republic"). And certainly there is nothing foolish in the political stance he adopts in *The Magic Mountain*, which will be discussed in the section devoted to the postwar literature that we now think of as the between-wars literature.

2

GERMANIC LITERATURE OF THE 1920'S AND 1930'S

The New Energy

Germanic literature blossomed after the First World War. There was a ferment in the defeated nation, protest against the defeat itself and against what seemed to be the rigid terms of the treaty of Versailles. But there was also an ecstasy of artistic expression as the country, now a republic, began for the first time to feel a sense of freedom. Individual authors such as Thomas Mann went on with their careers, following their own necessary development, but many other writers took part in the postwar Germanic movement of Expressionismus, or expressionism. The beginnings of this movement have been mentioned in connection with some of the earlier plays of Gerhart Hauptmann and those of R. J. Sorge, who was killed in the war. The official start of the expressionist movement may be traced, perhaps, to the Stormbühne Theater which, in 1910, announced that it would produce "expressionist drama in expressionist style." One of the Stormbühne playwrights (under the leadership of Herwarth Walden) was the great modernist painter Oskar Kokoschka.

Expressionism, with its explosive syntax, its disintegrating forms, and its panoramic simultaneities, had a kinship with many other modern-art movements, including futurism and cubism; it borrowed from Rimbaud and the French symbolists, it was influenced by Dostoevsky and Strindberg, and it was motivated by Freud's explorations of the unconscious. Expressionism in turn influenced the American playwright Eugene O'Neill.

The expressionists felt that they created rather than merely reproduced, and that they were reacting against what they regarded as the predominantly surface approaches of such nineteenth-century movements as naturalism and impressionism. For the most part, these were concerned, for all their differences, with material aspects; the expressionists regarded themselves as concentrating upon the spiritual. Therefore they could throw out the customary realistic devices of representation and could violate grammar as well as the theatrical conventions of verisimilitude: in the expressionist drama the thoughts of a character could be presented by soliloquy or by slides thrown upon a screen. There were of course variations of these techniques, and the expressionists themselves were somewhat informally divided into schools such as the activist, which believed in affirmative political assertion, and the passivist, which did not go beyond the projection of skepticism or despair. Some of the expressionist plays were of the type that later might have been classified as existentialist, emphasizing the aloneness of man upon earth, while other dramas in the movement manifested a religious impulse.

The New Germanic Theater

Expressionism, more popular in Germany than in Austria, was the principal mode of German drama after the war, and the movement found its most ardent adherents in the theater. Concurrently with this, the productions of Max Reinhardt (1873–1943) illuminated classic and modern drama as nowhere else in the world in that period; and Reinhardt staged a number of expressionist plays.

In Berlin, Reinhardt founded the Kammerspiele and the Grosse Schauspielhaus, and from 1905 until driven out by Hitler's anti-Semitic campaign in the 1930's, he managed the Deutsches Theater zu Berlin. He also staged plays in Vienna and in Salzburg, where his presentation of Hugo Hofmannsthal's version of the medieval morality *Jedermann* (*Everyman*), in the cathedral plaza, was particularly notable. In his repertory, Reinhardt had the greatest actors in Europe, including Alexander Moissi, Albert Bassermann, and Conrad Veidt, but because he was a régisseur in the style suggested by Gordon Craig, he put on spectacular productions that often tended to dwarf the actors.

In Berlin two other notable producers operated at this time, Erwin Piscator at the Volksbühne (People's Stage) and Leopold Jessner at the Staatliches Schauspielhaus (State Playhouse). Piscator (1894–1966) was the forerunner of the epic-theater style later developed by Bertolt Brecht. Jessner was noted for productions such as *Richard III*, with Fritz Kortner, in which the adherents of Richard were dressed in red, representing evil, and those of his supplanter, Henry Tudor, Earl of Richmond, were clad in white, representing good. Jessner in his plays made spectacular use of steps, which became known as Jessnertreppe.

In Vienna, the other Germanic theater capital, the dominating playhouse was the Burgtheater, which had its own standard speech known as Burgtheaterdeutsch. There were many dialects in Germany and Austria but, except when stressing regional accents, the Burg actors used a model and uniform pronunciation.

Expressionism as a technique often went in the direction of wildness; as noted earlier, even its syntax was chaotic. The dominant playwright in the movement between the wars was Georg Kaiser, a native of Madgeburg, who settled in the country near Berlin. For a time he was a businessman; he spent three years in South America. In 1921, although he was already a distinguished writer, he served a prison sentence in Munich for stealing furniture from a villa he sublet; his excuse was that he could not live without the luxuries to which his family's wealth had accustomed him—wealth lost in the postwar inflation. Besides, an artist was a special human being and needed luxuries. This prison escapade and other unusual events of Kaiser's life give it almost an expressionistic tinge.

His most notable contributions to the movement are *Von Morgens bis Mitternacht* (1916; *From Morn to Midnight*) and his trilogy, comprising *Die Koralle* (1917; *The Coral*), *Gas I* (1918) and *Gas II* (1920). All these plays are in one way or another attacks upon capitalism which use, as one of their chief weapons, the very mechanism induced by a capitalist society.

The robot-like leading character in *From Morn to Midnight* (produced on the stage by Max Reinhardt) is really not a character at all. This is emphasized because he is given no name; he is called the Bank Cashier. At the bank one morning, he mistakes the friendliness of a foreign woman for a flirtation and embezzles enough money to elope with her. When she refuses to go with him, he indulges in a fling which ends with his suicide at midnight after a Salvation Army girl, who had pretended to be his friend, betrays him to the police.

From Morn to Midnight is full of tricks; it depends more upon displays of technique than upon human interest, so that the audience watches the Bank Cashier's adventures from the outside without becoming involved. These adventures are presented effectively enough, as the Cashier visits dancing halls, gambling rooms, and brothels, as well as attending a bicycle race at which he gives an enormous prize.

The content of fantasy in the play is high; the crowds that jostle the protagonist are made up of automata, and at one point he discovers that a girl with whom he has taken up is a pasteboard figure with a wooden leg. In another scene, when the Cashier stretches out his arms as if crucified, Kaiser is apparently attempting to say that mechanism and artificiality are the Golgotha of modern man. This is a drama of the kind making use of Stationen (stages, or phases in the hero's development), typical of expressionism and used abundantly in the plays of Ernst Toller.

Kaiser sets the scene of *The Coral* (also produced by Reinhardt) in an enormous factory whose billionaire owner is the son of a former laborer there. He envies the happy childhood which had been spent by his Secretary, the Billionaire's physical double, who can be distinguished from him only by a piece of coral which the Secretary wears on his watch chain. Although the Billionaire feels sympathy for the workers, he is afraid of them, and they despise him. His son, in revolt from the father, shows his own sympathy for the workers by taking a job as a stoker on a cargo boat when his father actually thinks he is a passenger on a luxury ship. In the course of the play the father becomes estranged from both his son and his daughter, after which he murders the Secretary, taking the coral from him in order that he may be mistaken for him. He is, but the police arrest him and he is executed for his own murder.

The next two parts of the trilogy, *Gas I* and *Gas II,* also take place in the factory. The first play shows the Billionaire's son operating it on a coöperative basis which permits the workers to share in the profits. The factory, which provides gas for the industry of the entire world, is one day destroyed by an explosion. The Billionaire's son, in a powerful scene which alternates individual speech and repetitive choruses, suggests that the ruins be cleared away and green lands cultivated on which the workers will be given farms. But the men, who had been clamoring against the factory Engineer, suddenly begin to pay heed to him when he urges them to rebuild the factory rather than let its site be turned into farmland. A war is threatening, and the government encourages the Engineer and the workers, who happily return to the factory, which will undoubtedly blow up again. Meanwhile, the Billionaire's son dies from the effects of a stone hurled at him by one of the workers.

In *Gas II* the central figure is the great-grandson of the Billionaire of *The Coral*. Both worker and manager, he is called the Billionaire Worker. When the Engineer shows the men at the factory a container of gas which will destroy the enemy, an idea which is greeted with enthusiasm, the Billionaire Worker seizes the container and smashes it, annihilating the factory and all its people.

These idealistically anti-war, anti-capitalistic plays were enormously successful despite the fact that the human figures in them were for the most part merely types or automata. Kaiser believed that a play should be a Denkspiel, a drama of ideas, rather than a kind of Schauspiel, the type of spectacle usually produced by Max Reinhardt. Kaiser's language was a particularly striking feature of his work; it was stenographic or telegraphic in nature. This accorded with the violent juxtapositions of scene in the plays themselves, the rapid shuttling of ideas and people.

Some of Kaiser's other works include *Kanzlist Krehler* (1922; *Clerk Krehler*), the story of a little Bürger who tries to escape from everyday life by ignoring it and concentrating intensely on the problems of existence. But, aware that he is beginning such activity too late, he lapses into madness and kills himself.

In *Nebeneinander* (1923; *Side by Side*), Kaiser presents the reverse of this theme when he shows his hero realizing his sense of responsibility to his fellowmen. The story, set in the period of Germany's postwar inflation, contains three "side-by-side" plots which, although related to one another, never flow together. This too is a play about self-annihilation: a man kills himself after his failure to interest others, including the police, in attempting to prevent a girl's suicide. Another of the plots shows the girl finding happiness and not killing herself after all; a third division of the story deals with the girl's seducer. Neither he nor she is aware of the experiences of the man who found the girl's note and supposed she planned to commit suicide.

Kaiser's last play in the expressionist vein was *Gats* (1925), which failed in its attempt to recapture the spirit of revolutionary utopia as projected in the *Gas* dramas. Kaiser was more successful with *Oktobertag* (1928), produced in London in 1939 as *A Day in October*, a play with a familiar Kaiser theme on those occasions when he turned to romantic drama—a pair of lovers against society. By the time he wrote *Lederköpfe*

(1928; *Leather Heads*), derived from a story of Herodotus which became, in Kaiser's hands, an attack on militarism, the playwright had adopted most of the conventional techniques of the theater; the syntax of the speeches approximated that of normal conversation, the plot was not an abstraction, and the characters were individualized and given names.

Besides taking plots from such sources as Herodotus, Kaiser sometimes used events of the day, as in *Mississippi* (1930), suggested by the 1928 floods; the plot concerns the conflict among the riverside farmers who want to strengthen the Mississippi dikes so that New Orleans—to them a place of sin—will be flooded rather than their farms.

The Nazis banned Kaiser's plays from the German stage after 1933; five years later he moved to Switzerland, where he continued writing until his death in 1945. He turned out several romantic dramas, such as *Der Gärtner von Toulouse* (1938; *The Gardener of Toulouse*), *Alain und Elise* (1940), *Rosamunde Floris* (also 1940), as well as some satirical plays, such as *Der englische Sender* (1940; *The English Radio*) and *Klawitter* (again 1940), vigorously anti-Nazi in tone. *Der Soldat Tanaka* (1940; *The Soldier Tanaka*) is an anti-militarist story set in Japan; Tanaka, who has protested against the inhumanity of the social system, is told, after being condemned to death, that he may ask the emperor for mercy; when Tanaka at once replies that the emperor should be the one to ask forgiveness, for his crimes against mankind, Tanaka is led out to be shot. *Das Floss der Medusa* (1943; *The Raft of the Medusa*) takes place in a lifeboat occupied by thirteen children who act out a grim drama of morality. Shortly before his death, Kaiser completed a trio of plays taken from Greek mythology and published in 1948: *Zweimal Amphitrion* (*Double Amphitrion*), *Pygmalion,* and *Bellerophon.*

Since his death, Kaiser's earlier plays have from time to time been revived in Germany, and because of their oddity they often create theatrical interest, but for the most part they are too closely bound to the mannerisms of their own time to be of permanent interest. Indeed, no expressionist play by anyone has really survived the collapse of the movement in the mid-1920's, but all of them are of intense historical interest—they provided a fascinating interlude in the history of the theater.

One of the outstanding expressionist plays almost forgotten today is Reinhard Göring's *Seeschlacht* (1917; *Naval Battle*), staged by Max Reinhardt for Das Junge Deutschland (The Young Germany), an advance-guard group in Berlin. The setting of *Naval Battle* is the armored turret of a battleship during the conflict at Jutland. Seven sailors comprise the cast, and they feel the dread and tension of battle. The fifth sailor, whose growing antagonism to the idea of war itself seems mutinous under the circumstances, proves to be the bravest fighter of all, and he gives a dying speech that reflects the futility of all they had done; and before the play ends they are all killed. The force of the drama is intensified by the heavy battle music that accompanies it. Göring wrote another, less exciting expressionist drama about naval warfare, *Scapa Flow* (1919), which dealt with the scuttling of the German fleet. Before lapsing into silence, he wrote two more plays, *Die Retter* (1919; *The Saviors*), which had an anti-revolutionary tone, and *Des Südpolexpedition des Kapitän Scott* (1930; *The South Pole Expedition of Captain Scott*).

Sternheim and von Unruh

Carl Sternheim, who had a somewhat telegraphic style and was a disciple of Wedekind, was actually a more important forerunner of expressionism than some of the more clamorous members of the movement. Born in 1881, Sternheim satirized the bourgeoisie in *Bürger Schippel* (1913), a comedy set in a provincial town in which the working-class Schippel rises, after some comic difficulties, into the bourgeois category. In the trilogy *Aus dem bürgerlichen Heldenleben* (*From the Burgher Hero's Life*), consisting of *Die Hose* (1911; *A Pair of Drawers*), *Der Snob* (1913; *The Snob*, also translated as *A Place in the World*), and *1913* (1915), Sternheim dealt with three generations of an outrageously middle-class family. In *A Pair of Drawers*, Frau Moske loses her underpants on the street, and this excites a poet and a hairdresser into taking up lodgings in her house, where they hope to profit erotically. But it is Frau Moske's husband, Theodor, a petty clerk, who uses their rent money to good advantage; it helps him start a family and rise in the world. *The Snob* continues with the story of Moske's son, Christian, who wants to climb above his father's merely bourgeois ambitions onto a higher social plateau. He is so successful that in the third play, *1913*, he is shown wearing a new title—but the very name of the play suggests the end of the old order, the last year of peace before the war in which the last Hohenzollern emperor became engaged. Indeed, the play, which is concerned mostly with the struggle between the aging Christian and his children, ends with a mocking masquerade that suggests a kind of Totentanz, death dance, of the old order.

Sternheim, who considered himself a later-day Molière, continued his anti-bourgeois satires up through and beyond the expressionist period in such works as *J. P. Morgan* (1930). In *Aut Caesar, aut Nihil* (1931; *Either Caesar, or Nothing*), he prophesied the rise of the Nazis. He subsequently became a voluntary exile from Germany, but is said to have returned there for a time before his death in Brussels in 1943.

The expressionist plays of Fritz von Unruh reflect the conflict in the man himself between his military background and his anti-militarist ideals. Before the First World War, Unruh wrote *Offiziere* (1912; *Officers*), a picture of army life with no anti-militarist overtones, a play successfully staged by Max Reinhardt. After Unruh resigned from the army he wrote *Prinz Louis Ferdinand von Preussen* (1913; *Prince Louis Ferdinand of Prussia*), the production of which was prohibited although in that year Unruh won the Kleist Prize. Both these plays were written in the older, pre-expressionist manner. After Unruh went back into military service during the war, he became involved in censorship troubles over the novels he wrote at the front. In 1920, Gerhart Hauptmann nominated Unruh for the Schiller Prize, but this nomination by the President of the Schiller Prize Committee was turned down by the Prussian Minister of Culture; in 1927, however, Unruh was awarded this prize along with Hermann Burte and Franz Werfel.

Meanwhile Unruh had become a leading expressionist playwright. In *Ein Geschlecht* (1916; *A Family*) and in its sequel *Platz* (1920; *Town Square*), Unruh followed the fortunes of a family through the war and the subsequent revolution.

In the first of these plays, as in most expressionist drama, the characters are types rather than developing persons; the action occurs during a single night at the entrance to a graveyard where the Mother is burying one of her sons who has been killed in a battle that is taking place nearby. Her Daughter and her Youngest Son are with her; the other two sons appear during the course of the play—one of them has refused to join in the battle, and the other has tried to rape a woman; both these sons are tied to the cemetery gate by soldiers. The Mother, her sons and the Daughter are united by their mutual hatred, and their wrangling in front of the dead soldier's grave gives the play something of an Æschylean intensity: the Eldest Son even attempts incest with his sister. Later, the Mother is killed by officers whom she defies when they order the removal of her son's body. She has cried out a protest:

> How can we continue to suffer such madness
> That crazily shatters and drags to the grave
> The temple of man which we created!

In *Town Square*, the sequel to *A Family*, the setting is a public place surrounded by government buildings. In this play, in which the characters have names, Dietrich, the hero—he is the Youngest Son of the earlier play—seeks the regeneration of mankind. He tries to find it in love, rejecting both revolution and democracy for the girl Irene. For all its topical interest, *Town Square* lacks the dramatic intensity of *The Family*.

These two plays are caught too rigidly in the grip of their own propaganda, and although they make use of some of the expressionist techniques, they lack the energy and variety of Georg Kaiser's dramas. Like Kaiser, Unruh usually projected abstract characters rather than living human beings, but Kaiser was at least able, through a more vital use of expressionist technique, to make his plays livelier and more interesting. In *Bonaparte* (1927) Unruh attempted to warn his country-men of the coming dictatorship. In the satiric *Phaea* (1930) he portrayed the futility of a man trying to produce idealistic films in an industry dominated by conformity and commercialism.

After the Nazis came to power, Unruh moved to France so that he could turn his pen against them. They asked him to come back, offering to make him "the modern Schiller," and when he rejected the offer they burned his books and took away his citizenship. At the beginning of the war the French put him in a concentration camp. After the surrender of France, Unruh was able to escape, and he made his way to the United States with his wife. He returned home after the war, advising his fellow Germans to admit their guilt in Nazism; the latter part of his career was given over to writing novels rather than plays, his most notable con-tribution in the fiction area being a story of St. Catherine of Siena.

The Early Werfel: Revolutionist and Expressionist

Two prominent members of the expressionist movement were natives of the old Austro-Hungarian province of Bohemia, which was to become part of Czechoslovakia, Karel Čapek and Franz Werfel. Although Čapek wrote in the Czech language, he has a kinship with the Germanic ex-pressionists because his plays were produced alongside theirs in German' theaters and, in English translation, they were also highly successful in London and New York.

R.U.R. (1921; *Rossum's Universal Robots*) introduced the word robot (derived from *robotit*, meaning to drudge) into English. In this play, Čapek projected a future in which workers would be robots or auto-mata, and he showed them in revolt in an attempt to acquire souls and become individuals. Parts of the play are too superficially didactic, and its dramatic effectiveness is somewhat reduced by its optimistic ending. *Ze Zivota hmyzu* (1921; *The Insect Play*, also known as *The World We Live In*), which Čapek wrote with his brother Josef, shows man's foibles in terms of the insect world. *Věc Makropulos* (1922; *The Makropoulos Secret*) attempts to make a comedy out of the idea that it is perhaps not good to attempt to live forever. Čapek, who fretted himself into illness after the Munich pact in the autumn of 1938, died of pneumonia on Christmas Day of that year.

If, like the Hungarian Ferenc Molnár, Čapek seems by adoption to belong to Germanic literature, Franz Werfel belongs to this category by choice. Although born and brought up in Prague, he moved to Vienna in his youth and lived there until the Nazis took over the country in 1938. Unlike Čapek, but like Molnár, Werfel came from a Jewish family.

Werfel began by writing poetry before the First World War, producing such volumes as *Der Weltfreund* (1911; *Friend of Mankind*) and *Wir sind* (1913; *We Are*). While serving at the front on the side of the Central Powers, Werfel continued composing; at this time he produced the poetry for two other books, *Einander* (1915; *One Another*) and *Gerichtstag* (1919; *Day of Judgment*). *Friend of Mankind* and *We Are* used the dawning technique of expressionism to project an attempt of the individual to find his place in society and religion. The poems Werfel composed in the trenches were anti-war in spirit, particularly "Der Krieg" ("War"), which was written as early as August 1914. In this poem, which was an accusation of the warmongers ("Die Wortemacher des Krieges"), Werfel envisioned the war as destroying the idea of the brotherhood of man as expressed in his earlier verses.

The poems in *The Day of Judgment* describe Werfel's present despair and his yearning for a better life which would contain some of the innocence of childhood. In this protest, Werfel was a spiritual cousin to such English poets as Siegfried Sassoon, who were similarly sending anti-war poems back home from the trenches. At the same time a group of pacifist writers gathered together in Switzerland, where they produced a journal called *Die weissen Blätter* (*The White Papers*), which published writings by Werfel, Heinrich Mann, Carl Sternheim, Leonhard Frank, René Schickele (its founder), and other Germanic authors as well as those of the Frenchman Henri Barbusse, who in 1916 wrote the famous French war novel *Le Feu* (*Under Fire*).

Werfel in the first chaotic days after the war was an active social revolutionary, but he soon settled down to imaginative writing, first the drama and then the novel. His social conscience remained awake, however, as his later opposition to the growth of Nazism shows. His last years were spent in the United States as a world-famous novelist; he died there in 1945.

In 1915 Werfel published the first full version of *Die Troerinnen*, his adaptation of Euripides' tragedy *The Trojan Women*. If this is an expressionist play, it also somewhat foreshadows the existentialists in showing that man is doomed to suffer in a world which the gods have guiltily and stupidly created; but the duty of mankind, emblemized by the character Hekuba, is to give meaning to the world by living and suffering. Produced first at the Lessing Theater in Berlin, the drama was an enormous success, but was attacked by one of Werfel's fellow expressionists, Kurt Hiller. A leading member of the activist group of the expressionists, Hiller found Werfel too passive. Werfel entered into the controversy, defending his point of view and opposing Hiller's belief that the salvation of the individual was to be obtained in the sacrifice of individualism itself by amalgamation into the masses.

Werfel's "magic trilogy," *Spiegelmensch* (1920; *The Mirror Man*), is an expressionist drama obviously influenced by Goethe's *Faust* and Ibsen's *Peer Gynt*. The leading character, Thamal, is accompanied by Spiegelmensch, his mirrored self, who acts as a kind of Mephistopheles to his Faust. Thamal had attempted to retire to a monastery, whose abbot told him that he should first experience more of life. Thamal shoots at his own reflection in a mirror and in doing so releases his other ego, the mirror man who represents his lower instincts. After going through a series of adventures in which Spiegelmensch continually leads Thamal into evil, Thamal finally breaks away from him and turns himself over to the authorities, accepting responsibility for his crimes. Although Spiegelmensch tries to tempt Thamal back into a life of pleasure and power, he swallows a cup of poison. Miraculously, this frees him from Spiegelmensch, who returns to the mirror, as Thamal returns to the monastery, with visions of a finer life. *The Mirror Man*, which was one of the few expressionist plays admired in Austria, had the distinction of being produced at Vienna's Burgtheater.

In *Bocksgesang* (1921; *Goat Song*), Werfel by his very title suggests that he is going to the roots of tragedy: the Greeks were supposed to have derived the word tragedy from a term meaning goat song, and the Dionysiac chorus in early Hellenic tragedies is thought to have been dressed in goatskins because Dionysius was the goatfoot god. In Werfel's play a monster born to an eighteenth-century Slavonic peasant couple becomes the leader and emblem of a group of revolutionists. Although the army defeats them, destroying the monster and restoring the old order, there is an augury of the future in that the monster has impregnated one of the women in the play, and the implication is that the primeval and revolutionary terror will continue. *Goat Song*, although not successful in its first production at Frankfurt, Germany, was at the same time given a resounding reception at the Raimundtheater in Vienna; subsequently, it was an international success, and was staged by the Theatre Guild in New York.

The Later Werfel: Exile and World Fame

Werfel soon broke away from expressionism and began writing plays of a more conventional type. Such dramas as *Juarez und Maximilian* (1923; *Juárez and Maximilian*), *Paulus unter den Juden* (1926; *Paul Among the Jews*), and *Das Reich Gottes in Böhmen* (1930; *God's Kingdom in Bohemia*, translated as *The Eternal Road*)—the last a dramatization of Old Testament events from the time of Abraham to that of the Prophets—were popular successes in the theater but were less effective than Werfel's earlier dramas.

As a novelist Werfel generally wrote large-sized volumes which had enormous international sales. *Verdi: Roman der Oper* (1924; *Verdi: A Novel of the Opera*) dealt with the musical figure Werfel had long admired and whose letters he had edited. *Barbara oder die Frömmigkeit* (1929; translated as *The Pure in Heart*) is a psychological study, and *Die Geschwister von Neapel* (1931; *The Brothers and Sisters of Naples*, translated as *The Pascarella Family*) explores the tyrannical influence of a Neopolitan father over his sons and daughters. In these books, Werfel continually sounds the note of world brotherhood. This is seen in terms of justice in *Der Abituriententag* (1928; *The Class Reunion*), which shows a judge in Vienna confronted by a prisoner who has the same name as a classmate whom he allowed to take the blame for a crime the judge himself had committed.

Werfel's greatest popular success as a novelist came with *Die vierzig Tage des Musa Dagh* (1933; *The Forty Days of Musa Dagh*), which again treats two of his favorite themes, race and religion. Musa Dagh is a mountain on which the Armenians take refuge during their opposition to the Turks in the First World War. After withstanding a forty-day siege, the Armenians were rescued by the French navy, but it is ironic that their leader, Gabriel Bagradian, who was born in Paris but has

TWENTIETH-CENTURY GERMAN LITERATURE

returned to his native country, has fallen into an exhausted sleep during the rescue and is left behind, to be killed by a Turkish bullet.

Werfel's growing sympathy for Catholicism was evident in *Der veruntreute Himmel* (1939; *Embezzled Heaven*) and *Lied der Bernadette* (1941; *The Song of Bernadette*). In America these widely read religious confections were both selections of the Book-of-the-Month Club.

Werfel had a last theatrical success with *Jacobowsky und der Oberst* (1944; *Jacobowsky and the Colonel*), a comic dramatization suggested by some of his own experiences while escaping from occupied France. (This farce, adapted for the American theater by S. N. Behrman, featured Oskar Karlweis as Jacobowsky. A star of the Viennese theater, Karlweis was an old friend of Werfel, whose wife, Alma, had earlier been married to the composer Gustav Mahler.) In the play, the anti-Semitic Polish colonel flees from Paris at the time of the fall of France. He travels in the company of his French mistress Marie-Anne and a worldly-wise little Polish Jew, Jacobowsky, who by a miracle in the crisis had picked up an automobile. It is a comedy of suspense, but the travelers finally reach the French coast, where Jacobowsky alone, because of his resoucefulness and his *joie de vivre*, is deemed worthy enough to escape to England to start a new life. It was an amusing little play, topical, and predominantly superficial. In 1965, *Jacobowsky* was made into an opera in Germany.

Werfel, toward the end of his life subject to critical heart attacks, finished his last novel, *Stern der Ungeborenen* (1945; *Star of the Unborn*), a story of life a hundred thousand years in the future. In this book Werfel projects a long-established world state, with a small and stable population and longer life for human beings, who have enormous material advantages. In the story, this civilization is threatened by surviving "jungle" people, who represent throwbacks to twentieth-century mankind. They finally conquer the "Astromental" world, most of whose citizens then commit suicide. This book makes interesting comparisons with Aldous Huxley's *Brave New World* (1932) and Hermann Hesse's *Das Glasperlenspiel* (1943; *The Game of Beads*). But what Huxley and Hesse manage to convey in small compass, Werfel cannot seem to accomplish in anything less than pretentious epic space. As is true of all his fiction, *Star of the Unborn* is prolix; it is the kind of huge, overgrown novel which subscribers to popular book clubs seem to favor. *Star of the Unborn* has some interesting concepts, but it is full of hollow places and low-pressure writing. Werfel was a good-hearted, well-meaning citizen of the world, but his only works that remain impressive now are his early poems and parts of his expressionist plays.

Hasenclever and Toller

Another expressionist playwright who was also a poet, Walter Hasenclever was born in the same year as Werfel (1890), but died five years earlier (1940). Hasenclever, who after the coming of the Nazis had exiled himself to France, was a suicide.

Born in Aachen, Hasenclever studied at the universities of Oxford, Lausanne, and Leipzig. He was wounded while fighting on the German side in the First World War and spent more than a year in the hospital. He had published his first volume of verse, *Der Jüngling (The Youth)*, in 1913, and his first play, *Der Sohn (The Son)*, in 1914. Written just before Hasenclever went into service, *The Son* became the manifesto of his generation. It is the story of a boy of twenty who fails his examinations and, defying the despotism of his old-fashioned father, leaves home to become a social and political revolutionary. After being initiated into physical love, he is captured by the police and brought before his father, whom he threatens with a pistol; in his furious response to this, the father suffers a stroke and dies.

The fresh treatment of familiar situations accounted for a good deal of the popularity *The Son* enjoyed in the decade following its first production in 1916. In some parts of the play, verse breaks in on the prose, and music is called upon for help—Beethoven's Ninth Symphony and even "The Marseillaise." As in the plays of Kaiser and other expressionists, the characters have no names; they are known merely by such designations as the Father, the Son, or the Girl.

Two of Hasenclever's plays written during the war, the dramatic poem *Der Retter* (1915; *The Savior*) and *Antigone* (1917), were both suppressed. In *The Savior* a poet who believes in the brotherhood of man tries to stop the war and is brought before a firing squad. Creon in Hasenclever's adaptation of Sophocles' *Antigone* was obviously Kaiser Wilhelm II, opposing the pacifism and democratic idealism of Antigone.

In *Die Menschen* (1918; *Mankind*), the central character, Alexander, is a corpse who returns from the next world in an attempt to atone for the suffering and grief he has caused others during his stay upon earth. A murderer gives him a sack with his victim's head in it, and Alexander carries this with him as a mark of expiation. After a mélange of scenes showing Alexander going through various adventures, the murderer comes back from the grave in order to let Alexander return to it in peace. In this play Hasenclever often uses a telegraphic style like that of Georg Kaiser, frequently employing only monosyllables.

A figure from beyond the grave again dominates a Hasenclever play in *Jenseits* (1920; *Beyond*), produced by Max Reinhardt. In this drama a dead husband haunts his widow and her new lover; he is never seen except when the fire takes the shape of his face; his presence is felt, however, as doors keep opening and closing for his entrances and exits. He finally drives the lover into killing the woman and himself. In *Gobseck* (1921), Hasenclever drew upon Balzac's story of that name, the tale of the usurer Gobseck and of the unhappy marriage of the Countess de Restaud.

Abandoning expressionism, Hasenclever turned out such comedies as *Ein besserer Herr* (1927; *A Gentleman*) and *Ehen werden im Himmel geschlossen* (1929; *Marriages Are Made in Heaven*). Still another comedy, *Napoleon greift ein* (1930; *Napoleon Enters the Scene*), was, like Carl Sternheim's *Either Caesar or Nothing*, prophetic of the Nazi dictatorship. In Hasenclever's play, however, the strutting Napoleon, who reappears in a later, supposedly less romantic world than the Corsican conqueror originally knew, is confined to an asylum.

Another member of the expressionist group, Ernst Toller, who wrote plays usually quite different from those of Hasenclever, nevertheless had certain points in common with him, not the least of them biographical. Like Hasenclever, Toller was wounded while fighting on the German side in the First World War and, again like Hasenclever, he took his own life —he committed suicide in New York in 1939.

Toller belonged to the activist wing of the expressionist movement, the phase which believed in pragmatic social reformation. Toller's first play, *Die Wandlung* (1919; *Transfiguration*), was written while he was serving a jail sentence for taking part in a pacifist demonstration in 1918. *Transfiguration* indicates how far Toller had fallen away from the enthusiasm with which he had joined the armed forces of the Kaiser several years earlier. It is a somewhat autobiographical play in that its central figure is a young sculptor who ardently welcomes the war which he believes will prove his nation's superiority. After receiving military honors, he becomes disillusioned when he hears a nurse rejoice over a victory that has cost the lives of ten thousand men. Subsequently, he destroys a patriotic statue he has made and goes out to lead the masses to revolution. In thirteen tableux (Stationen), Toller depicts the horrors of war.

He again used the tableau form in *Masse Mensch* (1920; *The Human*

Mass, translated as *Man and the Masses*), which also employs the expressionist Sprechchor (Speaking Chorus) as well as the assistance of music, dream projections, and poetic speech that sometimes becomes telegraphic in style. Toller, in a note to the producer of the play, said that "it literally broke out of me and was put on paper in two days and a half. The two nights which, owing to my imprisonment, I was forced to spend in 'bed' in a dark cell, were abysses of torment." Tortured by visions of demonic faces in grotesque postures, Toller in the mornings wrote feverishly until his fingers would no longer serve him; he allowed no one into the cell even to clean it, and he became enraged with those who questioned or tried to help him. After this, he spent a "laborious and blissful" year in revising the play. He felt that it represented the essential humanism of proletarian art, which could "only exist where the creative artist reveals that which is eternally human in the spiritual characteristics of the working people."

Not long after Toller put down that hectic first draft of his play, the Bavarian revolution broke out, and he was elected the first president of the Bavarian Soviet Republic (Bayerische Räterepublik). When the Social Democratic government repressed this workers' republic, Toller was again imprisoned. He was condemned to death, but the soldiers refused to fire upon him. His sentence was changed to life imprisonment. He was not released when the political prisoners of Bavaria were given amnesty, but he was finally set free in 1924. In the meantime his plays had been produced in Berlin and the other capitals of the world.

Die Maschinenstürmer (1922; *The Machine-Wreckers*) concerns the Luddite riots of 1812, when the Nottingham weavers, resenting the new looms which they feel will be destructive to their livelihood, rise up in rebellion to smash them. The hero of the play is an idealistic young worker, Jim Cobbett, whom the mob murders when he tries to stop the revolt. The prologue to the drama is a dramatization of Lord Byron's speech in Parliament defending the Nottingham workers; he is answered by the reactionary Lord Castlereagh, who says that Byron's words are those of a poet rather than a statesman. *The Machine-Wreckers* forms an interesting contrast with Gerhart Hauptmann's earlier play, *The Weavers,* which in effect praises the workers for destroying the machines.

Toller's *Hinkemann* (1924; translated as *Brokenbrow*) was very much in the spirit of the times in that its leading character was a soldier sexually wounded in the war. This relates him to the Fisher King who plays so important a part in T. S. Eliot's *The Waste Land* (1922) and he foreshadows Jake Barnes, the protagonist of Hemingway's *The Sun Also Rises*

(1926). *Hinkemann* is also notable because it represents Toller's one attempt to get away from the panoramic, mass-men type of play and create a sympathetic individual character.

In *Hoppla, wir leben!* (1927; *Hoppla! Such Is Life!*) Toller begins with a "cinematographic prelude" showing a number of social revolutionaries in a prison cell, among them Karl Thomas and Wilhelm Kilman. The latter has sent a petition to the president saying that he found himself among the revolutionaries against his will, and he is released. Karl Thomas, on the other hand, spends the years from 1919 to 1927 in a madhouse; a newsreel bannering the leading event of each of the intervening years is flashed on a screen. When Thomas is released, he discovers that Kilman is the prime minister. He intends to assassinate him, but instead the deed is carried out by a Nazi, who says he hates Kilman for being a Bolshevik. Karl Thomas is arrested for the crime. A court eventually exonerates him, but he has meanwhile hanged himself in his cell. *Hoppla!* is interesting as a spirited dramatization of life in Germany during the Weimar Republic, but it lacks profundity, and technically it shows no advance over Toller's earlier plays.

Similarly, there are no signs of growth in *Feuer aus den Kesseln* (1930; translated as *Draw the Fires*) or in the drama about Mary Baker Eddy which Toller wrote with Hermann Kesten. Shortly before his death, Toller visited Spain to encourage the Republican army there. The plays of this man who at one time showed such energetic promise are rarely produced nowadays.

The Early Plays of Bertolt Brecht

On the other hand, a somewhat younger contemporary of Toller's, Bertolt Brecht, who died in 1956, became one of the world's most popular playwrights in the decades following the Second World War. This holds true even in the democracies, despite the fact that Brecht had Communist affiliations and spent the last years of his life in East Germany. The point remains, however, that Brecht was too deeply committed to individualism to have been a very successful advocate of communism. As his biographer Martin Esslin notes, Brecht was unable to write a single play about the realities of life in the Soviet-dominated part of the world although he was living in the middle of it: "The authorities alternately begged and ordered him to try his hand. He did not succeed." Esslin further points out that the Communists feel that all Brecht's work fails "in conveying the message of hope in man's redemption by a radical change in the social order that he so earnestly and persistently sought to put into it. Yet the final effect of Brecht's negative picture of the human condition is not entirely one of despair," because of his sense of the tragic, of heroes and heroines who "redeem themselves by their courage in the face of overwhelming odds."

Brecht flourished in two periods, the years following the First World War as well as those coming after the Second, though his fame was not so extensive, internationally, in the earlier phase. His career therefore must be considered in two different sections of this book. The first part of it will be treated here, the second—which finds Brecht at the height of his powers and influence—later on.

Brecht, born in Augsburg, was a boy of sixteen when the 1914 war broke out. He has described how he was eventually mobilized and put to work in a hospital: "I dressed wounds, applied iodine, gave enemas, performed blood-transfusions. If the doctor ordered me: 'Amputate a leg, Brecht,' I would answer: 'Yes, your Excellency,' and cut off the leg." At this time Brecht wrote a poem, "Die Ballade vom toten Soldaten" ("The Ballad of the Dead Soldier"), which told of military medical officers digging up the dead soldier, pronouncing him fit for military service, and sending him back into the fighting. The poem for a while was very popular at the front, except with officers. Brecht wrote his own music to this ballad and would sing it in bars or coffeehouses, accompanying himself on the guitar or banjo; sometimes in the postwar years this aroused the wrath of ex-soldiers. Brecht included the poem in the first of his plays to be produced, *Trommeln in der Nacht* (*Drums in the Night*), written between 1918 and 1920 and staged in Munich and Berlin in 1922.

This is the story of a soldier coming back from a prisoner-of-war camp to discover that his fiancée is engaged to a war profiteer and expecting a child by him. The soldier and the girl quarrel against a background of small bars and Spartacist street riots, and in the early morning they become reconciled.

The Berlin drama critic Herbert Ihering went to Munich for the opening of *Drums in the Night* and wrote in his paper that a twenty-four-year-old poet had "changed the literary physiognomy of Germany overnight." He had brought to the time "a new tone, a new melody, a new vision"; he was "impregnated with the horror of this age in his nerves, in his blood," and this accounted for "the unparalleled force of his images." His language could "be felt on the tongue, on the palate, in one's ears, in one's spine." It was a language "brutally sensuous and melancholically tender," which contained "malice and bottomless sadness, grim wit and plaintive lyricism." Later that year, Ihering was one of the judges for the awarding of the Kleist Prize, given for the best display of young dramatic talent, and this was granted to Brecht.

An indefatigable reviser of his work, Brecht had originally planned to call the play *Spartakus*. He first designated it as a drama, but later as a comedy. He permitted *Drums in the Night* to be published in 1923, but four years later reissued it with many changes. He had written one earlier play, in 1918, *Baal;* this was first produced in Leipzig in 1923 and later, in 1926, in Berlin, with a cast including Oskar Homolka.

Max Reinhardt, who had enthusiastically attended rehearsals of *Drums in the Night*, appointed Brecht to the staff of the Deutsches Theater in Berlin, where his play *Im Dickicht der Städte* (*In the Jungle of Cities*) was produced in 1924, a year after its first staging in Munich as *Im Dickicht*. This play in eleven scenes is subtitled "The Struggle between Two Men in the Giant City of Chicago." Its action takes place between 1912 and 1915. The story principally concerns Shlink, a Chicago timber merchant of Malaysian origin. He quarrels with George Garga, who works in a lending library. Shlink, trying to dominate Garga, turns over his business to him, and Garga stages a fraud which makes Shlink out as a swindler. But at the last moment Garga takes the blame and serves the jail sentence in order to shame Shlink.

At the time of his release he sends a letter to a newspaper denouncing Shlink for having seduced two girls, one of them Garga's own sister, who was in love with Shlink. As a mob comes to lynch Shlink, he and Garga have a vision of man's essential loneliness. In this, the play foreshadows the theater of the 1950's and 1960's, which emphasizes the essential solitude of man. In Brecht's *Jungle* play, this solitude is so great that Shlink and Garga see that even such a struggle as theirs cannot bring human beings together. This is not the only time a relationship similar to that of Verlaine and Rimbaud enters a Brecht play (Garga even quotes passages from Rimbaud's *Season in Hell*). As the mob intent on lynching arrives, Shlink dies and Garga escapes, setting fire to the premises. Brecht included a note in all published editions of the play, advising the reader not to worry too much as to the motives in the incomprehensible struggle portrayed between two human beings.

By 1924, expressionism was going out of fashion in Germany, to be succeeded by the Neue Sachlichkeit, the new realism or matter-of-factness. This was a name given to tendencies rather than to any specific group; it represented an objectivity, an intensification of realism, that came into literature and the arts as the novelty of expressionism faded. Brecht as a writer of social dramas drew upon some of the new-realist characteristics. He was not yet dedicated to Marxism, but he was already turning toward didactic plays with social lessons—what he was to call Lehrstücke. Brecht's growing social awareness is evident in *Mann ist Mann* (1926; *A Man's a Man*), which its author called a comedy. It is a play about the destruction of the individuality of Galy Gay, an Irish dockworker in India. He becomes involved with four British soldiers who have robbed a temple. Three of the soldiers force him to impersonate the fourth, Jeriah Jip, which Galy Gay finally does with such conviction that he becomes Jip. After a series of fantastic adventures, he demonstrates bravery in action and even captures a fortress. He has so completely displaced Jip that Jip, when he tries to attach himself to his comrades again, is rejected and given Galy Gay's identity papers. The play shows how pliable men can be under the force of circumstance.

In 1928 Brecht and Kurt Weill, with whom he had collaborated before, first presented their modern adaptation of John Gay's *The Beggar's Opera* as *Die Dreigroschenoper* (or *The Threepenny Opera*). With its brilliant libretto and attractive music, *The Threepenny Opera* has been for more than three decades a favorite all over the world; it ran in New York, in an off-Broadway production, for the last half of the 1950's, with a cast featuring Lotte Lenya of the original company, who is Kurt Weill's widow.

It was also in 1928 that Brecht collaborated on the dramatization of the Czech novel by Jaroslav Hašek, *Osudy dobrého vojáka Svejka za světové valky* (1920–1923; *The Good Soldier Schweik*), the story of the comic adventures of a very bad soldier in the Austrian army. The play was staged at the Piscatorbühne, the theater operated by Erwin Piscator, mentioned earlier. He was a director of Marxist persuasion who had a great influence upon Brecht. Piscator's production featured the noted comic actor Max Pallenberg, and settings by the satirical German artist George Grosz.

The production of *The Threepenny Opera* marked the beginning of Brecht's association with the Theater am Schiffbauerdamm, in Berlin, where for a number of years he trained actors who later became widely known, including Curt Bois, Alexander Granach, Oskar Homolka, Peter Lorre, Lotte Lenya, and Helene Weigel, who became Brecht's wife.

At this theater, Brecht began to put into practice ideas he had already embodied in *A Man's a Man*, his theories of non-Aristotelian or "epic" drama. In this, narrative replaces the usual dramatic plot, which implicated the onlooker in the theatrical situation but wore down his power of action; the narrative in the epic theater was supposed, while making the spectator into an observer, to arouse at the same time his power of action. Where the older type of drama took the human being for granted, in the epic drama the human being became the object of enquiry; where in the older form he was unalterable, he was, in the newer, regarded as alterable and capable of altering. The conventional dramatic form, Brecht said, focused on the finish, while the new focused on the course itself. Where each scene created another in the dramatic form of theater, in the epic each scene stood for itself; and, in technique, montage supplanted the conventional forms of growth. Montage, as made famous in the Russian films of Sergei Eisenstein, formed a composite picture by crowding together a number of separate images, superimposing one upon another, blending them into a whole in which every single picture nevertheless remained distinct. As Brecht used it, montage was a technique which seemed somewhat akin to expressionism; he even projected subtitles onto the stage.

These characteristics manifested themselves in many of Brecht's plays of the time, such as *Die Mutter* (1932; *The Mother*), a free adaptation of Maxim Gorki's novel and a continuation of it. It is the story of a mother drawn into revolutionary activity by her son, who is arrested; after he has escaped from Siberia, he is captured and shot. Brecht's continuation shows the mother, Pelageya Vlasova, continuing in revolutionary activities through the 1914 war and into demonstrations shortly before the October Revolution. The play in fifteen scenes contains a number of songs; it is written in prose with some unrhymed irregular verse.

Brecht kept working in many dramatic forms, such as his "attempt at an epic opera" in *Aufstieg und Fall der Stadt Mahagonny* (1930; *Rise and Fall of the City of Mahagonny*), which had music by Kurt Weill; *Der Flug der Lindberghs* (1929; *The Flight of the Lindberghs*), a didactic radio play for children with music by Kurt Weill and Paul Hindemith; and *Die Heilige Johanna der Schlachthöfe* (1932; *St. Joan of the Stockyards*), originally performed over the radio in Berlin; its first stage production was in Copenhagen in 1935, when Brecht was a refugee there. During his exile he wrote a series of social dramas such as *Furcht und Elend des Dritten Reiches* (1937; *Terror and Misery of the Third Reich*), a sequence of brief scenes depicting life in Nazi Germany. It was first staged in Paris, with Brecht's wife, Helene Weigel, in the leading role. "Based on eye-witness accounts and newspaper reports," the play was produced throughout America and Europe, except of course in Nazi Germany. It contained twenty-four scenes, and was performed with music by Hanns Eisler.

Before going to Denmark, Brecht in his exile had lived in Austria and France. As war became imminent in 1939, he considered Denmark too close to the German border to be safe, and moved to Sweden. But after the Nazi invasion of Norway and Denmark, Brecht went to Finland, partly because this was an easy place to obtain an American passport. He left just before Hitler's invasion of Russia, which put Finland in the war as an ally of Germany. Brecht and his family went across Russia to Vladivostok, where he took a ship to the United States. During the greater part of the war he worked in Hollywood, writing plays and occasionally working for the films. (With Fritz Lang, he wrote *Hangmen also Die*, which had music by his old collaborator Hanns Eisler. The film, which starred Brian Donlevy, dealt with the assassination of Reinhard Heydrich, the Gauleiter of Prague. Brecht was so disgusted with the screenplay made from the story written by himself and Lang that he went to the courts to make sure that the screen credits differentiated it from the scenario itself.)

Brecht must be regarded as a lyric poet as well as a dramatist. His plays are full of ballads and other kinds of verse, but he also wrote a good deal of poetry independent of the theater, such as one which came out in 1927, the year after a slightly different edition of only twenty-five copies: *Die Hauspostille* (*The Domestic Prayer Book*, translated as *Manual of Piety*). One of its most famous items is the title-piece of its Appendix, "Von Armen B. B." ("Of the Poor B. B.") This title, using the author's initials, may also be a pun: Bébé (baby). In this poem, Brecht tells of being carried in his mother's womb from the black forests to the cities, in whose asphalt he has always felt at home. The people are animals with a peculiar smell, but so is he; he associates with them and follows their customs. After a night of drinking and smoking, he settles down into a nervous sleep:

> In the earthquakes that are to come, I hope
> I shall not let my Virginia cigar be crushed out by bitterness,
> I, Bertolt Brecht, brought to the asphalt cities
> From the black forests, inside my mother, long ago.

Personal as this is, there is a cool detachment in its grim humor. Brecht did not always remain so objective, as in the fairly late poem, "Böser Morgen" ("Evil Morning"), which deals with the aftermath of the Berlin workers' revolt of 1953. On the morning he writes of, the poet suddenly sees that a beautiful poplar has become a hag and that the lake has become dirty dishwater. He is still shaken by his night's dream, in which a broken and work-callous finger pointed at him as if he were a leper. He cries out against the ignorance that would accuse him, but his cry comes out of guilt. As a poet, particularly in the ballad form, Brecht has a striking importance not always recognized because he has become so well known as a dramatist.

The later phases of Brecht's career as a playwright belong to the period after the Second World War, and will accordingly be discussed later. As for the expressionist movement which, at least in its early phases, motivated a number of these German writers, it must be said that although this movement had for a while the excitement of revolutionary creativity it became entangled in its own mechanisms; its techniques have occasionally given life to later plays, when sparingly used, but for the most part they are bound to their own time. Perhaps the greatest limitation of expressionism was that its practitioners were for the most part men of secondary talents, such as Georg Kaiser; those of more assured gifts, such as Bertolt Brecht, took what they needed from expressionism and went their own way. So the movement remains, even to a limited extent, in the modern theater, and it furnishes an exciting chapter in the history of that theater itself.

The New Objectivism and the Zeitstück

If expressionism was the most exciting theatrical movement in betweenwars Germany, it was still not the only one; its partial successor, the Neue Sachlichkeit (new objectivism, or new matter-of-factness), has already been mentioned. There was also the Zeitstück, the play which dealt with contemporary issues. Later the Nazi plays came, official after early 1933.

The new objectivism, which was not an attempt to revive the naturalism of the 1890's, occasionally used expressionist techniques in its attempt to penetrate the skin of "reality"—a matter which makes difficult any attempts to pinpoint the Neue Sachlichkeit as a definite movement. In the main, the newer realism attempted to come closer to everyday speech than expressionism did in its often poetic utterances; and the succeeding movement presented characters which developed more in the traditional style than the types found in expressionistic drama; similarly, instead of generalized settings, the Neue Sachlichkeit plays featured scenery that imitated life, and their plots were more concrete than the abstract, often idea-controlled stories which occurred in expressionist plays. Expressionism as a movement ended about 1923, yet traces of it lingered, as we have seen. The new exponents of matter-of-factness, which at first had

programmatic tendencies, never really crystallized into a group; the objectivity was largely a reaction to the expressionist movement, even when
borrowing from it.

Consequently the term Neue Sachlichkeit can be applied to many German plays (and novels) of various modes from the early 1930's to the
advent of party-line National Socialist compositions. One of the forerunners of both the new objectivism and the issues-of-the-time plays was
actually written during the war and first published in 1918—Hans José
Rehfisch's *Heimkehr* (*Homecoming*) dealt with the problems of the
returned soldier, which later became a common theme. Rehfisch also wrote
Chauffeur Martin (1920), the story of a man's rebirth, and *Wer weint um
Juckenack?* (1924; *Who Weeps for Juckenack?*), another of the typical
ex-soldier stories of the time, this one concerned with a lawyer's clerk
who dies insane. He makes some futile humanitarian experiments after
awaking from a dream in which he had seemed to be dead; the Berlin
setting, full of types of the time, is rendered with compelling realism. In
the Volksstück, or popular-play medium, Rehfisch mixed in comedy with
his tragic theses, particularly in *Die Erziehung zu Kolibri* (1921; *Education at Kolibri*), which was set in a brothel; in *Nickel und die sechsund-
dreissig Gerechten* (*Nickel and the Thirty-six Just Men*), produced in
1925 by Max Reinhardt; and in *Duell am Lido* (*Duel at the Lido*), produced in 1926 by Leopold Jessner. Rehfisch was a good theater craftsman,
a neat juggler of contemporary themes, whose work is limited by the
topical subject matter that made them so popular in their own time.
Rehfisch died in Switzerland in 1960.

For all their concessions to realism, some of the new-objectivist productions were in the tradition of escape literature. Several of these plays
represented flights from civilization in the manner of Gauguin. One of them
was by an older dramatist, Wilhelm Schmidtbonn, who had made his
debut in 1901 with *Mutter Landstrasse* (*The Highroad; Our Mother*), a
modern version of the prodigal-son story. Schmidtbonn's escape-from-
Europe play was *Die Fahrt nach Orplid* (1922; *Journey to Orplid*), very
much in the spirit of the times. It was followed by Wilhelm Speyer's
Südsee (1923; *South Sea*) and Bernhard Blume's *Fahrt nach der Südsee*
(1924; *Journey to the South Sea*). Audiences stepping into the theater
from the gray streets of German cities were greeted with settings that
shone with fresh green, and were regaled with stories in which people
sank happily into a life of languor, far from wars and the problems of
inflation.

Gerhart Hauptmann made his contribution to this escape literature, though for the most part in high poetry rather than in the mode of the newer realism. *Der weisse Heiland* (1920; *The White Savior*) told in trochaic tetrameters the sad story of the noble and gentle Montezuma, whose idyllic country is invaded by brutal and cynical conquistadors. In *Indipohdi* (1922) Hauptmann took Prospero from Shakespeare's *The Tempest* but omitted Ariel and Caliban; in this story Prospero exhibits, on his island, a Buddhist urge toward nonexistence. And here it may be added that in 1928 Hauptmann wrote what he considered his finest poem, *Till Eulenspiegel*, whose beginnings are steeped in new-realist pictures of postwar Germany, though the language is cast in hexameters. In this epic-size poem, Hauptmann makes the legendary rogue into a military aviator of the defeated side, wandering through his native land in a wagon drawn by two horses; he has his magic tricks and wears his jester's cap and bells on his airman's helmet. Besides the Germany of dispirited ex-soldiers and shouting Bolsheviks, Till sees an older Germany, which comes dreamlike through the music of Bach; and later he spends an ideal and idyllic existence of a thousand years in Greece with Baubo, the hand-maiden of the gods. Till at last returns to the actual world and looks for death in a glacier in the Swiss Alps.

Among those who actually subscribed to the principles of the new objectivity, comedy was as much a medium as plays of disillusion or escape. In 1922 the physician Max Mohr wrote *Improvisationen in Juni* (*Improvisations in June*), which mixed the expressionistic and the realis-tic in a story of the complications that occur when an American mil-lionaire attempts to buy an old German castle.

An almost exact contemporary of Mohr's, Paul Kornfeld (born two years earlier, in 1889), was in the early part of his career an expressionist playwright, but he became one of the comedy writers of the newer realism. Kornfeld's first drama, *Die Verführung* (1913; *The Seduction*), centers about a young man appropriately named Bitterlich, whose function is to kill everyone who irritates his aesthetic or ethical sense; this activity is stopped only when Bitterlich's brother-in-law poisons him.

In the epilogue to the printed version of the play, Kornfeld said that the actors in it should not strive to imitate reality, but should take abstractions from reality and present only emotions, ideas, and destiny— a concept that matched the artificiality of the dialogue. Kornfeld wrote several other plays during the expressionist period, and in the time of the new realism turned to comedies such as *Der grosse Traum* (1923; *The Great Dream*), which made fun of the idealism of the revolutionaries, and *Kilian und die gelbe Rose* (1926; *Kilian and the Yellow Rose*), broadly extravagant in its humor.

Mohr and Kornfeld, those two outstanding writers of comedy in the new-objectivist period, met with fates rather typical of the times. After the Nazis came to power in 1933, Dr. Mohr felt he could not work under a dictatorship and so moved to Shanghai; there he wrote a letter to Thomas Mann in which he said: "When I arrived here last year with ten dollars in my pocket, I possessed my instruments, my medical training, a few photos of the family I had left behind in Germany, and the glorious feeling that I have finished with Germany." He died soon afterward, the victim of one of the Oriental diseases for which he was attempting to find a cure. Paul Kornfeld's death came in 1942, in a concentration camp in Poland.

A third playwright of this time, Carl (or Karl) Zuckmayer, left Germany before the Second World War, returning after it to West Germany to become for a while that new nation's most popular dramatist. The early phase of his career, to be considered now, was notable for his highly successful play, *Der fröhliche Weinberg* (1925; *The Happy Vineyard*). Realism marked this comedy, especially in its reproduction of Rhenish dialect. The play is a robust chronicle of life in the vineyards and taverns; as in other of Zuckmayer's works, the stiff soldier is a figure of fun, here represented by a chauvinistic corps student. Because *The Happy Vineyard* attacked anti-Semitism, it was disliked by the Nazis, whose storm troopers often caused riots at performances of the play. But it remained popular until the Nazis took over the country. The comedy's heroine was a particular favorite in the German theater of the time: because her father will not let her become betrothed until she is pregnant, Klärchen Gunderloch fools her suitor, the pompous Knuzius, in a way which enables her to marry the man she really loves, the sailor Jochen. The fruitfulness of the vines accents the robustness of this comedy.

Zuckmayer, born a Rhinelander, served four years in the German army in the First World War; like so many authors, he began writing during that time, poetry at first. In 1920, while he was studying biology at Heidelberg, the Staatstheater in Berlin brought out his first play, *Kreuzweg* (*Crossroads*), in which two chanting choruses represented the two halves of humanity. This was not a popular play, as *The Happy Vineyard* proved to be; among other satisfactions, *The Happy Vineyard* brought Zuckmayer the Kleist Prize. His *Schinderhannes* (1927), a play about a famous outlaw, was a succès d'estime. Zuckmayer, however, had a succès fou with *Der Hauptmann von Köpenick* (1931; *The Captain from Köpenick*), based on an actual occurrence. The scene is a Berlin suburb during the reign of Wilhelm II, when an ex-convict, a cobbler named Karl Vogt, bought a secondhand officer's uniform, commandeered a troop of soldiers, and bullied the mayor and other officials into letting him take over the town hall and even the municipal funds. The cobbler in the play is, more than anything else, fighting a battle against red tape, for he has not managed to get a working permit; in his coup, his object is to get a passport that will enable him to leave the country. He is thus a sympathetic figure, but also the center of a boisterous comedy as his shoutings and stampings terrify the burghers: the play is a healthy laugh at the Germans' tendency to let the military impose upon them, and in the days before the Nazis came into power the comedy set a great part of Germany to laughing. But the laughter did not last long, for when Hitler took over the country in 1933, he banned the plays of Zuckmayer, whose mother was of Jewish descent. Zuckmayer, who had been living in Austria since 1925, left that country at the time of the 1938 Anschluss; after a year in Switzerland he emigrated to America and settled in Vermont. His later career belongs with the discussion of Germanic literature following the Second World War.

The Zeitstück plays—the dramas with topical themes—were sometimes, as we have seen, expressionist or new-realist in tone. Many of them were Heimkehrer, or homecoming plays, named after the drama *Heimkehr* by Rehfisch, which was discussed earlier. Brecht's *Drums in the Night* and Toller's *Hinkemann* are in this category; so is the Austrian-born Arnolt Bronnen's *Die katalaunische Schlacht* (1924; *The Catalaunian Battle*), which takes its title from Attila's battle in which the spirits of the dead are supposed to have fought alongside the living. In *The Catalaunian Battle*, which opens during the First World War, a woman disguised as an orderly follows her husband into the trenches. He is killed there; his comrades, who escape with the wife, all obsessively want to possess her, and they are shown pursuing her after the war, in Paris and later on a ship heading for America; but like the slain soldiers of Attila, the spirit of the husband keeps interposing itself. At last the wife, after hearing a recording of her husband's voice, kills herself to end this crudely sensational play.

Bronnen (1895–1959) had earlier written one of the typical father-and-son dramas of the time, *Vatermord* (*Parricide*), first produced in 1920, a play in which the neurotic son, young Fessel (fetter), hating the domination both of his father and of the school authorities, becomes involved in homosexual difficulties with his classmates and incestuous complications with his mother, before murdering his father with a coal shovel. Today we regard the plays of Bronnen merely as a lurid manifestation of their time; Bronnen became a supporter of the Nazis, but after their ascent to power in 1933 he temporarily stopped writing. (In 1945 he became a Communist and was a resident of East Berlin at the time of his death.)

Leonhard Frank's *Karl und Anna* (1929; *Carl and Anna*) was an important Heimkehrer play, which was adapted from his own short novel published in 1927 (it has even been made into an American film, with Greer Garson; a poor film, with the setting for no good reason switched to France). In *Carl and Anna*, Anna's husband, a German prisoner of war in Russia, incessantly tells a fellow captive about his wonderful wife; when the friend escapes, he goes back to Germany and, because he can relate so many intimate details of her married life, he convinces Anna that he is her husband. Later, when the original husband reappears, Anna stands by the interloper, since he has been transformed into her real husband. This variant of the Enoch Arden theme, with all its improbabilities, appealed to postwar readers and theater audiences because it showed the confusions and emotional upheavals caused by the war itself.

In the theater, Heimkehrer plays continued to appear until the Nazis began clamping down on them in 1933. In 1928 there was Gerhart Menzel's *Toboggan*, in which a soldier reported dead cannot convince anyone, including the woman who loves him, that he is still alive, and when his advances chill her, he goes out to die in a winter night of heavily falling snow. In 1929 there was Eberhard Wolfgang Möller's *Douamont oder die Heimkehr des Soldaten Odysseus* (*Douamont, or The Return of the Soldier Ulysses*), in which a soldier who has had the unusual luck to survive the bombardment of Fort Douamont comes back home to find, like Odysseus, that men who have stayed behind are besieging his wife; at least two of them are. Unlike Penelope, however, the wife does not welcome her husband back, and he cannot find employment. The obsession of the war is still with him, and at the end of the play he is powerfully able to project the Douamont experience in a monologue which makes his wife's suitors believe that they are in the fort while it is being shelled. In their terror, the pair give up their courtship and, after the husband is reconciled with his wife, he is no longer haunted by war memories.

In 1929 another of the Heimkehrer plays was Hans Chlumberg's *Wunder um Verdun* (*Miracle at Verdun*). Set in the future—1939—it dramatized the resurrection of the war dead, French as well as German, who arise from the graves in a military cemetery and march home. In order to end the panic which this action brings about, the statesmen of the world beg them to return to their entombment. The first production of this drama was marred by an accident at the dress rehearsal in which the young author was killed.

Besides these Heimkehrer plays, the new matter-of-factness of the 1920's also produced various dramas about adolescence and school life. These were of course expressionist themes, too, from Wedekind on, but the later writings dealt with the disillusion and emotional chaos of young Germans who in the 1920's experienced something of the hopelessness and cynicism which the British and American youth were to know after the Second World War. One of the best and most famous of these German dramas of youth is Christa Winsloe's *Gestern und Heute* (1930; *Yesterday and Today*), better known as *Mädchen in Uniform* (one of the finest of all films). Christa Winsloe was actually the Baroness Hátvany; Hátvany was a friend of Klaus Mann, a son of Thomas Mann, and himself the author of *Anja und Esther* (1925; *Anja and Esther*), one of the most famous of the Neue Sachlichkeit plays about young people in school (Klaus Mann's sister Erika played one of the leading roles in Christa Winsloe's *Mädchen in Uniform*). In *Mädchen in Uniform* the humanity of one of the teachers, Fräulein von Bernburg, alleviates some of the harshness of a school for officers' daughters. The Oberin (headmistress) attempts, in the days of the Weimar Republic, to maintain the old Prussian discipline. The beautiful Fräulein von Bernburg, who comes into conflict with her, unconsciously inspires passionate love among the uniformed girls, particularly Manuela, a general's daughter who in a fit of youthful lesbian frustration kills herself, more than anything else a victim of the Oberin's attempt to crush all tenderness. *Mädchen in Uniform* was a successful international film in 1932, with Dorothea Wieck and Hertha Thiele; a quarter-century later it was again made into a motion picture, with Lili Palmer and Romy Schneider.

The Neue Sachlichkeit period also produced a good many social dramas representing both leftist and rightist points of view. Ernst Toller's *Feuer aus den Kesseln* (1930; *Draw the Fires*) has already been mentioned; it is a post-expressionist effort, a rather dispirited play dealing with the Battle of Jutland and the German sailors' subsequent mutinies. A drama of the same year, Friedrich Wolf's *Die Matrosen von Cattaro* (*The Sailors of Cattaro*), deals with another mutiny, that in the Austro-Hungarian navy just before the end of the war. This became a stock piece of the international proletarian theater. The last play Wolf wrote in Germany, *Tai Yang erwacht* (1931; *Tai Yang Awakens*), was produced by Piscator in his epic style as a straight expression of Communist propaganda, with the Piscatorian clichés of cinema bits, flaring posters, tendential bulletins, and other devices.

But soon there would be room in Germany for only one kind of propaganda. Already the Nazis were preparing to take over the state and, with it, control over all literature. By 1933 the German people—who had voted for it—saw the beginnings of the swastika censorship.

German Poets between the Wars

Gottfried Benn (1886–1956) is perhaps the typical poet to select for the beginning of a discussion of the verse which appeared in Germany in the years following the First World War. Benn was an expressionist who dedicated himself to the expression of horror. A physician who specialized in venereal diseases, Benn called his first volume of poetry *Morgue* (1912). Like Richard Dehmel a native of Brandenburg, Benn was the son of a Lutheran pastor who had married a Frenchwoman.

Benn served as a doctor in the war, but as the title of his first book indicates, he already had developed his sense of horror before he saw the battlefield dead and dying. One of the *Morgue* poems, "Schöne Jugend" ("Beautiful Childhood"), demonstrates this:

> The mouth of a girl who had for long lain among the reeds
> looked as if it were gnawed away.
> When the breast was slit open, the gullet was full of holes.
> At last in a hollow place below the diaphragm
> a nest of young rats was found. One of the littlest sisters lay dead.
> The others had fed on liver and kidneys,
> drunk the cold blood and had
> here enjoyed a lovely childhood.
> And beautiful swift also came their death:
> They were all thrown together into the water.
> Oh, how their little snouts squeaked!

That gives the reader some idea of what to expect from Gottfried Benn; where Georg Trakl was concerned with the "golden image of man," Dr. Benn was interested in the "purple body" of man on the dissecting table. His wartime book, *Fleisch* (1917; *Flesh*), and the subsequent *Schutt* (1924; *Rubble*), contained mostly poems of despair, often sketched out in hideous detail and, following the expressionist technique, stretching syntax to its limits and trying to reinforce their pictures by declamatory exclamations. The very rhythms were violent, somewhat resembling those of Swinburne in English.

Benn continued writing in his expressionistic manner through and beyond the Second World War, publishing a collection of poems, *Aprèslude*, in 1955, the year before he died. He also wrote a good many essays and polemics in rather striking prose, often celebrating Nietzsche and consistently emphasizing the isolation of the poet. Benn was a striking figure in his time, but he has hardly survived it in his work, although he has been a powerful influence on recent younger Germanic poets.

Karl Kraus, the Czech-born writer who settled in Vienna, is at the opposite end of Germanic literature from Gottfried Benn. A satirist and aphorist, Kraus in 1899 founded the surprisingly long-lived journal *Die Fackel* (*The Torch*), largely a one-man paper devoted to attacking the bureaucratic abuses of the Austro-Hungarian government and, later, the First World War itself. The journal died with Kraus in 1936.

Kraus, who gave public readings of his own works as well as those of the German classics and Shakespeare, is best known for his prose satires, but he attained a good deal of fame with his panoramic drama, *Die letzten Tage der Menschheit* (1918–1922; *The Last Days of Mankind*). His poems are found in *Worte in Versen, I–IX* (1916–1930; *Words in Verse*, selections translated into English in 1930 as *Poems*). Lyrical as well as satirical, they are an important part of Austrian history of the time, but have had little currency in the world outside since their idiom is so personal and epigrammatic that they are essentially untranslatable.

The Nuremberg poet Karl Bröger (1886–1944) was another who, like Dehmel and Werfel, wrote from the trenches. He expressed his war experiences in the poems in *Kamerad, als wir marschiert* . . . (1916; *Comrade, as We March* . . .) and *Soldaten der Erde* (1918; *Soldiers of the Earth*). Like so many poets who were converted to pacifism by the war, Bröger joined radical groups in the years of peace, though he never seems to have been a Communist. He wrote one of the grimmest of war novels, *Bunker 17* (1929; translated as *Pillbox 17*). A leader of youth movements in the time of the Weimar Republic, Bröger became known as one of the labor poets. That he was taken in by Hitler is demonstrated in his novel of 1935, *Nürnberg*.

Another of the so-called labor poets, Heinrich Lersch (1889–1936) was, like Bröger, a member of what might be called the workers' wing of the expressionist movement. A lyric writer, sometimes given to mysticism and sometimes to comedy, Lersch was also one of the poets who took part in the First World War, during which he brought out three books of verse—*Abglanz des Lebens* (1914; *Reflection of Life*), *Herz, aufglühe dein Blut* (1916; *Heart, Heat Thy Blood*), and *Deutschland* (1917; *Germany*). The last is a socialistic poem, though not one recommending revolution. His earlier volumes are somewhat experimental; Lersch finds himself and at the same time draws upon German tradition in such later works as *Mensch im Eisen* (1924; *Man in Iron*), *Stern und Amboss* (1926; *Star and Anvil*), and *Mit brüderlicher Stimme* (1934; *With Brotherly Voice*), the last written two years before his death.

Still another expressionist poet, Johannes Robert Becher (1891–1958), a native of Munich, brought out a collection of verse and prose in 1914: *Verfall und Triumph* (*Decay and Triumph*). His wartime poems included *An Europa* (1916; *To Europe*), *Verbrüderung* (1916; *Fraternization*), *Gedichte für ein Volk* (1917; *Poems for a People*), and *Päan gegen die Zeit* (1918; *Paens against the Age*). His postwar volumes include *Ewig im Aufruhr* (1920; *Forever in Tumult*), *Gedichte an Lotte* (1920; *Poems to Lotte*), *Um Gott* (1921; *About God*), *Am Grabe Lenins* (1925; *At Lenin's Tomb*), *Maschinenrhythmen* (1925; *Machine Rhythms*, and *Der grosse Plan: Epos des sozialistischen Aufbaus* (1931; *The Great Plan: Epic of Socialist Building*). The titles of the latter volumes indicate Becher's consuming interest in social-political themes, which he often treated ecstatically. At the time the Hitler regime began, Becher exiled himself to Russia where he started writing in a more simplified style, in keeping with Soviet ideals, as in his *Neue Gedichte* (1933; *New Poems*) and *Sonette* (1939; *Sonnets*). After returning to Germany at the end of the Second World War, he took part in left-wing politics.

The Rhinelander Carl Zuckmayer was a dramatist and novelist as well as a poet, particularly known for his comic play *Der Hauptmann von Köpenick* (1931; *The Captain from Köpenick*), which made fun of German militarism. Zuckmayer, who in 1925 moved from Berlin to Salzburg, left Austria in 1938 after the Nazis arrived. His poems are for the most part written in a colloquial style with a deceptive ease. But he is best known as a playwright and is discussed at length among the sections devoted to German dramatists.

The poets of the between-wars period produced a few remarkable lyrics, although none of them, whether in or out of expressionism, approach the achievement of Rilke or Stefan George. But one more poet of the time deserves at least passing mention—Oskar Loerke (1884–1941). He was an expressionist with classic discipline; his pictures are often symbolic, often forceful in their imagery, but the language remains under strict control. Loerke resigned his poetry secretaryship of the Prussian Academy of Art after Hitler took over the government. The poet did not leave, but stayed on in Berlin in silent protest; he died in self-imposed loneliness. His *Gedichte und Prosa* (*Poems and Prose*) are now being brought out in a collected edition; the first volume appeared in 1958.

3

THE LATER
RILKE

In February 1922, which Rainer Maria Rilke later called his "great time,"
he was at last able to complete the *Duineser Elegien* (1922; *The Duino
Elegies*, also translated as *Duinese Elegies*) and he was also inspired to
write *Die Sonette an Orpheus* (1923; *Sonnets to Orpheus*), the latter
comprising fifty-five poems. This was perhaps the greatest blaze of
creative energy any poet has known in our century.

Rilke, as mentioned earlier, began the *Duino Elegies* in 1912. He was
visiting at the castle of Duino on the Adriatic near Trieste. Left alone one
troubled January day, he was walking on the windy cliffs above the sea
when he "heard" the words that begin "First Elegy": "Who, if I cried
out, would hear me amongst the orders of the angels?" He finished the
"Elegy" that day, and the second shortly afterward. A few more frag-
ments came before the power left him, to reappear intermittently; he
wrote parts of the "Elegies" in Spain in 1913, and finished the third
(begun at Duino) in Paris in that same year. But he could not recapture
the full force of the first inspiration until after the war, when at last he
completed the *Elegies*, which became ten in number.

The years of battle were a tormenting time for Rilke. At the outbreak
of hostilities, he was for a short while the victim of nationalist fervor, as
his letters of the time show; they also indicate that their chauvinism soon
turned sour. He was called up on January 1916, disastrously for himself,
as he wrote to his publisher Kippenberg, in one of his most revealing
letters (February 15): "I was in a rapid ascent of work. . . . I already

thought the freest prospects were ahead, when the gray army cloth fell
before my clarified vision." After some wretched experiences in the
barracks, Rilke was assigned to the War Archives in Vienna. But the hack
work involved in "hairdressing the hero" proved upsetting and frustrat-
ing. When he was released from the office at three each afternoon, he
could not "give the remainder of the day its own stamp and meaning."

Friends have reported how baffled and bewildered Rilke seemed in
military uniform; fortunately for himself and for the future of poetry,
he was soon taken out of that uniform. Frau Kippenberg circulated a
petition among leading German intellectuals, and because of this Rilke
was given permanent leave from military service. He went to Munich, but
at the end of the war when the troubles in Bavaria made daily living
there too hectic he moved to Switzerland. He had always, he told a
friend in one of his incomparable letters, through all the years of "the
affliction, the confusion, and disfigurement of the world," retained his
faith "in the great calm of the inexhaustibilities of life." And before long
his writing bloomed again in Switzerland.

In the summer of 1921, he discovered the towered old Château de
Muzot, which a friend bought and placed at his disposal. It was here that
the great inspiration came to him and he was able to finish the *Elegies*
and write the *Sonnets to Orpheus.*

The angels of the *Elegies,* as Rilke once explained, are not the angels
of the Christian heaven, but are closer to those of Islam. "The angel of
the *Elegies* is the creature in whom that transformation of the visible
into the invisible we're performing already appears complete"; this angel
is "terrible" because we still depend so largely on the visible, while the
angel stands for creative recognition of reality in the invisible. The
angels, superhuman, godlike, are the principal symbol in the *Elegies,*
pointing up the deficiencies of human nature. These angels are introduced
in the "First Elegy," as are the human lovers, who in their intensity
should be able to see the higher reality of life, but are too bound together
to do so. The lover becomes the central figure of the "Third Elegy." He
is balanced by the girl, who in turn becomes the mother, a controller of
experience and the one who drives away the child's fear, bringing him
inner peace.

The "Fourth Elegy" begins, "O trees of life, when comes your winter?"
But unlike the trees, the birds, and the rest of nature, man does not
recognize his winter when it arrives. Our enemy is what comes next, and
lovers continually find precipices in each other instead of safe spaces, the
freedom of the hunt, or home itself. The poet addresses his own father,

who would find bitterness in the necessity of the poet's life. But Rilke asks whether he was not right in looking for a meaning in life through the medium of poetry. He introduces, in conjunction with the symbol of the angel, the image of the doll, combined with the idea of a marionette controlled by the angel. A child is introduced, with the vision of death; indeed, death and life are brought together in the child himself.

The next "Elegy" was written last, but was moved up into fifth position. It is to a great extent inspired by Picasso's painting "Les Saltimbanques," which hung in a house in which the poet lived in Munich (1915). Rilke describes the acrobats as standing upon their "tattered carpet," in a circle of onlookers. The carpet signifies the rootlessness and the loneliness of the troupe. These people, "even a little more fleeting than ourselves," symbolize the instability of human life. They become most real in their moments of pure equilibrium in their performance.

The "Sixth Elegy" focuses upon the figure of the hero and those who are doomed to die young. But, despite its elegiac obsession with death, this poem flows into the seventh, which is a glorification of life itself. The world of reality is shown here as an inner entity, and it is here that the great temples and statues of our time are built. This is the most affirmative of the *Elegies*, but its note of the celebration of existence is lost in its successor. This eulogizes the animal side of man, but at a very high level. The animal lives an "open" existence, differing from our awareness of an "opposite." The animals have their terrors, but human beings are by their very nature in an even more unfortunate position. If the animal has a home in the world, man has none, subject as he is to the always "opposite." And at the end of the poem, Rilke re-emphasizes in an elegiac mood that all things must pass away.

In the "Ninth Elegy" Rilke asks why man, knowing of the sadness to which he is doomed, does not wish to abandon life. But he shows that only through its very transitoriness can the visible world be made into an invisible one, embodying the higher reality. Man must face the very concept of the finite. In this, death itself becomes friendly. In the tenth and last "Elegy," Rilke shows that life is the city of pain, and death the land of pain. Rilke projects a landscape which belongs both to this world and the next; toward the end of the poem the youth who was an allegorical traveler through these lands confronts the Sphinx with new stars above it. The poem shows the mystical happiness of the dead:

Alone, he climbs to the mountains of primal pain,
And not once are his steps heard from out of that soundless destination.

And yet, the timeless dead were creating a symbol within us,
See! they would point, perhaps, to the catkin hanging
From the empty hazel, or they would show us rain
Falling on the dark earth in early spring.

And we, who have always thought of happiness
As climbing, we would know the emotion
That almost astonishes us
When happiness falls.

The *Elegies* cannot successfully be synopsized; the only purpose in
such summarizing as that above is to point toward an understanding of
the poems by a reader newly approaching them. But with their symbols
and allegories, their great angels, their confrontation of the theme of
death-in-life, the *Elegies* are a creation that can be absorbed only after
long study. The result is worth the effort, for they greatly enrich the
reader's vision of life.

The *Sonnets to Orpheus*, written in that same burst of inspiration
which enabled Rilke to finish the *Elegies*, had as their immediate source
the death of an attractive young girl whom Rilke had known, Wera
Ouckama Knoop. Her mother had sent Rilke a note at the time her
daughter had died of a mysterious illness which caused her great suffering and physical disfiguration without damaging her spirit. Shortly after
receiving the note from Wera's mother, Rilke saw in a shopwindow a
print representing Orpheus with his lyre, and he suddenly knew that the
Orphic myth had a message for him. He began writing the *Sonnets* immediately.

If the *Elegies* are often laments, the *Sonnets*, despite their involvement
with Wera's pathetic death, are a consistent and exuberant affirmation of
life. If these *Sonnets* celebrate the Orpheus who had had a glimpse of the
after-life, they also celebrate the musician who with his lyre charmed men
and beasts. The poet, of course, is often Rilke also. Concrete, dealing
vividly with the visible world, these poems with their background of
Greek mythology represent a serenity in their acceptance of the world.

In the *Sonnets*, the song of Orpheus has no emphatic message; it
exults in pure being. Orpheus, who was not only the poet but poetry
itself, exists both in our realm and that of the beyond. The poet ranges
over earthly experience, delightedly naming the fruits of the earth in lines
that almost seem to finger them.

The first part of the *Sonnets* consists of twenty-six poems; the second series, written later, consists of twenty-nine. These are longer-lined, and freer in rhythm. The last of them is Rilke's confession of faith, ending:

> And if what is earthly has forgotten you,
> Say to the still earth: I flow.
> Say to the rapid water: I exist.

Rilke lived for another four years after completing the *Elegies* and the *Sonnets*, and wrote many shorter poems, some of them in French. And he continued to write the letters that are among the greatest by any author. During the last part of his life he suffered from ill-health and was in and out of sanitoriums. In October 1926 the thorn of a rose injured his left hand, which would not heal; in December, at the Valmont Sanitorium, the doctors found that Rilke had leukemia. As he wasted away, he told his physicians not to deaden his consciousness with pain-killing drugs. Rilke died on December 29, 1926, and was buried where he had wished to be, in the little cemetery adjoining the old church at Rarogne. He said that its enclosing wall was one of the first places from which he had received the wind and light of that landscape, along with all the other promises which it and his new home in Muzot were later to help him realize. At his funeral, without "sacredotal intervention," a Rarognan custom was observed when young girls in Valaisanne peasant dress followed his coffin up the rocky hill. Rilke's gravestone reads:

> Rose, O pure contradiction, delight
> To be the sleep of no one beneath so many
> Eyelids.

THE LATER
THOMAS MANN

The Mountain of Magic

During the First World War Thomas Mann wrote *Der Zauberberg*, first published in 1924; three years later it appeared in English translation as *The Magic Mountain*. It is beyond dispute the great philosophical novel of the twentieth century so far, the type of book the Germans know as a Bildungsroman, or educational novel. In his foreword, Mann says of the story: "We shall tell it at length, thoroughly, in detail—for when did a narrative seem too long or too short by reason of the actual time or space it took up? We do not fear being called meticulous, inclining as we do to the view that only the exhaustive can be truly interesting." Some readers find the book too exhaustive in detail; others relish the complications and depth of Mann's insights, penetrating a wide range of surfaces.

The Magic Mountain is the story of a young engineer, Hans Castorp, and of the seven years (1907–1914) he spends at the Berghof Sanitorium in Switzerland. He goes there from Hamburg to visit his cousin Joachim, a young officer who has developed a lung infection while on maneuvers. Hans, arriving in the magic upland world of the Berghof, feels dizzy with the altitude as he enters into the fantastic community. He soon meets Settembrini, a spinsterishly fussy Italian liberal, and from a distance he sees the slant-eyed, Tartar-faced Russian woman Clavdia Chauchat, married to a Frenchman who is not at the Berghof. In a fevered dream recalling his youth, Hans remembers his boyish attachment for a schoolmate with an exotic face very much like Clavdia's. The shy Hans dared approach this schoolmate once only, to borrow a somewhat emblematic red-and-silver pencil. The grown-up Hans suddenly begins to have fevers at the Berghof, and when he goes to the head doctor, Behrens, he discovers that he is tuberculous and prepares for a long sojourn at the sanitorium where he will be near the attractive Slavic woman. As in the case of his schoolyard romance, however, Hans does not dare approach Clavdia.

Hans and Joachim become the frequent conversational targets of Settembrini and, later, of a man named Naphta, a Jew who has been brought up by the Jesuits. Joachim apparently understands little of their arguments, or at least he remains aloof as Hans becomes the battleground for the clashing ideas of the two older men. Ironically, Settembrini, who is the embodiment of humanism and political liberalism, is narrow-minded, self-indulgent, and cranky; Naphta, who represents authoritarianism, both in his church background and in his subservience to communist doctrine, is on the other hand spiritually generous, tolerant, aesthetic. Hans, who has had an engineer's training, is for the first time battered by political and liberal-arts ideas, and in the long periods of rest at the sanitorium he becomes a voracious reader on virtually every subject relating to both humanism and science.

A year passes before Hans approaches Clavdia, and he does this only on a carnival night, when gaiety and pretense reign. During a game in which the revelers in paper caps are drawing pictures, Hans shyly goes to Clavdia and borrows another of those symbolic red-and-silver pencils which are so important in this novel. Hans and Clavdia begin to talk; not daring to speak to her in his own language, he addresses her in French, the language not only of diplomacy but of romance, a tongue native to neither of them: they meet on a middle ground. Here Hans feels bold and, calling upon his recent reading of books on anatomy, he exalts the human body in a Whitmanesque rapture. Clavdia tells him he is "joli bourgeois à la petite tâche humide." He proposes that they go to Clavdia's room. At the end of the striking scene, there is a subtle but unmistakable suggestion that they do go there. Clavdia, leaving her pencil, departs, but stops in the doorway and says softly over her shoulder: "N'oubliez pas de me rendre mon crayon."

Clavdia goes away from the sanitorium the next day and does not return until sometime later, and then in the company of a gigantic Dutch planter, Pieter Peeperkorn. He is a genially demonic figure, apparently introduced by Mann at this point to take some of the strain away from the intense concentration on intellectual matters. Peeperkorn is almost inarticulate and can rarely utter a coherent sentence, but he has everyone hanging in attendance upon him. He represents not only the mysterious and instinctual life force, but also, at another level, he is a Resurrection figure perhaps combining both Christ and Pan; there is even a Last Supper scene.

Peeperkorn dies, as do several other characters in the novel, which has a background chorus of pulpy coughs and continual reminders of the presence of death. But Peeperkorn is a suicide. Naphta likewise takes his own life—in the middle of a duel with Settembrini. Joachim, who has against the doctors' orders returned to his military duties in the flatlands, comes back to the sanitorium ravaged by his illness and soon dies; and various other figures in the book are carried down the mountainside in coffins. At the end of the story, war has broken out, and the reader's last glimpse of Hans is as a skirmisher advancing toward the enemy through a wood. Typically, the book ends with a question mark.

Since Mann's method is so detailed, his reader is given an education almost as thorough as Hans's. From medicine to music, from literature and philosophy to politics, many modern points of view are dramatically analyzed. Psychology, too, comes in for a diagnosis, although at the time he wrote the book Mann was not so well acquainted with the doctrines of Freud as he was to become later; but what he did not know he apprehended intuitively. Some of the most striking passages in the book, which is full of such comic grotesqueries, concern the Saturday-morning sessions of the doctor who is second in command to Behrens, Krokowsky; he compels the patients to listen to his theoretic exposition of the idea that illnesses are psychosomatic and that his listeners are present on the mountaintop not because they merely have a physical disease of the lungs, but because they have been disappointed in love or have erotically frustrated themselves. As he gloats over them, the patients listening to the lectures sit writhing in a kind of unhappy joy.

Hans, in the great chapter "Snow," in which he is lost in the mountains and has a terrible vision, comes to the conclusion that "it is love, not reason, that is stronger than death." And on this occasion Hans also realizes that "all interest in disease and death is only another expression of interest in life"—which might be taken as the motto of the book.

Mann frequently speaks tenderly of his hero as a mediocre young man, but in coming to understand the arguments on the magic mountain, Hans becomes what Mann calls a "lord of counterpositions," and a "genius of experience." The ending shows the enlightened Hans, "Life's delicate child," taking Joachim's place in the army:

Farewell—and if thou livest or diest! Thy prospects are poor. The desperate dance, in which thy fortunes are caught up, will last yet many a sinful year; we should not care to set a high stake on thy life by the time it ends. We even confess that it is without great concern we leave the question open. Adventures of the flesh and in the spirit, while enhancing thy simplicity, granted thee to know in the spirit what in the flesh thou scarcely couldst have done. Moments there were, when out of death, and the rebellion of the flesh, there came to thee, as thou tookest stock of thyself, a dream of love. Out of this universal feast of death, out of this extremity of fever, kindling the rain-washed evening sky to a fiery glow, may it be that Love one day shall mount?

This translation (by Helen Tracy Lowe-Porter) of that paragraph, which is properly faithful, unfortunately has an antiquated effect in English because of the use of the second-person familiar locution, so appropriate in the German original. But the passage gives some idea of the scope of the book, the vastness of the ideas encompassed. Perhaps *The Magic Mountain* is not so widely read as it was years ago, but surely it will stand high among the novels of the century; it is Goethean and Tolstoyan in the grandness of its conception and in the elaborate skillfulness of its writing.

Mario and Joseph

In 1930 Thomas Mann published another of his remarkable short novels, *Mario und der Zauberer* (*Mario and the Magician*), the story of a sensational event at an Italian seaside resort where a German family is on holiday. Although in *Mario* the element of pure story is as strong as the allegorical, this novella should have made it clear to the Nazis who later tried to assimilate Mann that he was extremely antagonistic to the kind of authoritarianism embodied in fascism. Cipolla, the arrogant magician and hypnotist who makes the simple waiter Mario look ridiculous at a public demonstration, is a figure emblematic of fascism, and is not unlike Mussolini himself. *Mario*, a story of the dignity of freedom in the face of oppression, is told with all of Mann's narrative and dramatic skill, and is invested with his supreme ability at capturing atmosphere. Although, almost until the time of the Second World War, Mann regarded himself as somewhat of a political innocent, this story puts him in the class of prophetic authors. It is the first attempt in imaginative literature by a major writer to show the evils of twentieth-century totalitarianism.

Between 1933 and 1943 Thomas Mann wrote the tetralogy *Joseph und seine Brüder*, translated into English as *Joseph and His Brothers* (in England, *The Tale of Jacob*). The individual volumes are: *Die Geschichten Jaakobs* (1933; *The Tales of Jacob*), *Der junge Joseph* (1934; *Young Joseph*), *Joseph in Ägypten* (1936; *Joseph in Egypt*), and *Joseph, der Ernährer* (1943; *Joseph the Provider*). Mann once traced the original inspiration for these books to a series of illustrations for the story of Joseph for which he was asked to write an introduction shortly after he had completed *The Magic Mountain*; he had always been interested in the Egyptian past, and he recalled Goethe's statement that although the Joseph story in the Bible was charming it seemed too brief and called for more detailed treatment.

Mann had thought that his own version of the story would, as he had first envisioned *The Magic Mountain*, be a short novel, but the tetralogy spread to more than twenty-one hundred pages. Again in a Mann novel, the treatment is exhaustive: archeologically, anthropologically, religiously, and psychologically. The outlines of the Joseph story are so well known that they do not need summarizing here; it is enough to say that Mann developed the characters, not only Joseph—who is seen from early youth into maturity—but shrewd old Jacob, as well as Rachel and Leah, Potiphar and his wife, and a gallery of others, some of them Mann's own invention, all of whom help give life to the crowded panorama. As in *The Magic Mountain*, theories about time are important. The narrative is often laboriously philosophical and requires a devoted reader who, however, will find the story intensively rewarding if he stays with it.

Mann wrote this book across a decade during which he was uprooted like Joseph. But the calm and stateliness of the writing are an unusual tribute to the profound concentration of an artist caught up in the turmoil of events of the 1930's and 1940's.

Because Mann did not openly denounce the Nazis when they were rising to power, they thought that they might win the Nobel Prize winner of 1929 to their side, and they were apparently willing to overlook the fact that his wife was Jewish. But Mann never spoke or wrote in favor of Nazism. In the spring of 1933, when he and Frau Mann were on vacation in Switzerland, they received a telephone call from Munich from their son Klaus and their daughter Erika, who told the elder Manns that the weather was bad in Munich and that they had better remain where they were. The younger Manns arrived in Switzerland the next day and explained to their parents that they would be in danger if they returned to Germany. Later, Erika Mann stole back to the family home near Munich and rescued the manuscript of *Joseph and His Brothers*, dodging the Nazis and slipping over the border into Switzerland.

Mann waited until 1936 to attack the Nazis as enemies of Christian and Occidental morality and civilization, after which the German government deprived him of German citizenship and even of his honorary degree from the University of Bonn. Mann then wrote to the rector of Bonn a denunciation of fascism published in *Ein Briefwechsel* (1937; *An Exchange of Letters*). And from then on Mann was known as one of the champions of liberty in the Western world.

The Faustian Questions

In 1938, Mann moved to the United States, living first at Princeton, New Jersey, and later at Pacific Palisades, California. It was there that he wrote *Doktor Faustus* (1947; *Doctor Faustus*), which ranks with *The Magic Mountain* and the *Joseph* series among his greatest novels. Mann worked on this book during the distraction of the war years, of lecture tours, and of a critical operation on his chest, all described in an absorbing narrative of more than two hundred pages, *Die Entstehung des Doktor Faustus* (1949; *The Story of a Novel: The Genesis of Doctor Faustus*).

Doctor Faustus is the Faust legend applied to the destruction of Germany under the Nazis. Mann's Faustus is the composer Adrian Leverkühn who, like his forerunner, sells himself to the Devil. Other details of the Faust legend appear in the story, in contemporary guise, and some of Leverkühn's experiences are taken from the life of Nietzsche. The action is seen through the eyes of Leverkühn's lifelong friend, Serenus Zeitblom, who watches with horror as both Leverkühn and Germany sink deeper into Satanism. A great part of the book is devoted to technical discussions of music, and Leverkühn composes somewhat in the fashion of Arnold Schönberg (who, incidentally, was infuriated by the book).

Full of Mann's usual irony, *Doctor Faustus* also has a demonic quality which no one else since Dostoevsky had captured so successfully in literature. The people and events in the story are illuminated with a terrible reality, and altogether *Doctor Faustus* is the greatest imaginative depiction of the frenzied events that led to the Second World War. Indeed, the novel is the masterpiece among all books so far written since that war; there are fine novels by Albert Camus and others, and several striking plays, but for scope, intensity, and the ring of true greatness, nothing since it appeared has surpassed *Doctor Faustus*.

Mann's Last Works

But if *Doctor Faustus* was the crown of Mann's career, it was not quite the end of it, for he still had several more books to write. While working on the *Joseph* stories, he had brought out an amusing novel about Goethe, *Lotte in Weimar* (1939; translated as *The Beloved Returns*), an ironic comedy of the visit of one of Goethe's sweethearts (the model for the heroine of *Werther*) who comes to visit him in his age. After *Doctor Faustus*, Mann wrote *Der Erwählte* (1951; *The Chosen One*, translated as *The Holy Sinner*), *Die Betrogene* (1953; *The Deceived One*, translated as *The Black Swan*), and *Bekenntnisse des Hochstaplers Felix Krull: Der Memoiren erster Teil* (1954; *The Confessions of the Swindler Felix Krull: the First Part of the Memoirs*, translated as *Confessions of Felix Krull*). *The Holy Sinner* is a short novel which reworks the old legend of Pope Gregory and amusingly mixes in some incest. Another short novel, *The Black Swan*, tells of the love of a middle-aged German woman for a young American; it is probably the extreme point of Mann's irony, for the flow of blood which the woman mistakes for a resurgence of youth is the beginning of the death process. *Felix Krull* was the revision of an earlier novella, the comic story of a confidence man. Mann had published only the first part of it and intended to write a sequel, but before he could do this he died in 1955 in Switzerland of a brain hemorrhage at the age of eighty. His reputation has somewhat diminished since then, as is often the case of authors who are famous in their own lifetime, but Mann's work will certainly stand among the highest mountain ranges of twentieth-century literature.

5

OTHER GERMAN
AND AUSTRIAN
NOVELISTS

Hermann Sudermann: Magda *and Beyond*

Hermann Sudermann, the oldest of the twentieth-century Germanic novelists (born in 1857), was also in his time a playwright, but since his death in 1928 his fiction has proved of more enduring value than his dramatic work. Indeed, his greatest success as a dramatist was in the nineteenth century; the plays he wrote in the twentieth were insufficiently adapted to the new theater to win over the younger generation of the time.

With *Heimat* (*Home,* translated into English as *Magda*), Sudermann in 1893 followed up the success of his earlier work, such as his first play, *Die Ehre* (1889; *Honor*), and became a world-renowned dramatist. He then wrote *Johannisfeuer* (1900; *St. John's Fire*), *Es lebe das Leben* (1902; *The Joy of Living*), *Stein unter Steinen* (1905; *A Stone Among Stones*), *Blumenboot* (1905; *The Flowerboat*), *Der Bettler von Syrakus* (1911; *The Beggar of Syracuse*), and *Der gute Ruf* (1912; *A Good. Reputation*)—but with these plays Sudermann failed to repeat his earlier success; he came particularly under the fire of Germany's most prominent drama critic, Alfred Kerr, who pointed out that Sudermann's plays were tricksy and merely technically smooth. Today he is best remembered for his *Litauische Geschichten* (1917; *Lithuanian Tales,* translated as *The Excursion to Tilsit*).

This book reflects the atmosphere of the broad plains and the land-locked waters of his East Prussian homeland, also found in his novel

Die Frau des Steffen Tromholt (1927; *The Wife of Steffen Tromholt*), which as a film, starring Peggy Wood and Lewis Stone, was one of the first Hollywood talking pictures. Sudermann had begun as a novelist with *Frau Sorge* (translated as *Dame Care*) in 1887, whose value was not recognized until after he had attained fame as a playwright. *Bilderbuch meiner Jugend* (1922; *Picture of My Youth*) was straight autobiography, while *Der tolle Professor* (1926; *The Mad Professor*) contained some autobiographical elements; these portray Sudermann's experiences at the University of Königsberg, showing him as a poor, intellectual student who was, however, a dueler and an ardent dancer.

Germany's Leading Woman Novelist

The woman novelist Ricarda Huch, a native of Braunschweig and seven years younger than Sudermann, was a far more remarkable writer. Indeed, Ricarda Huch, who died at eighty-three in 1947, was the leading woman novelist of Germany in her time and one of the finest woman writers of the modern world.

Her fame began in 1893 with *Erinnerungen von Ludolf Ursleu dem Jüngeren* (*Recollections of Ludolf Ursleu the Younger*) which has correspondences with Thomas Mann's somewhat later *Buddenbrooks*. In *Recollections,* Ludolf Ursleu looks back upon the tragic destiny of his patrician Hamburg family, centering around the fatal love of Ezard and Galeide, who meet in secret. The deterioration of Galeide leads to her debasement of love.

Frau Huch (her second marriage was to a cousin of the same last name) wrote novels which fall essentially into three categories: romantic and idealistic; biographical stories about the Italian Risorgimento; and philosophical. One of her most impressive historical works was *Der grosse Krieg in Deutschland* (1912–1914; *The Great War in Germany*).

Schnitzler and the Spirit of Vienna

Arthur Schnitzler is known mostly as a dramatist, but in many of his novels he caught the Viennese spirit of his plays. Perhaps his most notable novel is *Der Weg ins Freie* (1908; *The Road to Freedom*). Its leading character, Georg von Wergenthin, has a love affair with Anna Rosner, who has hopes of going on the stage. When she becomes pregnant, they go to Italy together, where their child is born dead. Georg, who after the death of his father has given up his law studies, wants to enter the musical world. He suggests to Anna that they resume their love affair, which she does not wish to do without marriage; he leaves, on the road to freedom, to become an orchestral conductor in an Austrian town. Georg feels no remorse, particularly after a philosophical friend tells him that Anna was perhaps intended to be his mistress, but never his wife. And in other novels, novellas, and stories, Schnitzler again caught the worldliness of Vienna; in *Casanovas Heimfahrt* (1918; *Casanova's Homecoming*), he dipped into the eighteenth century to project the wry account of a love affair in which Casanova indulged in the twilight of his life. Schnitzler, dying in 1931, outlived by fifteen years the Dual Monarchy of whose declining days he provided the most typical pictures.

Jakob Wassermann: Ersatz Dostoevsky

Jakob Wassermann, who died three years after Schnitzler, took a more serious view of life in Austria and Germany in the first decades of the twentieth century; and he attempted greater profundity. Wassermann who, like Schnitzler, was a Jew, was born in a factory town near Nuremberg. In his youth he worked there, as well as in Munich and Vienna, settling finally in a farmhouse in Styria after marrying a Viennese girl. Wassermann's first novel, *Geschichte der jungen Renate Fuchs* (*The Tale of Young Renate Fuchs*), appeared in 1900. His first great success was *Caspar Hauser* (1908), a sympathetic treatment of a famous historical case. *Das Gänsemännchen* (1915; *The Little Goose Man*) took as its central symbol a famous statue in Nuremberg. Wassermann's most ambitious book was the two-volume novel *Christian Wahnschaffe* (1918; translated as *The World's Illusion*), a story of a wealthy, idle young man who is first seen engrossed in a love affair with the famous dancer, Eva Sorel. Later he gives up his worldly life and goes to live in poverty in the slums, where he falls in love with a Jewish girl, Ruth Hoffmann. She is brutally murdered by a Jack-the-Ripper type, whom Christian forgives for his deed. At the end of the story, which had so realistically described so many strata of European society, Christian is heard of as a wandering, rather Franciscan figure, appearing in different parts of the world to help those in trouble.

This novel made Wassermann internationally renowned, and he was often considered the peer of Thomas Mann. Wassermann was, however, essentially superficial and sentimental, a kind of ersatz Dostoevsky; and his books are neglected today. In *The World's Illusion*, however, he was the literary ancestor of the later Austrian novelists Hermann Broch, Robert Musil, and Heimito von Doderer.

Franz Kafka: The Incredible Adventures of K

The writer who comes the closest to challenging Thomas Mann for first position among the Germanic novelists of the era is Franz Kafka (1883–1924), son of a Jewish family in Prague. As a student at the German University there, Kafka met the novelist Max Brod, who was to become his biographer and literary executor. After taking his doctorate in jurisprudence in 1908, Kafka went to work for a government insurance bureau in Prague, where he remained until forced to retire by ill health shortly after the First World War. Not long before that conflict began, Kafka had started to write stories. A sufferer from tuberculosis, he finished none of his three novels, all of which were published after his death in 1924: *Der Prozess* (1925; *The Trial*), *Das Schloss* (1926; *The Castle*), and *Amerika* (1927).

Kafka also left behind a number of short stories, journals, letters, and epigrams. He had wanted to have all his manuscripts destroyed, but fortunately Max Brod took the responsibility of giving them to the world.

The Trial is the story of a man named Joseph K, a bank employé who one morning is mysteriously arrested in his rooming house by two strangers. After a series of odd examinations in which the charges against him are never quite specified, Joseph is brought before a judge and undergoes a nebulous trial. Not confined to jail, Joseph wanders about the city, but can find no one able to enlighten him as to the reasons for his arrest; a priest tells him he will probably be convicted of the crime of which he is accused, although neither the priest nor Joseph knows what the crime is. But finally two men in frock coats appear at Joseph's rooming house and take him to a quarry, where they stab him in the heart.

Even in bare outline, the story will be seen as an allegory. What it means, however, is in dispute among Kafka's interpreters, who continually battle as to whether Kafka was primarily an artist or a metaphysician. His work undoubtedly has philosophical, even religious elements, but Kafka was essentially an artist, a very great one.

As a novel *The Trial* is full of realistic details and convincing psychological development; whatever its meaning, *The Trial* reveals itself to the reader as a compelling story of modern man. The same holds true of *The Castle*, whose central figure is a land surveyor known only as K.

Engaged to work in the grounds of the castle of Count West-west, K arrives at the adjoining village and discovers that he cannot get into the castle grounds. Those connected with the castle admit that he has been employed there, but he still cannot gain admittance. K settles down in the village, becoming the janitor at the local school. He involves himself in love affairs with two girls in the town, but all his efforts to get into the castle are frustrated. There are indications that Kafka, if he had finished the book, intended to let K get into the castle.

This novel has been called a *Pilgrim's Progress*, and some students of Jewish theology have even found it to be the projection of cabalistic doctrines. Various critics have spoken of it as one of the monuments of the modern symbolist school, and the Freudians have had many a turn at it. Certainly, among other things, Kafka must have been making fun of the bureaucracy of the Dual Monarchy, which he knew so thoroughly. The village in the story is supposed to be based upon one which he had lived in during a period of recuperation from a bout of illness, but the reader should always remember that Kafka grew up in the fabled city of Prague, which is full of fantastic castles. Despite the story's various levels of symbolic meaning, it is never unreal, but is full of verisimilitude. There have been many imitations of the technique of *The Castle*, but none of them has even come near to matching it in effectively showing the struggle of modern man against the compulsive forces of his world.

Kafka's other novel, *Amerika*, is a fantastic comedy about a land its author had never visited. A young German named Karl Rossman goes to America, where he lives with his millionaire uncle, meets a number of odd representatives of the country, and falls in love with a girl named Clara. After wandering across the land, Karl becomes happily involved with the Nature Theater of Oklahoma, at which point this unfinished story breaks off. Done in a lighter vein than most of the rest of Kafka's work, *Amerika* has a series of sharper and more provocative characterizations.

Among Kafka's shorter works, the novella *Der Verwandlung* (1916; *The Metamorphosis*) is the most famous and typical. It begins with the description of a young clerk waking up in the morning; he has been transformed into a man-sized cockroach. Gregor Samsa, who has been the main support of his family, is suddenly treated by its members as a thing of horror. He is locked in his room, and occasionally his sister who was very fond of him will, with a look of distaste, leave him a plate of food and then flee. Once Gregor gets out into the other rooms of the apartment; his father in terror throws an apple at him which becomes embedded in his roach's crust and festers there. Poor Gregor, shoved back into his room, eventually dies in it. *The Metamorphosis* is another example of Kafka's ability to write a story at once realistic and allegorical, lending itself to many possible interpretations but showing, as always, the degraded position of modern man.

In his life, Kafka was regarded as a cheerful companion. He had several love affairs, but refused to marry the girl he was engaged to. Cadaverous and feverish, he died in his early forties. He has often been regarded as a forerunner of the existentialists, in the way in which he presents the dilemma of mankind in an alien world.

Hermann Hesse and the Oriented Vision

Another novelist who deserves mention along with Mann and Kafka is Hermann Hesse, born in 1877 in the Black Forest region of Germany; from 1912 until his death in 1962, he lived in Switzerland, of which country he became a citizen. He began his writing career as a poet, with *Romantische Lieder* (1899; *Romantic Songs*), but achieved his first great success with a novel, *Peter Camenzind*, in 1904.

In this story, Peter, a rather cloddish young man from the uplands, after encountering the sophistication of the younger student-and-artist set of the cities, returns to his native Nimikon with his almost Franciscan simplicity reawakened. This and Hesse's other early writings marked him as a member of the school of Heimatkunst, which was preoccupied with regional or local themes and scenery.

The son and grandson of missionaries, Hesse in 1911 went to India, which appears from time to time in his subsequent work. This was first manifested in *Aus Indien* (*From India*) in 1913.

Many of Hesse's German friends broke with him because of his refusal to support the cause of the Central Powers in the First World War. In 1914 he published an essay which takes its title from a line of Schiller which Beethoven used in his Ninth Symphony: *O Freunde, nicht diese Töne* (*O Friends, Not These Sounds*). The essay attacked the German chauvinism of the time.

Living in Berne, a center of Freudian studies, Hesse became interested in psychoanalysis, as shown in his novel *Demian* (1919). This is the first-person story of a hypersensitive young man, Emil Sinclair, who was originally put down as the author of the book; it was not until the tenth edition that Hesse's own name appeared on the title page. *Demian* presents the double nature of man in terms of Cain and Abel, of the bright world of home and security as against the dark world of poverty and evil. The story is essentially a Bildungsroman of Sinclair's efforts to adjust himself to both worlds. He is partly awakened to intellectual realization by his somewhat older friend, Max Demian, and eventually he becomes acquainted with Demian's mother, a mystic known as Mother Eve. In addition to experiencing trouble with a blackmailer, Sinclair meets members of various sects: vegetarians, Tolstoyists, and devotés of the Eastern religions. Like Hans Castorp in Thomas Mann's *The Magic Mountain,* Sinclair is dragged into the war just as he completes his education. But *Demian* does not end with a question mark as *The Magic Mountain* does, with Hans Castorp a skirmisher advancing through a wood. Sinclair is actually wounded and, as he recovers, he continues his quest for self-realization in both the bright and the dark worlds.

Hesse's *Siddhartha* (1922) is an epic of India, a full dramatization of the father-son relationship, the quest of a son seeking his spiritual self in the world as he gradually moves away from paternal influence.

If *Demian* was a novel of Dostoevskian intensity, so was *Der Steppenwolf* (1927; *The Wolf of the Steppes,* translated as *Steppenwolf*). Hesse had examined Dostoevsky in his volume consisting of three essays, *Blick ins Chaos* (1920; *Looking into Chaos*), which helped influence T. S. Eliot when he was composing *The Waste Land. Steppenwolf,* Hesse's best-known novel throughout the world, concerns an odd figure named Harry Haller, who keeps in perennial disorder the attic room which he has rented in a lodging house. One day he disappears, leaving behind a manuscript which he has written. It tells how Haller has become a split personality, and how his ordered bourgeois self has been invaded by the spirit of a wolf from the steppes.

Haller becomes involved with two women. One of them, Hermine, to whom he has told his secret, attempts to help him; he suspects her of having a lesbian relationship with the other woman, Maria. Another friend of Haller's, Pablo, is a saxophonist who is also a drug peddler; he sympathizes with Haller's liking for Mozart and even with his dislike of jazz. At the end of the story Pablo takes Haller and Hermine, who has been dressed as a man and dancing with women, to a magic theater where in a corridor of mirrors Haller sees his various selves. In a fantastic scene in which he finds Hermine and Pablo naked together, Haller stabs Hermine; but when brought into court he is assisted by Mozart and is sentenced to eternal life. Pablo chides Haller for having spoiled the comedy of his magic theater by stabbing Hermine and by

spattering their illusory world with the mud of reality. At this, Pablo
takes up the body of Hermine, who shrinks to the dimensions of a doll
which he immediately puts into his pocket: "Suddenly Haller understood
everything, understood Pablo and understood the Mozart whom he had
found playing Handel on the radio. One day he knew he would learn
how to laugh; Pablo was waiting for him, and so was Mozart."

Synopsis does scant justice to the power of Hesse's writing, the power
with which he can grip the reader as he takes him through the dark,
chaotic side of existence which Hesse believes must be absorbed before
there can be a true realization of the other, more peaceful side. *Steppenwolf* is, among other things—like Thomas Mann's *Doctor Faustus*—a
symbolic picture of the Germany in which the Nazis rose. Haller may
be partly saved because he wants to understand laughter and because
of his enduring love of Mozart; but there is much in the book that
remains dark and given over to depravity.

In *Narziss und Goldmund* (1930; translated as *Death and the Lover*),
Hesse tells the story of a scholarly abbot, Narziss, whose pupil, Goldmund, goes out into the world to experience the dark side of life in the
sensuality of Vienna. This book has been called by Thomas Mann "a
poetic novel unique in its purity and fascination" and "a spiritual paradox
of the most appealing kind," the paradox being the spiritual union of
Narziss and Goldmund, despite their differing concepts of human
existence.

Das Glasperlenspiel (1943; *The Game of Beads*) was particularly
mentioned by the Swedish Academy in awarding Hesse the Nobel Prize
in 1946, the same year in which the staunch opponent of Nazism went
to Frankfurt to accept the Goethe Prize, which he hoped did not mean
that "the official Germany" recognized him: "My relationship to that
enigmatic people has always been thorny and intricate, two-edged and
difficult."

Das Glasperlenspiel, originally translated into English as *Magister
Ludi*, is a utopian novel set in a balanced future which, nevertheless,
contains some elements that may upset its equilibrium. Hesse's own time
is spoken of contemptuously as the age of digest or the journalistic age,
a period of intellectual triviality. The Castilian order, a sacred and semi-
secret group which preserves what is good from the heritage of the past,
educates the hero, Joseph Knecht, at its monastery, and at last he becomes
Magister Ludi, the Master of the Game. This game is centered in the
glass beads which represent the highest artistic and religious thought.
But Knecht, eventually wearying of the high and pure Castilian atmos-

phere, goes out into the world; he soon drowns while swimming in a lake in Switzerland. Knecht's death, like his life, becomes a lasting inspiration to the pupil he has brought with him from the ideal community.

The Game of Beads is a difficult allegory carried on largely through high-level discussions, and with almost no action. The book has, nevertheless, been popular in Germany; Thomas Mann told Hesse that he felt strongly "how much the element of parody, the fiction and persiflage of a biography based upon learned conjectures, in short the verbal playfulness, helped keep within limits this late book, with its dangerously advanced intellectuality, and contributed to its dramatic effectiveness."

Not so profound in his philosophical novels as Thomas Mann, and not so deeply involved in the tragedy of existence as Kafka, Hesse is nevertheless a writer of stature because of his synthesis of ideas, his evocation of atmospheres and, above all, his highly charged prose.

Two Remarkable Austrians: Broch and Musil

Hermann Broch (1886–1951) and Robert Musil (1880–1942) are two Austrian novelists who have become famous throughout the world since the Second World War. World recognition of Broch's work came for the most part before that of Musil, whose *Der Mann ohne Eigenschaften* (translated, in part, as *The Man Without Qualities*) has made its way slowly, particularly in the non-Germanic countries.

Broch was born in Vienna, the son of a manufacturer who hoped the boy would engage in the family business. He studied mathematics and philosophy at the University of Vienna and, in France, at Mulhouse; as an apprentice engineer he visited the United States in 1906 to learn American technics. In Austria he became a high-ranking executive, and by 1916 was general manager of the Austrian Textile Concern. He also became involved in Viennese literary circles and spent much of his time with avant-garde writers at the Café Zentral. Broch was waiting his moment; assured that he and his wife were financially secure, he broke away from his business interests and between 1930 and 1932 wrote a trilogy, *Die Schlafwandler* (1930–1932; *The Sleepwalkers*), which brought him immediate fame in Austria and Germany and, in translation, in the English-speaking countries.

The Sleepwalkers, which Broch called an essay in philosophy, begins with *Pasenow*, the story of Lieutenant Pasenow in 1888: it has been translated as *The Romantic*. The second part, *Esch*, concerns a clerk of that name in 1903 and has been translated as *The Anarchist*. The final section, set in 1918, is *Huguenau, or The Realist*. The three stories, in which some of the same characters keep recurring, is a picture of the decay of modern Germany and a prophecy of the kind of life the Nazis would produce.

In *The Romantic*, Joachim von Pasenow is the friend of Eduard von Bertrand, who resigns from the army to enter business. But Pasenow remains in the army despite his father's wish that he should retire to look after the family estate. Pasenow has formed a liaison with a Czech girl, Ruzena, who alternates between prostitution and the chorus line. Believing that Bertrand is an evil influence on Pasenow, Ruzena shoots and wounds him slightly. Both Bertrand and Pasenow are in love with Elisabeth Baddenson, who finally marries Pasenow. Yet the man who has had a mistress cannot bring himself to make love to his wife on their wedding night; he is more frightened and shy than Elisabeth. The book ends with the simple statement that, nevertheless, they had a child a year and a half later. In this first part of the story, it is Joachim von Pasenow who is the romantic, regarding the military uniform as the priest's robe of the later world. But Eduard von Bertrand, increasingly successful as a cotton importer, knows how precarious this world is, knows how much peril lies beneath its romantic façade.

In the second section of *The Sleepwalkers*, a lower order of society comes into view; only Eduard von Bertrand, from the opening part, plays an important role in the second. (Ruzena appears in one striking scene.) Bertrand has now become an important figure in the world of finance and, as head of a shipping company, he travels up and down the Rhine in a yacht manned by handsome young sailors. One of the company's clerks, August Esch, digs up evidence that Bertrand is a homosexual, but even the socialist newspaper will not print this. After Esch has confronted him, Bertrand commits suicide. Esch, who has no standards and cares little for anyone, is an anarchist in more than one sense; among other things he is an emotional anarchist. He swings between the lower levels of the business world and the outer edges of theater life—two of his friends are a dagger-thrower and his target, and another is a low-grade manager. Esch, who is married by the end of the book, can always get a job: the world of anarchy thrives underneath the façade of apparently successful capitalism which, however, is always at the edge of suicide.

In the concluding part of the trilogy, the desperate anarchy of 1918 is in the ascendant. Esch is now a public spokesman, for in the area of Kur Trier he edits the *Herald*. He later loses the paper by the trickery of Wilhelm Huguenau, who has deserted from the army; he even fools Joachim von Pasenow, a major stationed in the town, who half-consciously realizes that Huguenau is a fraud. Huguenau is also an emotional anarchist, one capable of outdoing Esch along these lines; indeed, he is a realist who knows how to seize the main chance. An Alsatian, he can speak either German or French—the author states that the family name was probably Hugenau before the French took Alsace in 1692—and in his slippery way he can go from one dialect to another, as he can go from one attitude to another. He is the man who triumphs in the 1918 riots, which drive Pasenow into madness: Huguenau rapes Esch's wife and stabs Esch to death. Huguenau later marries well, his business thrives, and he will probably become Bürgermeister.

Few authors in this century have written so prophetically. Broch foresaw the disease that was to eat its way through Germany. His trilogy is impressive, despite many circumlocutions and intricate philosophical passages, and the introduction of such lyric interludes as "Story of the Salvation Army Girl in Berlin." There are also discourses on the decay of values. If these sections arrest the narrative, particularly in the third part, they also broaden and deepen the theme. Broch becomes almost expressionistic in his technique as the novel goes on. Through a few representative characters, he shows at various levels, and usually with great effectiveness, how millions of people sleepwalked their way toward disaster while a few "realists" without conscience, such as Huguenau, cheated and murdered their way to security and power.

Broch's next novel was shorter, more conventional in form and tone, and rather flat. *Die unbekannte Grösse* (1933; *The Unknown Quantity*) is the story of Richard Hieck, a mathematician and astronomer who lives amid a smug Bürger family and is emotionally closed off in his own abstract problems. But two events bring him closer to human feeling: the suicide of his younger brother, Otto, and his growing love for one of his colleagues, Ilse Nydhalm. Hieck at last learns the meaning of what he had once said to a professor—that mathematics and reality are mixed together. Broch has some interesting points to make, but *The Unknown Quantity*, as a novel, represents low-pressure writing.

Die Entsühnung (*The Expiation*), Broch's play, was published in 1934, and he wrote several short stories. The Nazis imprisoned him for a time, but by 1939 Broch succeeded in getting to America, where he died in New Haven in 1951 at the age of sixty-four. Born a Jew, Broch converted to Catholicism, but toward the end of his life he planned to return to the religion of his fathers. In the United States, where he was awarded Guggenheim and other fellowships, he researched at Princeton and lectured on German literature at Yale. The most important work of his last years was *Der Tod des Vergil* (1945; *The Death of Virgil*, which will be discussed in the following paragraphs). Subsequently he brought out *Die Schuldlosen* (1950; *The Innocent Ones*), which combines some earlier stories and sketches with new materials to make up another panoramic novel, covering the years 1913, 1923, and 1933; the total effect is rather scattered and far less satisfactory than *The Sleepwalkers* in its use of simultaneity and of surrealist elements. Broch's posthumously published *Der Versucher* (1953; *The Tempter*) is more satisfactory in its concrete depiction of the evils wrought by a vagrant fanatic in the Austrian Alps, a novel which in theme somewhat resembles Jean Giono's *Joy of Man's Desiring;* in *The Tempter*, left in rough draft at the author's death but reconstructed from his papers, Broch returned to traditional narrative.

He had gone further away from it in *The Death of Virgil* than most novelists of his time had gone. The announced theme of the book was that of the great poet looking back from his deathbed on the meaning of life in the ancient world, and forward to its significance in the world to come. There is in it little that can be called a story, for it is really a poem (part of it written in verse), and the progression is more along the musical than the customary narrative line. Much of the space is taken up with Virgil's philosophic confrontation of death; the action occurs in a very limited time, barely more than a few hours, and there are several flashbacks: Virgil's past life projects itself into his dying mood as a present thing that sometimes whispers to him about events of the moment. There are of course some fairly realistic passages, one of which describes the arrival of Augustus's fleet at Brundisium and tells how the ailing poet is taken off one of the ships in a litter and carried through Misery Street. This is tangible, and it shows that Broch could have written a convincingly realistic book. The interview between Virgil and Augustus is a clever tête-à-tête about the problems of the *Æneid* and of statesmanship; during it, Virgil, as if anticipating his reputation in the Middle Ages, prophesies the coming of a savior. The scene is somewhat in the vein of Walter Savage Landor's *Imaginary Conversations* and it is rather mechanically put together. Writing about such men as Virgil and Augustus has its pitfalls: Shakespeare got beyond this problem, aided by his own age's general ignorance of the past, by making his historical personages unhistorical Elizabethans whose problems he could understand; hence his men and women are not strained through a gauze of rhetoric and labored re-creation.

In this novel Broch seems happiest in the long metaphysical passages, which are often turgid. Some of them have sentences that go on for pages, and often they break into poetry. A good deal of all this is abstruse or heavily Teutonic, and yet the book manages to present ecstatically a vision of a poet's destiny. With *The Sleepwalkers* it ranks at the apex of Broch's fictional projections of his ideas.

There is an element that is common to the work of both Musil and Broch—their principal novels have a massiveness through which the reader must scheme his way as through a labyrinth. Musil is less overtly philosophical than Broch, and less inclined to obtrude fantastic or poetic sequences, yet the Viennese world of Musil's *The Man Without Qualities* in many ways resembles the Berlin and German-provincial world of Broch's *The Sleepwalkers*.

Robert Musil, actually he was Robert Edler von Musil, was born at Klagenfurt, Carinthia, of an Austrian-Czech family. After a few years at a military academy in Eisenstadt, in the Burgenland, he went to the school for future soldiers at Weisskirchen (now Hraniče), in Moravia, the institution at which Rainer Maria Rilke had only a few years before been so unhappy. Musil was sturdier, yet the atmosphere of the place had a profound effect upon him, as may be seen in his first novel, *Die Verwirrungen des Zöglings Törless* (1906; *The Aberrations of the Student Törless*, translated as *Young Törless*). This is a story of the brutality and terrorism of schoolboys, who have an underground control of the academy that virtually makes it into a concentration camp. *Young Törless* was notable also for dealing in explicit terms with homosexuality, a subject literature avoided in those days. In this later age the book stands out as one of the most incisive and effective of all boarding-school novels.

The success of *Young Törless* made it possible for Musil to devote his time to writing and avoid the teaching career that was the alternative. After nearly accepting an army commission upon graduating from a military school in Vienna, Musil had studied civil engineering and invented a chromatometer that is named for him. He subsequently turned to philosophy and took a degree in 1908 at the University of Berlin, which offered him an instructorship (as the University of Munich also did), but by that time his novel had sold well enough to make him independent. He discovered that he could not write even while holding down a part-time job as a librarian in Vienna (after his marriage in 1910). He went to Berlin in 1913 and became one of the editors of the *Neue Rundschau*

(*New Panorama*), but found this even more distracting. Then the war came, and Musil served for four years as an officer in the Austrian army. For a while after the armistice he was press officer for the Foreign Ministry and subsequently a scientific adviser to the War Ministry.

He had in 1911 brought out a volume titled *Vereinigungen* (*Unifications*), which consisted of two stories. In 1921 he published an expressionist drama, *Die Schwärmer* (*The Enthusiasts*), which was weighed down by too much subtle intellectualism—Musil was already veering toward the complicated long novel which was to be his lifework. He objected so strenuously to the production techniques and the quality of acting in the first performance of *The Enthusiasts* that the producers withdrew the play after that first performance. But in 1924, Berthold Viertel successfully staged Musil's farce, *Vinzens*. Musil also wrote stories such as "Grigia" (1923) and those in *Drei Frauen* (1924; *Three Wives*), but he was soon devoting all his time to the long work which remained unfinished at the time of his death in 1942. The first volume of *Der Mann ohne Eigenschaften* (*The Man Without Qualities*) was published in 1930 in two parts, *Eine Art Einleitung* (*A Sort of Introduction*) and *Seinesgleichen gescheiht* (*The Like of It Now Happens*). The second volume, published in 1933, was called *Ins Tausendjährige Reich* (*Die Verbrecher*), which has been translated as *Into the Millennium* (*The Criminals*). This was continued in a third volume, posthumously published in Switzerland, which also contained some unrevised sections taken from Musil's manuscript. That the novel remains unfinished is not a reason for readers to neglect it, for actually it seems virtually as complete as it ever could be; it is in any case rather formless, and perhaps never could actually have been finished.

The man without qualities is Ulrich; the story, such as it is, covers the year just before the outbreak of the First World War, the last year of the Old World. Ulrich is called the man without qualities because all modern characteristics are concentrated within him to such an extent that no single one of them is outstanding; hence he has no special qualities. After having, like his creator, lived through various careers—military, mathematical research, engineering—Ulrich finally becomes involved in a zany activity which provides just the right place for a man lacking qualities. This is the so-called Collateral Campaign, organized for the purpose of celebrating 1918, Franz Joseph's seventieth year on the throne (what the author knew, which the people in the story could not know, was that Franz Joseph would die in 1916, and that 1918 would ironically mark the displacement of his successor and the end of the

Habsburg rule). Musil, who as we have seen worked in several ministries as the war ended, was in the Collateral Campaign creating one of the greatest of jokes on bureaucracy, the same Austro-Hungarian bureaucracy which Kafka mocked at in another way.

In Musil's book a group of secondary characters give substance to the social milieu in which Ulrich finds himself. For example, there is Tuzzi, a relative of Ulrich's, who is married to the high-ranking civil servant; Ulrich, with his ability to make ironic classical references, calls this intellectually aspiring woman Diotima, as he calls one of his own mistresses—who is a nymphomaniac—Bonadea. There is also Ulrich's sister Agathe, whose classical name dates from her christening; she and Ulrich, who look alike, decide that they are really Siamese twins; in their narcissistic relationship they grow increasingly close, and some of the last passages Musil wrote indicate that brother and sister were having a love affair. The wife of Ulrich's friend Walter, the slightly mad Clarisse, wants Ulrich to give her a child, an honor he refuses. Clarisse, obsessed with an imprisoned sex-criminal, the carpenter Moosbrugger, in her frenzy sees some relationship between him and Ulrich; after she helps Moosbrugger to escape from jail, he promptly murders another victim, and Clarisse goes completely mad.

Moosbrugger dominates the background of the story, but Musil introduces other important male characters, such as Imperial Liege-Count Leinsdorf, promoter of the Collateral Campaign, who becomes increasingly senile and less efficient. He does, however, enmesh some victims in the organization, including General Stumm von Bordwehr, supervisor of the army's participation, who sees the celebration in terms of military strategy. Another member of the group is the foxy international financier Paul Arnheim, whose motives arouse some suspicion. The young Hans Sepp opposes the campaign because it is not anti-Semitic (Arnheim, though Prussian, is partly Jewish)—yet Sepp's own mistress is Jewish. The idealistic poet Feuermaul, who appears from time to time, is evidently a caricature of Franz Werfel.

The exasperating futility of the whole enterprise is intricately prophetic of the fading days of the Habsburg monarchy which, in his deep satiric-artist's way, Musil knew was a time of twilight; in this he was as visionary about the Austria-to-be as Broch was about the future Germany. But Musil is more of a comic satirist, although not in the Kafka vein, in which the symbolism of fantasy predominates. There are symbolic overtones in *The Man Without Qualities,* but most of the novel is done in a tone of playfully ironic realism—the Collateral Campaign, for example.

Musil's force lies in his projection of the modern intellectual man, so well informed that he can give himself to nothing, is good only for such enterprises as the Campaign, and even this he regards with cool aloofness. Musil's triumph is in capturing the essence of this character, really the modern Faust who knows all and can really do nothing; he is as much a part of the great portrait gallery of modern fiction as Proust's closed-in and embedded Marcel, as the existential heroes of a somewhat later French phase, and of the lower-depths figures of the kind found in the novels and plays of Samuel Beckett. Ulrich belongs rootedly to the history and spirit of the twentieth century. Musil's technique was an attempt to avoid what he felt was unlifelike, events merely reflected inside the heads of men and of literature itself, a dim transfer and a threadbare convention; Musil wanted to give readers "the original."

While devoting more than ten years of his energy to *The Man Without Qualities*, Musil drew money for living expenses from a fund his admirers organized, known as the Musil-Gesellschaft (the Musil Society). He had no objections to living in this manner, for he felt that artists should be supported. Despite his early involvement with militarism, he detested the Nazis and after they took over Austria in 1938, Musil and his wife moved to Switzerland. His works were banned in Germany and Austria and were unobtainable in those countries even as late as the 1950's.

Musil died in Geneva early in 1942. He had just put in a morning's work that had satisfied him and, when death overtook him abruptly, he wore an expression of ironic astonishment. So *The Man Without Qualities* remains unfinished; though, as noted earlier, it is perhaps as much completed as it ever could have been.

Other German Novelists

Among the other novelists here considered, the two eldest are Alfred Döblin (1878–1957) and Hans Carossa (1878–1956). Both men were trained as physicians, but there are few further resemblances between them, for Döblin was an expressionistic novelist and Carossa a writer of traditional fiction and poetry. Döblin, a Jew, left Germany after the Nazi ascension and did not return until after the Second World War; Carossa, an "Aryan" who gave the Nazis no trouble, remained securely in Bavaria.

Döblin, who was born in the Baltic seaport of Stettin, moved with his mother to Berlin when he was ten. He attended the universities of Berlin and Freiburg, took his M.D. in 1905, and then went to Regensburg to work on a newspaper. He had been writing since 1900, and contributed to the expressionist magazine *Der Sturm* (*The Storm*). By 1912 he was married and practicing psychiatry in the Berlin workingclass district known as Alexanderplatz. His first novel, *Die Drei Sprünge des Wang-lun* (1915; *The Three Leaps of Wang-lun*), was a long book about Taoist doctrine and about a Chinese reformer in conflict with the state. The novel was well received although not so widely read as it might have been had the country not been fighting a war. Döblin himself soon was in the war, spending three years as a medical officer at the front. In 1918 he brought out the novel *Wadzeks Kampf mit der Dampfturbine* (*Wadzek's Battle with the Steam Turbine*), a vision of machines overwhelming mankind. The two-volume historical novel *Wallenstein* (1920) was a detailed story of the Thirty Years' War. *Berge, Meere und Giganten* (1924; *Mountains, Seas and Giants*) is another visionary, expressionist view of the triumph of machines, this time in an age of supermen set far in the future.

In his best-known book, *Berlin Alexanderplatz* (1929; translated as *Alexanderplatz Berlin*), Döblin wrote of the city proletariat in a huge novel that made use of the techniques of expressionism. Newspaper articles, popular songs, weather reports, vital statistics, legal reports, and similar devices obtrude upon the narrative in somewhat the same fashion as in the novels of John Dos Passos. Döblin tells his story through the consciousness of one character, Franz Biberkopf, who at the beginning of the book is leaving prison. The essentially simple-hearted Franz has to undergo a period of readjustment to the new attitudes and conditions in the slum world, and after some harrowing experiences he finally becomes a porter. Through most of the tale he is at the mercy of outside forces: the novel contains elements of materialistic determinism that makes it as much naturalistic as expressionistic. Today, the techniques of *Berlin Alexanderplatz* seem dated in a way which the works of Dos Passos and Joyce—with whom Döblin has also been compared—do not; but the book holds up remarkably in its picture of Berlin working-quarter life in the pre-Nazi era.

During his exile Döblin lived in both the United States and Palestine. After his return to Germany in 1945 he became involved in the publication of a literary magazine in Baden-Baden. He had brought out several novels while away; his last important work, published after his return, was *Trilogie: November 1918*, whose three volumes appeared in 1949–1950. This is a collective or roman-fleuve type of novel set in Berlin in the aftermath of the First World War, with a number of historical figures taking part in the story, which once again is technically similar to the work of Dos Passos, particularly *U.S.A.* But although Döblin's trilogy has some compelling scenes, it does not hold together so well as *Berlin Alexanderplatz*.

Hans Carossa, Döblin's contemporary and a fellow doctor, was born at Tölz, Bavaria. He was the son and grandson of physicians of Italian descent. Upon receiving his medical degree at Leipzig in 1903, he began practicing in Passau, where he married. After moving to Munich in the year following the outbreak of the First World War, Carossa went as a doctor to the Rumanian front (1916), later going to France where he had briefly served earlier; after being wounded he was invalided home and resumed his medical practice in Munich, later moving to the country-side. He continued practicing medicine, even though he had established himself as a writer before the war. After publishing some poetry, Carossa brought out a novel, *Doktor Bürgers Ende* (1913; *Dr. Bürger's End*), whose hero, upset by the suffering of his patients, takes his own life when he is unable to save his fiancée from death. In a later novel also based on his medical experiences—*Der Arzt Gion* (1931; *Doctor Gion*) —Carossa tells the story of a servant girl who insists on giving birth to her baby, although she knows that having a child will kill her. In this book Carossa again stresses the role of the physician amid human suffering.

Most of his books are autobiographical. They include: *Eine Kindheit* (1922; *A Childhood*), *Rumänisches Tagebuch* (1924; translated as *A Roumanian Diary*), *Verwandlungen einer Jugend* (1928; *Boyhood and Youth*), *Führung und Geleit* (1933; *Guidance and Companionship*), and *Das Jahr der schönen Täuschungen* (1941; *The Year of Beautiful Delusions*). These are the quiet and reflective confession of a poet who also kept turning out verse, including the *Gedichte* (*Poems*) of 1948. Carossa remained in Germany, writing for the public, during the Nazi regime. He tried to explain his attitude in *Ungleiche Welten* (1951; *Contrasting Worlds*), which at least outlines the predicament of the literary man in Hitler's time; the book has not persuaded all the German writers who went into exile, voluntarily or otherwise, that an artist could remain in Nazi Germany and maintain his integrity.

Other writers at least roughly contemporary with Döblin and Carossa also wrote of their experiences in the First World War. The one who attained the greatest fame was Erich Maria Remarque (born in 1898 as Erich Paul Kramer), with *Im Westen nichts Neues* (1929; translated as *All Quiet on the Western Front*). A story of a group of very young soldiers in the German army as it was losing the war, *All Quiet* appeared at a time when reaction to the conflict of ten years earlier had led to widespread pacifism. The book sold a million copies in Germany and, in translation, reached the bestseller lists of other countries; it was also a great success on the screen with Lew Ayres and Louis Wolheim in leading roles. As a book, *All Quiet*, episodic and in first-person narrative form, has some effective naturalistic scenes of the war, balanced by sentimentalized homefront sequences. The novel's sequel, *Der Weg zurück* (1931; translated as *The Road Back*), is far less effective. *Drei Kameraden* (1937; *Three Comrades*), another "road-back" story, is somewhat more interesting. It deals with three young veterans in the postwar years, emotional anarchists who believe in nothing, although when one of them is killed the other two do not pursue the matter legally, as they might have, but take matters into their own hands—in the style of the new brownshirt groups whose methods the comrades believe that they detest. Interestingly, their own closest bond is a machine, their automobile Karl. *Three Comrades* was also filmed, with Margaret Sullavan, Robert Taylor, Franchot Tone, and Robert Young.

Remarque's *Flotsam* (1941) is the story of a group of refugees fleeing from the Gestapo, a tale never properly focused. In *Arc de Triomphe* (1946; *Arch of Triumph*), Remarque, in the manner of many intellectuals of the time, showed that he had abandoned his between-wars pacifism; it tells of a refugee surgeon in the Paris of 1939–1940 who kills a Gestapo agent. (The motion-picture version featured Charles Boyer, Ingrid Bergman, and Charles Laughton.) Remarque's *Der Funke Lebens* (1952; *Spark of Life*) shows a small group of people surviving the brutalities of a concentration camp.

Liberal critics find it hard to disparage the work of Remarque, as is sometimes the case with John Steinbeck—the author's attitude is fundamentally liberal, revealing a man of good will, but the writing often has a best-selling glossiness, given a special sheen by the tearful and inevitable sentimentalism. An author who followed Remarque's *All Quiet* with his own war book produced a far better one; this was Ludwig Renn with *Krieg* (1928; *War*). Ludwig Renn is the pseudonym of Arnold Friedrich Vieth von Golssenau, born in 1889. An officer before the war, Renn drew upon his battle experiences for his novel, which was written in a stark, terse idiom that heightened the story's effectiveness. Renn has never equaled his performance in *War*. *Nachkrieg* (1930; *After War*) is a large and confounding story of the confusions of the Weimar Republic. Renn, who had become a Communist, published in 1932 a book about

his travels in Russia; and he taught at the Marxist Workers' School in
Berlin. Arrested at the time of the Reichstag fire in 1933, he was
imprisoned for two years, and after his release escaped to Switzerland,
where in 1936 he brought out *Vor grossen Wandlungen* (*The Great
Changes*, translated as *Death Without Battle*). Renn fought on the Loyalist
side in the Spanish civil war, during which he made an American lecture
tour; during the Second World War, he remained chiefly in Mexico, later
returning to East Germany. But, whatever Renn's attitudes or the comparative failure of his later work, *War* is one of the most gripping combat
novels of this century.

Two somewhat younger novelists who wrote about special aspects of
the First World War are Paul Alverdes, born in 1897, and Ernst Glaeser,
born in 1902. Glaeser's famous war novel was appropriately called
Jahrgang 1902 (1928; *Class of 1902*), which did not deal with combat
but rather with the effect of the conflict upon the generation growing up
in the country that was losing the war, the generation whose illusions
were shattered (interestingly, after criticizing the Nazis and leaving Germany, Glaeser returned to live under Hitler). The most famous book by
Alverdes does not deal with combat either, but rather its results. *Die
Pfeiferstube* (1929; *The Whistlers' Room*) is set in a hospital ward
inhabited by three Germans and an Englishman who, because they all
have throat wounds, can only communicate, in their strange comradeship,
through metal tubes ("whistles") inserted in the wounds.

Not all the books of the time concerned the war. Hermann Kesten, for
example, who was born in 1900, wrote of the struggles of youth to tear
itself away from family and even from national ties, in *Joseph sucht die
Freiheit* (1927; *Joseph Breaks Free*) and *Ein ausschweifender Mensch*
(1929; *A Roving Man*). In *Glückliche Menschen* (1931; *Happy People*),
the happy man, Max Blattner, begins unhappily as an unemployed brick-
layer full of self-dissatisfaction. There is a moment of rueful comedy
early in the story when the father of Max's girl, Ilse, finds Max in bed
with his daughter; but Max maneuvers out of this trouble as he manages
to twist himself out of most difficult situations in his animal-like quest for
easy contentment. Eventually, poor Ilse throws herself under a subway
train, making Max briefly unhappy; but he soon marries a wealthy young
woman and becomes one of the monstrous Bürgers of the late phases of
the Weimar Republic who lent themselves so readily to the caricatures of
George Grosz, who illustrated *Happy People*. Its author next wrote *Der
Scharlatan* (1932; *The Fake*), an anti-Nazi satire which made it necessary
for Kesten to leave Germany when Hitler took over. Kesten, who came to

live in America, summed up the recent experience of his native Germany in *Die Zwillinge von Nürnberg* (1947; *The Twins of Nuremberg*), the story of two sisters, one of whom marries a writer who is forced to leave Germany and lives in Paris, the other of whom has a husband in Gœbbels's propaganda office. The novel contains much satire, but there is a poignantly dramatic scene when the woman who remained in Germany and supported Hitler's aims meets her son in the ruins of Nuremberg—her son has become an officer in the American army.

The First World War gave Arnold Zweig the subject matter for his most famous work, which is one of the finest of all modern war novels— *Der Streit um den Sergeanten Grischa* (1927; *The Case of Sergeant Grischa*). Arnold Zweig (not to be confused with the Viennese writer Stefan Zweig) was born in Silesia in 1887 and began writing before the war, when his *Novellen um Claudia* (1912; *Novellas of Claudia*, translated as *Claudia*) scored a hit. Zweig also wrote plays, one of which was *Grischa*, first composed in dramatic form in 1921. Six years later, when it appeared as a novel, *Grischa* made Zweig a world-famous author. He followed the success of this book with several others concerned with the war, including *Junge Frau von 1914* (1931; *Young Woman of 1914*), *Erziehung vor Verdun* (1935; *Education Before Verdun*), and *Einsetzung eines Königs* (1937; *The Crowning of a King*). The young woman of 1914 is Leonore Wahl, in love with Werner Bertin, one of the friends of Sergeant Grischa; Bertin appears again in *Education Before Verdun*, a novel about the useless slaughter of battle and particularly about the deaths of two young German officers with whom Private Bertin serves. *The Crowning of a King* is, like *Grischa*, set on the Eastern front; it deals with the ridiculous internal warfare among the German higher officers as to which of them will be crowned king of Lithuania!

Zweig wrote this and the preceding novel in exile—actually dictated them, since a wound suffered in the First World War had left him virtually blind. He lived in various parts of Europe, then in Palestine, and after the Second World War finally settled in East Berlin.

For the best of Arnold Zweig, it is necessary to go back to *The Case of Sergeant Grischa*, with its dramatic force heightened by humanitarian themes. It is the sad story of a simple man caught in the military-bureaucratic trap. Grischa Paprotkin, an escaped Russian prisoner behind the German lines, takes on the identity of another Russian soldier and is caught. He is suspected of being a spy and is tried and condemned to death. Even when Grischa proves his identity and his innocence, General Schieffenzahn, commandant of the military police in the Eastern

Front town where Grischa was arrested, insists on carrying out the death
sentence which had earlier been passed upon Grischa. Schieffenzahn is
opposed by the commandant of the fighting forces in the area, General
von Lychow, a strict Prussian disciplinarian who has in his makeup a
streak of justice and humanity; he tries to save Grischa's life. Grischa, a
pawn in the generals' quarrel, is at last led out to dig his own grave
and be executed. In his anger, General Lychow brings the case personally
to the attention of the Kaiser, who in ordinary circumstances might have
taken drastic action against General Schieffenzahn: the Kaiser cries out
in annoyance that he had had enough Cavell cases, referring to the
execution of the English nurse Edith Cavell, in Belgium, an act which
created worldwide unfavorable criticism. But the Kaiser's irritation over
the case of Sergeant Grischa soon passes after he receives a glittering
present—a gold field-flask with a diamond-studded monogram and gold
cork, all in a blue silk case. Yet the book ends on a note of hope, with a
suggestion of the revolution exploding to the east. And so, in 1927, when
this novel first appeared, the Russian Revolution seemed to many writers
an outbreak of hopefulness, as it apparently still does to Arnold Zweig.

Not so the other Zweig, Stefan, a man who wanted no kind of totalitarianism. Like André Maurois, to some extent his French counterpart,
Stefan Zweig wrote both novels and biographies (though it may be said
in passing that Maurois has in his old age become a far greater biographer, with his books on Proust, Hugo, and George Sand, than Zweig
had been).

Zweig was born in Vienna in 1881, and in his youth was a poet. In
his posthumously published autobiography *Die Welt von Gestern* (1943;
The World of Yesterday), he wrote charmingly and modestly of his early
days in Vienna. During the First World War Zweig was assigned to the
war archives, as Rilke was—and like Rilke, he could not bear the work;
as a pacifist he spent the last years of the war in Switzerland. Then, in
the 1920's, his biographies made him world-famous: the short sketches of
Balzac, Dickens, Dostoevsky, Tolstoy, Casanova, Mary Baker Eddy, Sigmund Freud, and others, the longer biographies of Marie Antoinette and
Mary Stuart and especially the man he closely identified himself with,
Erasmus—*Triumph und Tragik des Erasmus von Rotterdam* (1934;
Triumph and Tragedy of Erasmus of Rotterdam, translated as *Erasmus of
Rotterdam*). As the Nazis spread over the German world, Zweig went into
exile from his permanent home in Salzburg, Austria, going first to the
United States and then to Brazil. One of his finest books was a ringing
cry for freedom: *Castellio gegen Calvin* (1936; *Castellio against Calvin*,

translated as *The Right to Heresy*), the story of a man who defied the tyrant of Geneva.

In fiction, Zweig was a fine craftsman in the novella, notably in *Amok* (1922), the story of a fierce passion that lasts beyond death, and in the posthumously published *Schachnovelle* (1944; *Chess Story*, translated as *The Royal Game*). This tells of a chess match aboard an ocean liner going from New York to Brazil; an unknown opponent wins the first game from the world champion but goes to pieces in the tension of the second game as a horrible experience out of the past puts a spell over him. It is one of the most dramatic stories of refugees from Nazism.

Zweig, who had divorced his wife of more than twenty years (with whom he kept on friendly terms), married his young secretary and in 1941 went to Brazil to start a new life, but came to feel that he could not go on. In February 1942 he and his wife were found dead in each other's arms, the result of a suicide pact. The force of the Nazis had proved too strong; and the death of Stefan Zweig ended an epoch in Germanic literature.

6

LITERATURE UNDER THE NAZIS

The Novel

Even before the outbreak of war in 1939, authors in Germany (and after the spring of 1938, in Austria) were put on a wartime basis. They were the ideological soldiers of the state. Many of them went into exile; most of these were Jews, but there were also many non-Jewish writers, such as Thomas Mann, who chose to live abroad—the Nazis once offered to make his Jewish wife an "honorary Aryan," but Mann rejected Hitler and his followers.

Thus far, the writings of German authors in exile usually have been discussed along with the work of such writers as Mann, Stefan Zweig, Fritz von Unruh, and others; here Heinz Liepmann, author of a compelling narrative of the secret resistance to Nazism (*Fires Underground*, 1935), should be mentioned. There was also Odön von Horváth, German-Hungarian (not Jewish) novelist, who, as a voluntary exile from the Third Reich, wrote two important books, *The Age of the Fish* (1938) and *A Child of Our Time* (1939). Before he reached forty Horváth met an unexpected death in Paris in 1938 when, as he walked along the Champs-Élysées, a sudden burst of wind blew down part of a tree that crashed onto his head.

Something should also be said, at this point, about the work of those who remained in Germany and continued writing, such as the earlier-mentioned Hans Carossa. What kind of literature was produced in Germany during the war-state phase of existence of the 1930's and 1940's? Some of the books written before Hitler's takeover fitted in neatly with the Nazi program, especially the literature of the new nationalism. There is, for example, the work of Hans Grimm, particularly his novel *Volk ohne Raum* (1926; *A People without Space*). Grimm, a master of the shorter form, as in his *Südafrikanische Novellen* (1913; *South African Novellas*), wrote a huge novel in *A People without Space*. It is the story of German settlers in Southwest Africa, particularly the peasant Cornelius Friebott. The emigrants leave an overcrowded Germany for Africa in the late nineteenth century, to become the victims of the hardships of the Boer War and, later, to have their land taken away from them by the Treaty of Versailles, which degrees that they must return to a still more overcrowded Germany. Grimm, who wrote of the superiority of the Nordic man over the Negro, was admired by the Nazi race theorists; besides, his novel, which sold more than a million copies between the time of its appearance in 1926 and the outbreak of the war in 1939, also embodied the Nazi theory of Lebensraum—living space—for the Germans. But even if Grimm was for a while a hero to the Nazis, he later opposed them.

So, or at least partly it seems, did Ernst Jünger; his attitude was somewhat ambiguous. Jünger, born in 1895, had an adventurous youth, first in the French Foreign Legion and soon afterward on the Western Front as a member of the German army. He was wounded several times and decorated for bravery. Between the wars he wrote several books which the Nazis liked, beginning with *In Stahlgewittern* (1920; *Storm of Steel*), a glorification of the military man. Jünger's admiration for military discipline somewhat mitigated his generally nihilistic attitude. In *Das abenteuerliche Herz* (1929; *The Adventurous Heart*), he explores nature and his own dreams, again idealizing the military type as the one organized against life's irrationalism and absurdity. *Der Arbeiter* (1932; *The Workingman*) celebrates the technician, who operates in somewhat the same spirit as the trained military man and, with him, will replace the Christian-sentimental Bürger. *Afrikanische Spiele* (1936; *African Diversions*) describes the author's youthful experiences in France and North Africa in somewhat the manner of André Malraux or Antoine de Saint-Exupéry, in prose with many of the striking qualities that characterize the work of those authors.

Although his writing had been taken up by the Nazis, Jünger refused to be drawn into their sphere and had moved out of Berlin. Surprisingly, the censors permitted publications of his *Auf den Marmor-Klippen* (1939;

On the Marble Cliffs), a novel about an ancient civilization that falls before the forces of destruction; it seems to be a veiled attack on Nazism. Surprisingly also, when war broke out in that same year, Jünger showed his willingness to fight on the side of the Nazis, who commissioned him as a captain in the army. In 1943 he circulated an unusual pamphlet, under the protection of General Karl Heinrich von Stülpnagel, who in 1944 was to join in the assassination plot against Hitler. This wartime book, *Der Friede* (*The Peace*), written after Jünger's son had been killed in the Italian campaign (finally published in 1948), showed its author becoming oriented to a Christian position and speaking out in favor of peace and a united Europe. Many such ideas are also found in Jünger's diaries of the Second World War, which he published as *Strahlungen* (*Radiations*) in 1949, the year of his utopian novel *Heliopolis*, the projection of an imaginary city of the future. Written in Jünger's usual masterly prose style, at one level this book seems an attack upon Nazi ideals but at another level is—as Edouard Roditi points out— "unconsciously still permeated with many notions that, although harmless in themselves, can fit dangerously well within the patterns of a totalitarian theology."

In Jünger, ideas are always predominant; indeed, it is questionable whether he is actually a novelist or a writer of philosophical dialogues. In *An der Zeitmauer* (1959; *At the Time Wall*), he discusses the problems of humanity in the Space Age and in the time of persistent revolutions. He is perhaps most at home in essay material of this kind.

Among the writers who stayed in Germany and openly opposed Nazism, Ernst Wiechert (1887–1950) is outstanding for his courageous attitude. Born in the forests of East Prussia, he was always close to nature, and often his writing suggests Rousseau. Wiechert tells of his youthful experiences—he was educated at Königsberg—in *Wälder und Menschen* (1936; *Woods and People*) and in *Jahre und Zeiten* (1949; *Years and Tides*). The hero of his first novel, *Die Flucht* (1916; *The Flight*), was a suicide. Wiechert, who had been for some years a secondary school teacher, gave up that occupation after the First World War and returned to the woods of his homeland to write. *Der Wald* (1922; *The Forest*) and *Der Totenwolf* (1924; *The Death Wolf*) reflect the chaos and brutality of the postwar years, but *Der Knecht Gottes Andreas Nyland* (1926; *God's Servant Andreas Nyland*) is considerably different: Nyland, who attempts to lead a Christ-like existence, finally abandons civilization to seek refuge in the depths of the forest.

Primitivism is the prevailing mode in *Die Magd des Jürgen Doscozil*

(1932; *The Maid of Jürgen Doscozil,* translated as *The Girl and the Ferryman*). In this crudely plotted story a young girl named Marte comes to the hut of the ferryman Jürgen, whose wife has just died. Jürgen and Marte develop their love against the background of the villagers' hatred. Marte is going to bear him a child, but first she serves a term of imprisonment for murdering the satanic minister Maclean, who has cast over the community an evil spell that only Marte has the courage to break. *Die Majorin* (1934; *The Major's Wife,* translated as *The Baroness*) tells of a war-wrecked soldier, who is regenerated by an officer's widow. His readjustment to his native soil, narrated in a rhapsodic, imitation-biblical style, plays a large part in this renewal of life and self, as it does in *Das einfache Leben* (1939; *The Simple Life*), where a former naval officer engages in a rather oversimple process of self-discovery on a small East Prussian island.

Wiechert during all these years did not remain politically inert, as his *Reden an die Deutsche Jugend* (1934, 1938, 1945; *Speeches to German Youth*) testify. Heinrich Himmler is supposed to have attended one of his lectures and subsequently ordered Wiechert's five months' detention in Buchenwald in 1938. After the war, Wiechert brought out two impressive novels, *Die Jerominkinder* (1945–1947; *The Jeromin Children*) and *Missa sine nomine* (1950). *The Jeromin Children* is a trilogy dealing with the rigors of poverty in a small town, and the experiences of a young man who, after serving as a medical orderly in the First World War, becomes the local physician; the story ends in 1939, with a new war about to bring new hardships to the town. *Missa sine nomine* tells the story of three brothers in a postwar setting: Erasmus attempts to help refugees, Ägidius discovers peace in farming, and Amadeus overcomes the bitterness and misery of four years in a concentration camp and works his way through to a rehabilitation and a love of his fellow men. Wiechert completed this book in Switzerland, where he had moved after the war.

One of the novelists who contributed to the tribal mysticism and mystique that underlay Nazi philosophy—the kind of Germanic-gods revival in which that proto-Nazi General Erich Friedrich von Ludendorff was especially interested—was Hans Friedrich Blunck, born in 1880. Soon after the First World War, Blunck, a worshipper of the primitivism of the Baltic peasants, brought out a trilogy, *Das werdende Volk* (*The Dynamic People*), composed of novels about three men: *Heinz Hoyer* (1920), *Berend Fock* (1921), and *Stelling Rottkinnsohn* (1923). Because of the influence upon Blunck of Selma Lagerlöf and other Scandinavian writers, his people seem less German than Scandinavian. In his second trilogy, *Drei Bücher aus der Frühgeschichte* (*Three Books of Early History*), he deals with actual prehistoric ages: *Streit mit den Göttern* (1926; *Quarrel with the Gods*), *Der Kampf der Gestirne* (1926; *The Battle of the Stars*), and *Gewalt über das Feuer* (1928; *Fire Subdued*). In these volumes, Blunck again seems Scandinavian rather than German; in them he is obviously under the influence of Johannes V. Jensen, the Danish novelist who evoked prehistoric ages. The Nazis rejoiced over Blunck's *Der einsame König* (1936; *The Lonely King*), a carefully documented and not too blatantly propagandistic story of Geiserich, king of the Vandals, a great leader of a warlike and pure-minded people. For such work Blunck received the Goethe Medal in 1938.

The novelist best known in the world outside Germany who remained in that country during the entire Nazi regime was Hans Fallada (pen name of Rudolf Ditzen). Fallada, after years of poverty and struggle, wrote an international bestseller during the Depression: *Kleiner Mann, was nun?* (1932; *Little Man, What Now?*). Born in 1893, Fallada was a spare-time writer whose first novels were ignored; then *Bauern, Bonzen, und Bomben* (1930; *Boors, Top Dogs, and Bombs*) was a critical success. *Little Man, What Now?* was the pathetic story of a young couple and their child in the world of depression and rising Nazi power. Hitler took over Germany shortly after the book appeared, and Fallada had to ask himself the question: Little man, what now? He decided to stick it out, but retired to the country. His autobiographical *Heute bei uns zu Haus* (1943; *Today at Our House*) is a rueful account of the author's difficulties at trying to be a farmer; it is almost a parody of the Blut und Boden (blood and soil) books the state wished its authors to produce. Nor did Fallada's novels, despite their lack of offensiveness to the Nazis, ever really celebrate the ideals of the Hitler regime; indeed, Fallada's imaginative works were often books of terror, with macabre settings and ideas. For example, *Wir hatten mal ein Kind* (1934; *Once We Had a Child*) is the story of the brutal methods Hannes Gäntschow uses to get back his family farm. In the two-volume novel *Wolf unter Wölfen* (1937; *Wolf among Wolves*), Fallada took a backward look at the frenzied period of inflation in Germany in the early 1920's. It is remarkable that this book does not attack the Weimar Republic which Hitler overthrew or that it does not extol the Nazis. *Kleiner Mann—Grosser Mann, alles vertauscht* (1939; *Little Man—Big Man, All Switched About*) is the story of an insurance man who inherits great wealth, which causes him misery, confusion, and mockery; he is not happy again until he gives up the money. Fallada was arrested in 1944 on a charge of attempted murder, but he was not convicted; while awaiting trial, he wrote in prison the story of a man's escape from reality through alcohol—*Der Trinker* (1950; *The Drinker*). In 1943 the Nazis at last banned his books; in 1945, the new city government of Berlin stopped the circulation of *Der Eiserne Gustav* (1938; *Iron Gustav*). After the war, in the year he died, Fallada published *Jeder stirbt für sich allein* (1947; *Every Man Dies Alone*). Fallada had by this time taken to writing a novel about a middle-class couple's futile and pathetic struggle against the Nazis. While correcting proofs on this book, Fallada died in a suburban Berlin hospital at the age of fifty-three.

A woman writer who spent the Nazi years in Germany and continued publishing, though without celebrating Hitler, was Gertrud von Le Fort (born in 1876). She was brought up in Calvinism but became a Catholic convert in 1926. In an essay discussing Germany's possible war guilt, "Unser Weg durch die Nacht" (1949; "Our Way Through the Night"), Baroness von Le Fort protests against the idea of blaming Germans collectively; some were, admittedly, capable of hideous crimes (the stench from the corpse camps still hung over the land), but others, she says, were able in those crimson years to perform acts of humaneness and generosity. And Christians must learn to forgive sin, she believes; her readers may wonder, however, whether she would expect the millions of tortured and exterminated Jews to be "forgiving." (The most gruesome book about Buchenwald, brought out in 1964 by a Czech scientist living in England, is Rudolf Vrba's *I Cannot Forgive*.)

Gertrud von Le Fort's imaginative writings continually embody ideas of forgiveness; many of them are set in the remote past, such as her huge, panoramic story of the eleventh century, *Der Pabst aus dem Ghetto* (1930; *The Ghetto Pope*). She used modern Rome for the setting of her two-volume novel *Das Schweisstuch der Veronika* (1927, 1946; translated as *The Veil of Veronica*), in which four attitudes toward the Church are displayed within a single German family living there: one woman member of the family is devout, another an unbeliever, and there are two conversions. The central character, Veronica, has been brought up without religion, but in the Rome of the years preceding the First World War, the testimony of her imagination and the testimony of her faith lead her to Catholicism. The second part of the novel takes place in Heidelberg after the war, where Veronica becomes engaged to an embittered young Nietzschean, Enzio. Despite the recommendation of a humanistic professor that Veronica break off her relationship with Enzio, she marries him. In *Die magdeburgische Hochzeit* (1939; *The*

Magdeburg Wedding), Gertrud von Le Fort again dealt with a historical theme.

Her novels are somewhat loose and sprawling; her finest work is in the medium in which Germanic authors have been so successful, that of the novella. Her first attempt at this form was *Die Letzte am Schaffott* (1931; translated as *The Song at the Scaffold*), which has had an unusual success. Translated into French by Georges Bernanos, it became the basis of an opera by Francis Poulenc, and of a French film in 1960 (screenplay by Bernanos). It is the story of a young Carmelite nun who, at the time of the French revolution, overcomes her terror of the guillotine and goes bravely to her death. Baroness von Le Fort's novella *Das Gericht des Meeres* (1944; *The Judgment of the Sea*), a medieval story, was translated into English in 1962 and published together with three of the author's other short novels: *Am Tor des Himmels* (*The Gate of Heaven*), *Der Turm der Beständigkeit* (*The Tower of the Constant*), and *Plus Ultra*. *The Gate of Heaven* (1954) is a story of Galileo and his troubles with the Inquisition, told against the background of a Second World War air raid in Germany. *The Tower of the Constant* relates the difficulties of the Huguenots in eighteenth-century France (Gertrud von Le Fort's ancestors were Huguenot members of the nobility who emigrated to Germany). Gertrud von Le Fort's other work includes the four historical tales with Italian settings in *Die Tochter Farinatas* (1950; *The Daughter of Farinata*) as well as the two short stories in *Gelöschte Kerzen* (1953; *Extinguished Candles*)—"Die Verfemte" ("The Outlawed Woman") and "Die Unschuldigen" ("The Innocents")—which link the recent war with the Thirty Years' War. Besides her fiction, Gertrud von Le Fort has written the remarkable *Hymnen an die Kirche* (1924; *Hymns to the Church*) and *Hymnen an Deutschland* (1932; *Hymns to Germany*), a Christian appeal to Germany which was not heeded by the people among whom Gertrud von Le Fort continued to live.

Subtle opposition to Nazism came from various writers inside the Catholic fold, such as the novelist and poet Elisabeth Langgässer (1899–1950), whose first novel, *Proserpina* (1932), is a somewhat surrealist story of the battle between good and evil in the soul of a small girl. The same concern between these warring forces is manifest in this author's other novels, including *Triptychon des Teufels. Ein Buch von dem Hass, dem Börsenspiel und der Unzucht* (1932; *Triptych of the Devil: A Book of Hatred, Stock-Jobbing, and Prostitution*) and *Der Gang durch das Ried* (1936; *The Way through the Marshland*). Elisabeth Langgässer's most ambitious work, diffuse but powerful, was *Das unauslöschliche*

Siegel (1946; *The Indelible Seal*), the story of Lazarus Belfontaine, a converted Jew who in 1914 denies his faith and deserts his wife and child, and then is regenerated eleven years later, after the murder of his second wife. Surrealistic in manner, it projects hallucinations and deals in allegory. Langgässer wrote a somewhat simpler and more concentrated story in her last novel, *Märkische Argonautenfahrt* (1950; *Argonauts' Journey to the March*), the tale of seven people, unknown to each other, who leave ruined Berlin together for a monastery in the March of Brandenburg. The former soldier, Frederick am Ende, and his six companions cannot enter the monastery, but en route they have discovered their inner selves, their mutual guilt, and the impossibility of avoiding the power and presence of God. In her fevered prose visions of good and evil, Elisabeth Langgässer often resembles the French religious novelist Georges Bernanos.

Another German Catholic author who opposed Nazism was Reinhold Schneider (1903–1958), who investigated the problems of mortal sin and earthly power in historical novels such as *Die Hohenzollern* (1933; *The Hohenzollerns*) and *Las Casas vor Karl V* (1938; *Las Casas before Charles V*). Protestant morality was the mainspring of the work of Jochen Klepper (1903–1943), who in *Der Vater* (1937; *The Father*) presented a forceful portrait of the harsh but highly religious Prussian king who was the father of Frederick the Great. Klepper, who had a Jewish wife, killed himself during the war.

Still another of the Catholic writers who remained in Germany although antagonistic to Nazism, Werner Bergengruen, was born in Riga, Latvia, in 1892; he died in Baden-Baden, West Germany in 1964. A poet as well as a novelist, he wrote a book of verse which had an underground circulation in 1944 and was published in 1946—*Dies Irae*. Bergengruen was a master of the novella form and an expert practitioner of the historical novel. In the latter area, *Der Grosstyrann und das Gericht* (1935; *The Tyrant and Judgment*, translated as *A Matter of Conscience*) is the story of the ruler of a small Italian state at the time of the Renaissance who entangles his people in his own criminality but is finally bested by a man who is willing to accept punishment for what he is not guilty of and who, by so doing, rescues the community from the influence of the tyrant. In *Im Himmel wie auf Erden* (1940; *In Heaven as on Earth*), Bergengruen deals with another ruler (of Berlin and its territory) who acts arbitrarily, the Elector Joachim, who hears a prophecy to the effect that in 1524 the region will be destroyed by a flood. The Elector tries to stifle the prophecy despite his belief in the possibility of the flood. The terror of the elements in the story is intensified by the fear of leprosy's spreading through the land. One of Bergengruen's finest novellas is *Der spanische Rosenstock* (1940; *The Spanish Rosebush*), a love story. Bergengruen, who lived in Zürich during the Second World War, continued to produce distinguished poetry and fiction.

A good many of the novels that appeared in Germany and Austria during the Nazi regime were written under the limitations of censorship; many of them were silly propaganda, others were little more than expressions of bewilderment. Still others gamely tried to run the blockade, with varying degrees of success. Some of the less important fiction of this period will now be looked at briefly, as a matter of historical interest.

Some Other Novelists of the National Socialist Era

One of the popular novelists of the day was Kurt Eggers, admirer of the sixteenth-century soldier, poet, and patriot about whom he wrote the two novels *Hutten* (1934) and *Der junge Hutten* (1938; *Young Hutten*). Just before the Second World War, Eggers produced one of the classic stories of the German youth of the time, an oversized novel that is genuinely horrible in its picture of what could and did happen—*Tanz aus der Reihe* (1939; *Dance Out of Line*). Here we have an autobiographical "hero" (he even bears the author's own name). He is just too young to take part in the First World War but not too young to feel resentment at the German defeats and the Versailles Treaty. At school he hates the Jewish boys, and at college he becomes a divinity student who dreams up a new Nordic theology to replace the Christian religion, which has Mediterranean and Jewish roots. He becomes an ordained minister, but loses his assignment for preaching Nazi propaganda—an unfortunate reminder that in a few years pulpits as well as universities and newspapers would be under Nazi control. In Jakob Kniep's *Porta Negra* (1932), a young priest leaves his chosen vocation to fight on the German side in the First World War. In Kniep's *Feuer von Himmel* (1936; *Fire from Heaven*), this young man comes back home after the 1918 armistice and discovers that he must now battle against destruction and despair. Another story of a young minister occurs in Albert Lorenz's *Unter Gottes Gewittern* (1943; *Under God's Thunder*). In this story, Pastor Wietfeld, who refuses to accept National Socialism in its revolutionary days, sees himself as the leader of a new intensified Christian movement—while speaking fervently of this at a mass meeting at which he has shouldered aside the principal speaker, Wietfeld is knocked dead by a bolt of lightning, leaving open the question as to whether heaven was punishing him for not accepting Hitler or whether Nazism left no opportunity for another gospel, whose prophet must be symbolically destroyed.

The clergy was not the only profession to appear significantly in novels during Hitler's time. German readers had almost as great an interest in stories of doctors as the American television viewers of the 1960's. Some of the Nazi-period novels about doctors were historical, some modern. The sixteenth-century Swiss-German physician Philippus Paracelsus was a recurrent hero of such stories, which often presented a mystic approach to biology. A trilogy by Erwin Guido Kolbenheyer (1878–1962) was a forerunner of National Socialist thinking along these lines: his *Paracelsus* (1917–1925). His view of the famous physician apparently conditioned that of various historians and philosophers of medicine who also saw Paracelsus in terms of the mystique of a national hero with Faustian qualities. Pert Peternell, in his novel *Der König der Ärzte* (1941; *The King of Doctors*), manifests an admiration for Paracelsus, whose own writings he uses extensively, but he does not put him forward as the embodiment of a national myth.

Among the medical novels with a modern setting, Betina Ewerbeck's *Angela Koldewey* (1939) was one of the most popular, the story of a woman's sacrifice for the sake of the advancement of medicine. Because of its picture of stoical heroism, the novel was widely distributed through the armed forces in the early years of the war. Another woman writer, Hilde Walde, wrote in *Die andere Maria* (1940; *The Other Mary*) the story of a German girl in Italy whose Italian husband is an indifferent doctor who makes no attempt to study the pellagra common among his poorer patients. But his sympathetic wife, Marianne, makes some elementary discoveries about diet when trying to help these people, and her husband reaps all the glory when he publishes these findings in medical journals. Marianne, caring nothing for personal gain, does not mind, for she is interested only in helping to cure the pellagra. A childless woman, she realizes another destiny than motherhood: she is "the other Mary." This novel was far more convincing and psychologically sound than many others of its kind during the period. There is for example Hans Künkel's *Ein Arzt sucht seinen Weg* (1939; *A Doctor Seeks His Way*), in which the leading character, who has had some medical training, pays little heed to it and goes in for faith-healing in a mystic way that held a certain appeal for National Socialists, although they also admired the discipline of physicians, which to them was almost of a military kind.

One of the propagandist novels that pitted the virtues of the German Reich against the faults of other countries, Frank E. Christoph's *Sehnsucht nach der Heimat* (1943; *Longing for Home*), is the story of an Austrian couple in Venezuela. Among Jews, Negroes, and half-castes, the Austrians feel homesick and return to their native land despite the fact that the husband is facing a jail sentence. But this is set aside by the intelligent judges of the new system that reigns since Hitler has seized Austria and made it a happy home for respectable Aryans. A more extended xenophobia occurs in Rudolf Michael's *Roman einer Weltreise* (1940; *Novel of a World Tour*), actually more journalism than fiction. It is an account of a trip through the Orient and across the United States made by some German newspapermen, and it is a paean to Aryan, actually German, supremacy. America, with its Jews, seems decadent in comparison with the Third Reich. America was a frequent target for Nazi novelists, in such books as Erich Ebermayer's *Unter anderem Himmel* (1942; *Under a Different Sky*), which caricatures a Wall Street banker and his associates. His supposed daughter, who goes to school in Heidelberg, falls in love with Germany; her true father, with whom her mother had a secret love affair, was a German. But in some cases a Teutonic admiration for America appears, however unconsciously, in the novels of the time. In Hermann Strenger's *Strom aus der Erde* (1942; *Stream from the Earth*), for example, the hero leaves his small German town to become a scientist and a capitalist in the free society of nineteenth-century America.

A somewhat sympathetic picture of Russia is found in Edwin Erich Dwinger's trilogy *Die deutsche Passion* (*The German Passion*), comprising *Die Armee hinter Stacheldraht* (1929; *The Army Behind Barbed Wire*, translated as *Prisoner of War*), *Zwischen Weiss und Rot* (1930; *Between White and Red*) and *Wir rufen Deutschland* (1932; *We Call Germany*). Dwinger, the son of a German father and Russian mother, was fighting for the German armies in the First World War when he was captured by the Russians; his first volume describes his prisoner-of-war experiences, the second the battles between the Kolchak Whites and the Trotsky Reds, and the third the German soldier's return home. Although thousands of his fellow prisoners died; Dwinger, who could speak Russian, presents a sympathetic view of his captors. The prison-camp and battle scenes are vivid and graphic; the third volume of the trilogy, crying out for a new Germany and full of racial nonsense, is a letdown. Dwinger's next novel, *Die letzten Reiter* (1935; *The Last Horsemen*), is even less compelling. In the Spanish civil war he was a reporter with the Franco forces, as he was with the Nazi armies in the Second World War.

In the historical novel, no author was more blatantly simplistic than Mirko Jelusich, who before the war wrote novels about Caesar and Cromwell that made them protofascist chieftains. Just before the conflict broke out, he published *Der Soldat* (1939; *The Soldier*), a book about the German hero Scharnhorst, who had once defeated Napoleon; and in 1941 Jelusich's contribution was *Der Traum vom Reich* (*The Dream of the Empire*), a story of Prince Eugène of Savoy, who in the time of Louis XIV wanted to build a German empire across Europe. Jelusich's book, like all his work, was full of contemporary overtones; in it he invited the Germans to share in Prince Eugène's dream of power. Other novelists who celebrated Prince Eugène in their fiction were Ludwig Mathar and Walter von Molo. In 1937 two novels, each named *Wallenstein*, one by Gerhard Bohlmann and the other by Gerhart Ellert, dealt with the hero of the Thirty Years' War. Bohlmann's book attempted to show the famous general as essentially a man of peace, but such ideas ran against the current of Wallenstein's time as much as they did that of Hitler's. In most cases the historical reconstructions of the Nazi period, both fictional and supposedly factual, glorified the Third Reich and its militant ideals.

It is a relief to find novels of this period that are not tendentious. Two writers rather difficult to place are Hermann Stehr and Editha Klipstein; there is a content of independence in their work which is not of the Nazi type, and yet their books were published in the National Socialist years—indeed, Stehr was for a while officially encouraged by the Third Reich. Stehr, who died in 1940 at the age of seventy-six, was a village schoolmaster until he was nearly fifty, and at fifty-three he published his striking novel *Der Heiligenhof* (1918; *Saints' Farm*), which takes its name from the farm in the book. The story, which employs a realistic use of rustic dialogue, is of a mystic search for God and peace and happiness, seen in terms of the vision of Silesian peasants. *Peter Brindeisener* (1924) continues the story. Stehr's trilogy, *Die Familie Mächler* (1929–1944; *The Mächler Family*), the last volume of which (*Damian*, 1944) was published posthumously, dealt with German life from 1848 to the time of the Weimar Republic; as the author's style became somewhat clearer and his religiousness even firmer, his work fell somewhat out of favor with the Nazis. And the hero of *Damian*, in opposition to the prevailing morality of state depersonalization, asserts the sacredness of the ego. Also seemingly unorthodox, Editha Klipstein's *Der Zuschauer* (1942; *The Onlooker*) presents a hero who does not give himself up to causes, though he is not hesitant in expressing his views on various subjects. The book seems to be a defense of individualism, of rationalism, and of an intelligent approach to religion, hardly the kinds of opinions fostered by the Nazis; yet *The Onlooker* was permitted to be published during the war, another potentially independent book that somehow was accepted. But such works of intelligence were few enough, and were smothered under the crushing weight of propaganda.

Poetry in the Time of the Nazis

A great many German poets, as already noted, went into exile during the Third Reich. Some stayed behind to celebrate Hitler, his triumphs, his racial theories, and his glorification of Teutonism. Poets such as Baldur von Schirach, Gerhard Schumann, and Richard Euringer were rapturous on these subjects. Euringer was also a successful novelist whose *Die Fürsten fallen* (1935; *The Princes Fall*) was exactly what the Nazis wanted in their fiction and drama—a story of the failure of the European monarchies from the time of the French revolution to the rise of the new "superior" empire of Germany in the latter half of the nineteenth century. Euringer, who had been a pilot in the First World War and had written one of the better combat novels, *Fliegerschule 4* (1929; *Flying School 4*), in 1933 won the first national state prize of the Third Reich for his radio drama *Deutsche Passion* (*German Passion*). His verses in admiration of the new order appear in *Die Gedichte* (1937; *Poems*), which are undisciplined and filled with patriotic fervor and a raw vigor.

On the other side of the coin—it would not be too dramatic to say on the other side of the barbed wire and the gas ovens—we have Gertrud Kolmar, born in Berlin in 1894 to Jewish parents. Her family name was Chodziesner, from a town on the Polish border; Gertrud Chodziesner wrote under the name of Kolmar, which is simply the German name of that town. She had much of the shyness that was a characteristic of Emily Dickinson, to whom Gertrud Kolmar has often been compared. She did to some extent get out into the world, however, as a teacher of deaf-mute children. But again like Emily Dickinson, she published virtually nothing during her lifetime, small volumes in 1917, 1934, and 1938; the last was almost at once used for pulp when the Nazis forbade Jewish publishers to function. Gertrud Kolmar disappeared into the Nazi concentration-camp system in 1943 and was never heard from again. But her verse has lived, and she is now often spoken of as Germany's greatest woman poet. A cycle of poems, *Welten* (*Worlds*), appeared posthumously in 1947, and in 1955 the collection *Das lyrische Werk* (*Lyric Work*), the latter reissued in 1960 with editorial augmentation and an additional two dozen poems.

Her work is so richly varied that for full appreciation it should be read in its entirety; a single poem, "Der Schwan," ("The Swan") can only faintly suggest the delicate wonder of her imagination:

> O a swan!
> Unfolded grand and flexed.
> Was he cast out of the reed-forest by Pan
> As a white rose?
>
> Do not doubt!
> When over weary waves
> An unearthly light moves,
> He shields his own brightness.
>
> This vision reflects
> The tides more purely.
> Poppy-milk ripples, escapes,
> Where his wings touched.
>
> Picture of woman,
> He sings profoundest dying;
> From the glass-cool dew
> The sweet silence rings.
>
> Calyx of down,
> Defenseless, all exposed,
> The sound and dream
> He has given up to evening.
>
> Floating along,
> Changed to gold-gray,
> He is a song
> That ends in sadness.

This paraphrase in another language at least catches a little of the imagery of Gertrud Kolmar, as well as some of her response to animals, of which she wrote with sympathetic involvement. She had an enormous range of subject matter and of technique, using various meters and rhythms to express a variety of poetic subjects. She wrote one cycle of poems about the romance of Napoleon and the Polish countess Marie Walewska, and another to the coats-of-arms of Prussian towns. She could be specifically realistic or could draw upon myths; she wrote of nature with intimacy and could treat abstract ideas successfully. She was an expert at use of such disciplined forms as the sonnet, and yet she could write free verse with abundant excellence. She had just attained to a fluent mastery of her work when she was put into the barbed-wire stockade from which she never emerged.

Another writer who stayed in Germany but survived is Friedrich Georg Jünger (born 1898), brother of the novelist and essayist Ernst Jünger. Friedrich Jünger's survival was, like that of his elder brother, something of a miracle, for in 1935 Friedrich Jünger wrote an openly anti-Nazi poem. A fine if somewhat traditional lyrist, Jünger is the author of several books of verse, including *Der Westwind* (1946; *The West Wind*), *Das Weinberghaus* (1947; *The House in the Vineyard*), *Gedichte* (1949; *Poems*), *Iris im Wind* (1952; *Iris in the Wind*), and *Schwarzer Fluss und windweisser Wald* (1955; *Black River and Windwhite Forest*). Jünger's anti-Nazi poem, at first published and then given an underground circulation, is "Der Mohn" ("The Poppy"), which begins as an invocation to the scarlet poppy above graves. Then the cries for fame and heroic deeds and victory fill the air. Laurels grow but poorly in the north, so they must be brought from the warm southern countryside. "The tribe of orators disgusts me. Turkey hens / I hear gobbling in the marketplace, scratching in the plaza. / Fakers are full of oily words, as saviors they save falsehood, as doctors they fear death." The people are deceived, and the poet is sick of shouts for enthusiasm:

> Woe! Enthusiasm! Silver well of silence, you clear,
> You crystal spring, do not call it enthusiasm.
> The dead are more profoundly silent, they grieve,
>   they do not hear the noise,
> They do not hear the song of infamous drunkenness.

Some of the other poets who remained in Germany during the Hitler years have already been mentioned, a few of them among the novelists: examples of the latter are Gertrud von Le Fort and Elisabeth Langgässer, two Catholic writers. Gertrud von Le Fort's book of the Weimar Republic days, *Hymns to the Church* (1924), has already been referred to; a profoundly religious volume, it earned the admiration of Paul Claudel. Gertrud von Le Fort also wrote, as previously noted, *Hymns to Germany* (1932), which in Christian terms asked the Germans to turn their thoughts to the things of heaven rather than to the things of earth. After the war, this poet published her collected verse as *Gedichte* (1949;

Poems). That her work was outside the Nazi orbit is evident as the final stanzas of her poem "Die Heimatlosen" ("The Homeless") will show:

> The city lies waste, and courtyard and halls,
> The hand is empty,
> We have seen a world collapse in ruins—
> Nothing more can touch us.
>
> If hatred or mockery comes,
> What difference?
> We are God's homeless ones—
> He shelters us.
>
> Guilt has wept itself dry, we have come
> To the ultimate woe:
> Eternal Grace opens its fountains,
> Blood becomes snow.

Elisabeth Langgässer's best-known postwar poem indicates that she also had been always antagonistic to Nazism, as the earlier references to her novels suggest. Indeed, her daughter was sent to a concentration camp; it is this daughter's return whom Elisabeth Langgässer celebrates in "Frühling 1946" ("Spring 1946"), which also gives hints of a possible new Germany now that the toad is gone, and the gorgon, with spring once more over the earth:

> Gracious anemone,
> Have you returned
> And do you appear with bright calyx
> To requite me for my sufferings
> Like Nausicaa?
>
> Wind-stirred bowing,
> Wave, foam, and light!
> Oh, what joy from other spheres
> Has taken the weight off my shoulders
> Burdened with dust?
>
> From the domain of the toad
> I rise up,
> Pluto's redness still under my eyelids
> And the flute of the guide of the dead
> Still sounding hideously in my ear.
>
> I saw in the gorgon's eye
> The iron gleam,

The squirt of venom of lies
I heard whisper that it would
Kill me utterly.

Anemone! Let me
Kiss your face:
Unmirrored by the rivers
Styx and Lethe, lacking knowledge
Of "No" and "Not."

Without corrupting,
You are alive and you are here,
Quietly to touch my heart,
Without setting its fires blazing up—
Child Nausicaa!

National Socialist Drama

The drama, with its contagious appeal to the emotions, was one of the most forcible weapons of Nazi propaganda and was at the same time under more stringent control than poetry or even fiction. If a few novelists and poets wrote in a general way under the Third Reich, almost no dramatist did; the plays had a definite slant, and none of them of that period is worth preserving except as a historical curio.

Long before the Nazis came into power, drama helped chop out a path for them (as certain novels had). One of the forerunners among the playwrights is Hanns Johst (born in Saxony in 1890), who eventually stopped being a forerunner and became a Nazi celebrant. His early work included poetry and fiction as well as plays—the novels *Der Anfang* (1917; *The Beginning*) and *Der Kreuzweg* (1921; *The Crossroad*) and several volumes of verse that manifested Johst's expressionistic tendencies. After writing a one-act play at the beginning of the First World War, Johst in 1916 came up with *Der junge Mensch* (*The Young Man*), a Wedekindesque drama about the troubles of adolescence. Next he wrote *Der Einsame* (1917; *The Lonely One*), a drama about the nineteenth-century playwright Christian Dietrich Grabbe, ruined by drink and the contempt of his fellows. Grabbe, who was regarded by the expressionists as a kind of ancestor, is in Johst's play given such speeches as this:

Oh! This feeling! I wouldn't trade it for a throne! Heaven and earth become a plaything of my will! I am the cosmos! And without my words and without the shining garland of my poetry all this—history, reason, the present, and the soul of a thousand of God's acres—all this crumbles into meaningless dust.

This grandiosity is partly romantic, and Nazism played the romantic chord loudly. Its aestheticians even declared that romanticism itself was of German origin. Grabbe's utterance was of the kind that in only a few years the German people would be hearing Hitler make—Hitler who did not rise to power through a coup d'état but rather because of his strength in elections.

Johst went on writing such plays. *Der König* (1920; *The King*) projected the same kind of disillusion over the 1918 revolution that Hitler revealed in *My Struggle*. Johst, still writing in the expressionist vein, became emphatically nationalistic in *Propheten* (1922; *Prophets*), in which Jews appear as unwholesome usurers, and in which Martin Luther speaks of a reborn Germany. *Thomas Paine* (1927) is of course about the American Revolution, the creation of a new state, with George Washington as a good Nazi who says that the new state demands blood. In *Schlageter* (1933), Johst deals with an actual Nazi, a man whom the French put to death in 1923 for committing sabotage during the Ruhr occupation. In the play (dedicated to Hitler with affection, veneration, and loyalty) as Schlageter goes to his execution, he cries out: "Germany! A last word! A request! A command! Germany!!! Awaken! Flame up! Burn enormously!" These words rang on the ears of people soon to see the Reichstag fire and not long after to see Germany cast the brand of war across Europe.

Besides Johst, a number of other playwrights helped condition people to the ideas of National Socialism, some of them—like Johst—doing so even before the National Socialist Party was formed. These include the dramas of Paul Ernst, Hermann von Bötticher, Dietrich Eckhart, and Hans Franck. Some of the plays, like the pre-Nazi and Nazi novels, were historical, exalting such figures as Frederick the Great.

Other plays were of the blood-and-soil type, the Blut und Boden literature at the time facetiously known as Blubo. In the 1930's one of the popular dramatists of the latter school was the Austrian Richard Billinger, born in 1893, who wrote *Die Hexe von Passau* (1935; *The Witch of Passau*), which takes place at the time of the peasants' war; it concerns a girl who, although burned at the stake for witchcraft by the authorities, has so impressed a young officer that he joins the peasants in their revolt and leads them to victory. In Billinger's *Der Gigant* (1937; *The Giant*), the title refers to the city of Prague, portrayed as an evil place which ruins a peasant girl who learns that she should submit to the mystic spell of the land on which she had been born, rather than yielding to the "giant."

Besides the historical and Blubo manifestations, still another type of play emerged into popularity: the drama that dealt with the First World War, glorifying Germany's role on the Western Front. One of the most striking of these Fronterlebnis plays was *Die endlose Strasse* (1930; *The Endless Road*) by Sigmund Graff and E. C. Hintze. Graff subsequently wrote plays by himself, usually glorifying the Nazi creed. Another National Socialist dramatist, Eberhard Wolfgang Möller, born in 1906, wrote an anti-Semitic play, *Rothschild siegt bei Waterloo* (1934; *Rothschild Wins at Waterloo*). This appeared at almost the same time as George Arliss's Hollywood film *The House of Rothschild,* which praised rather than denigrated Nathan Rothschild for the way in which he used his intelligence service to get the first news in London of Napoleon's defeat. Möller also drew upon historical themes for *Das Frankenburger Würfelspiel* (1936; *The Frankenburg Dice Game*), a play about the peasants' war, and for *Der Untergang von Karthago* (1938; *The End of Carthage*), a verse drama purporting to show how the disciplined Roman officer Scipio defeated the materialistic Carthaginians. Still another propagandist through the use of the historical play was Hans Rehberg (born in 1901), who wrote a series of dramas about early Prussia and the rise of Frederick the Great. Like his illustrious predecessor Friedrich Schiller, but with a quite different intent, Rehberg turned to Spanish history for *Isabella von Spanien* (1938; *Isabella of Spain*) and *Karl V* (1943; *Charles V*). He dealt with English history in 1942 with *Heinrich und Anna* (*Henry and Anne*) and in 1949 with *Heinrich VII* (*Henry VII*) and *Elisabeth und Essex* (*Elizabeth and Essex*). But, with the Nazi momentum no longer impelling him, Rehberg failed with these last two plays. No dramatist from the Nazi entourage thrived in the later Germany; as noted earlier, the plays of that time remain mere historical curiosities.

Germany's most notable elder twentieth-century playwright, Gerhart Hauptmann, did not oppose the Nazis and kept bringing out plays during their rule. He had been honored by the Weimar Republic and scoffed at by the Fascists, but when the latter came to power Hauptmann was the only writer of great distinction to remain in Germany and attempt to live with them. Hermann Kesten, the German novelist and playwright who went to live in New York, spoke of Hauptmann as an "opportunist and perpetual conformist" who "became the echo of all the changing political regimes of his time." Erika and Klaus Mann, son and daughter of Thomas Mann, in their book *Escape to Life* (1939) tell of the end of the friendship between Hauptmann and Alfred Kerr, the most influential drama critic of his time, whose enthusiasm for Hauptmann's work greatly enhanced its reputation: "When the old poet [Hauptmann] made his pitiable bow to the Nazis, Kerr wrote him an open letter, bidding him farewell with anger and pain." This episode gave the American dramatist S. N. Behrman the germ of his 1935 anti-Fascist play *Rain from Heaven.*

Hauptmann in his later years turned mainly to older themes and settings, with the medievalism of *Ulrich von Lichtenstein* and *Die Tochter der Kathedrale* (*The Daughter of the Cathedral*), both dating from 1939, the latter taken from an old French legend in which the double wedding of twin girls to twin princes ends an ancient quarrel between two families. Hauptmann's *Hamlet in Wittenberg* (1935) is a prelude to Shakespeare's play which ends with the young prince, at the university, receiving news of his father's death. Between 1941 and 1945, Hauptmann (who died at eighty-three in 1946) rewrote the ancient Greek Orestes–House of Atreus plays as *Die Atridentetralogie* (*The Tetralogy of the Atrids*). This differs greatly from the humanitarian treatment of the story in Goethe's *Iphigenie auf Tauris* (*Iphegenia in Tauris*). Some critics regard the violence and doom of these last Hauptmann plays as the dramatist's shocked reaction to the Second World War or even as a form of protest against Nazism.

As for the German theater in the 1940's, its activities were increasingly curtailed. During the 1914 and 1939 wars, the Germans had set the brutal example of bombing cities filled with civilians. In the Second World War, although Air Marshal Hermann Göring had assured the German people that no enemy aircraft would cross the nation's borders, the Royal Air Force by night and the U.S. Air Corps by day blasted the German cities. After 1942 the number of theatrical performances was greatly reduced in Germany. (Meanwhile, the London theaters flourished, as the many Americans who attended many performances there can attest.) In 1944 an official edict closed all German theaters, so that among the smoking ruins the curtain comes down forever on Nazi drama.

7

THE LATER
CAREER OF
BERTOLT BRECHT

During the Second World War, when Bertolt Brecht was a Hollywood screenwriter, he remained for the most part in eclipse: since he was an outspoken anti-Nazi, the Germans did not produce his plays. Some of them, however, were put on in Switzerland. The professional theater in the United States ignored Brecht's work, but several of his dramas were staged by American college theater groups. Finally, in the summer of 1947, *Galileo* (*Leben des Galilei*) was produced in Los Angeles (with Charles Laughton), and later that year in New York.

This drama, which Brecht had first written in the late 1930's (it was originally staged in Zürich in 1943), concerns the Inquisition's smothering of Galileo's work, which the Church felt might prove uncomfortable, as indeed it has because Galileo popularized the Copernican discovery that the universe does not revolve around man's little drama of good and evil on this particular planet. One of the brilliant strokes in the play is its presentation of the central figure not as a saintly martyr but as a sensual man who enjoys the pleasures of life. Toward the end of the story Brecht shows him as old and virtually blind, but still watched closely by the Inquisition. He feels that his recantation was an act of cowardice which has set back the development of science by putting it under authoritarian control. Finally he lets a manuscript he has secretly written be smuggled out of Italy so that truth may be proclaimed.

The play obviously presents the case of the individual against the authoritarian state, the case for experiments to arrive at truths. Ironically, in the autumn of 1947 the House Un-American Activities Committee summoned Brecht to ask him about his beliefs. The head of the Committee at the time was Representative J. Parnell Thomas, who had not yet been imprisoned for fraud. Brecht admitted that many of his plays had a Marxist bias, but he defended his right to hold dissenting opinions. At the end, the Committee thanked him for having been a cooperative witness; he firmly denied that he had ever been a member of the Communist Party. By showing how greatly the translations of his works in the Committee's possession misrepresented what he had actually written, and by exposing the inability of various members of the Committee to understand complex ideas, Brecht had (in the common phrase) made monkeys out of them; as one of his friends said, the affair resembled the cross-examination of a zoölogist by apes.

When the proceedings were over, Brecht went back to Europe, where he eventually took out Austrian citizenship; this permitted him freedom of travel. He moved to East Berlin because he was given his own theater there. As explained earlier in this book, he never wrote plays celebrating life under Soviet domination: Bertolt Brecht remained an individualist in the Communist camp.

As also mentioned in the discussion of Brecht's earlier works, his 1928 adaptation of John Gay's *The Beggar's Opera*, with music by Kurt Weill, met with extravagant success in its second New York presentation. The off-Broadway production ran from 1954 to 1961, breaking all records for a musical play. An off-Broadway theater also produced, in 1961, Brecht's *Im Dickicht der Städte* (*In the Jungle of Cities*), first staged in Munich in 1923 (also discussed previously). In 1962, another off-Broadway theater honored the memory of Brecht by presenting *Brecht on Brecht*—an anthology of his works, in English.

Meanwhile, the capitals of the world have continually responded to his plays, and it is time to note several of the most important of them which have not been mentioned here before. *Mutter Courage und ihre Kinder* (*Mother Courage and Her Children*), which is frequently revived, is often considered Brecht's masterpiece. It was staged on Broadway in 1963 and, although the actors missed the spirit of the play, the production was commercially successful. Written at the end of the 1930's, *Mother Courage* deals with the experiences of a woman peddler during the Thirty Years' War. Mother Courage plies her wagon as well as her loyalties between the contending armies and loses several sons and a daughter in the process, engaging in cheap bargaining while they are dying. She was not an admirable figure to Brecht, for she represented the philosophy that business must go on; but she has become to modern audiences a stubborn symbol of the noncombatant victim of wars. The qualities her author did not intend to manifest themselves as admirable have somehow come through as merely roguish. The play, spiced with a rich variety of characters, is written partly in Bavarian idiom, with the seventeenth-century flavor in its coarse prose and ingenious lyrics. No historical drama of our time has so much power; and it is widely regarded as one of the greatest modern plays.

In *Der Gute Mensch von Setzuan* (*The Good Woman of Setzuan*), written between 1938 and 1941, Brecht presents a parable of modern China in which three gods descend to earth to see if they can find a good human being. They discover that there is one, a prostitute. Yet after she becomes head of a tobacco factory she turns into an exploiter of other human beings and loses her essential goodness. The play is left unresolved except for the author's suggestion that in this dog-eat-dog world it is impossible for anyone to remain good. In *Herr Puntila und sein Knecht Mattli* (*Mr. Puntila and His Man, Mattli*), written in Finland in 1940, Brecht presents contrasting characters: Puntila, who is friendly when drunk but mean when sober, and his folk-witty chauffeur, Mattli. The latter refuses to marry Puntila's daughter, Eva, who he thinks will not adapt satisfactorily to proletarian ways, and so he leaves the Puntilas and goes his own proletarian way.

The last full-length play Brecht wrote in America, *Der kaukasische Kreidekreis* (*The Caucasian Chalk Circle*), completed in 1945, is based on an old Chinese drama with the setting moved to Soviet Georgia. The core of the play is the dramatization of a legend sung by a folk singer, a legend that concerns Georgia in feudal times, and a child who is abandoned by his wealthy mother, the governor's wife, during a rebellion. A servant girl rescues him and takes care of him. Later, when the rebellion is over and the governor's wife tries to retrieve the child, the servant girl puts up a fight for him. The judge who arbitrates the matter sets up a Solomonic situation: the two women must engage in a tug-of-war for the child within a chalk circle; the one who first drags him out of the circle wins him.

When out of fear of injuring the little boy, the servant girl refuses to take part in such a contest, he is awarded to her; she is the true mother. In this play, in which the evil characters wear masks, the language— mostly prose, with several songs and some choral narratives in irregular verse—is forceful, and the action effectively stylized; all these elements make the play one of the outstanding examples of what Brecht meant by epic theater.

In Switzerland in 1948–1949, Brecht wrote *Die Tage der Commune* (*The Days of the Commune*), which is partly a commentary on Nordahl Grieg's Norwegian play *Nederlaget* (1937; translated as *The Defeat*). Grieg, disappointed over the collapse of the Spanish republic, had in his play about the Paris Commune of 1871 attacked Western pacifist humanism. (It is interesting to note that Grieg was anti-Fascist and pro-Soviet; he was killed in a British bomber over Berlin in 1943.) But Brecht apparently felt that Grieg had not sufficiently stated the case for the Paris Commune; he took over some of the Norwegian's characters, using them for his own purpose, which was in part to show the willingness of the bourgeoisie to make peace with a national enemy rather than to let the workingclass gain strength; the statesmen Thiers and Bismarck are important figures in this play, as are a group of Montmartre proletarians. The drama is tendential, warped by its propaganda.

After moving to East Berlin in 1948, Brecht put on and revised some of his old plays in the theater he had been given. He wrote nothing importantly new; he often worked on translations of the plays of others, including Shakespeare's *Coriolanus* and Sophocles' *Antigone*.

At a time when he was preparing his theater group, the Berliner Ensemble, for a 1956 season in London, Brecht died of coronary thrombosis on August 14 of that year.

His influence endures, and his plays, despite their frequent contradictions between Marxian mechanism of the self and individualistic assertions of the self, continually satisfy theatrical audiences. Like many prolific writers, Brecht borrowed from a variety of sources, and he wrote at multiple levels, in a language that even in translation can be exciting. Unlike so many other problem playwrights of recent years, Brecht never seems to be a novelist who has strayed into the theater; he is always the true dramatist except when doctrinal passages weigh down his plays; when he writes in straightaway fashion, he is always the vital dramatist. His writings continually manifest a tension Brecht was aware of in himself, which he called his *Widerspruchsgeist*—his contradictory spirit. This probably accounts for much of the heightening of drama in his work.

8

GERMAN LITERATURE AFTER THE SECOND WORLD WAR

Falling in Flames, Arising in Division

April and May 1945 witnessed Nazi Germany's Götterdämmerung amid artillery fire and aerial bombardment. A great deal of the trouble that has since plagued the world could have been avoided if General Eisenhower had taken the initiative to move the American and British armies toward and into Berlin before the Soviet forces occupied the city. It is necessary to mention this as part of an explanation as to why Germany itself has a literature that, like its land, is divided in two.

In the last weeks of the western phase of the world's biggest war, Eisenhower, inflated to mythical size by public relations officers, had absolute authority in the military campaign. The unfortunate political decisions dividing Germany into zones for postwar occupation had not included Berlin, and many British experts have criticized Eisenhower's failure to realize the importance of taking that city, among them Churchill and Lord Alanbrooke. The historian H. C. O'Neill, known as "Strategicus," author of a standard work on the First World War and of an eight-

TWENTIETH-CENTURY GERMAN LITERATURE

volume account of the Second, has lamented that President Roosevelt, in the physical weakness of his last days, "was responsible for an almost incredible political directive and Eisenhower was left to rationalize it in military terms. We should have preferred this great man [Roosevelt] to turn the last page of his life with a decision that better became him, and the causes for which he stood."

Eisenhower reported to the Combined Chiefs of Staff that he did not feel that Berlin represented an important military objective: "Military factors, when the enemy was on the brink of final defeat, were more important in my eyes than political considerations"—political considerations that were later to plague President Eisenhower.

Field Marshal Montgomery says in his *Memoirs* that Eisenhower wrote to him of Berlin: "That place has become, so far as I am concerned, nothing but a geographical location, and I have never been interested in these." Montgomery adds that the important thing at the time was "to ensure that when that day [of final defeat of the German army] arrived, we would have a political balance to help us, the western nations, to win the peace. That meant getting possession of certain political centers in Europe before the Russians—notably Vienna, Prague, and Berlin." Eisenhower had no true understanding of such matters, and one of the main reasons why he didn't try to take Berlin is that, as so often, his intelligence (the word is used here in the military sense) was faulty. He and his staff were in a flap about a supposed German plan to make a last stand in a "southern redoubt."

The southern-redoubt story, and the rumors of "werewolves" that would ravage the country, were Joseph Goebbels' last grim joke before he annihilated himself and his family in the Berlin bunker. And now the Berlin Wall divides the city as a permanent mockery.

German literature is partitioned, as the country itself is, into east and west, usually considered separately. And there are also, once again, the literatures of Austria and of German-speaking Switzerland, also essentially a part of Germanic literature.

After Chaos and Old Night: New Literary Beginnings

For a while after the shock of war, little writing came out of Germany except journalism. Then, as prosperity began to dazzle the western part of the country, most of the literature that began to appear dealt with immediate problems: sex; trying to make good in the new society; rebuilding on ruins that must be forgotten. With a few exceptions, such as Theodor Plievier and Karl Jaspers, it was nearly fifteen years after the war before German writers began probing the country's recent past and assessing its guilt. The American novelist Kay Boyle was considerably ahead of many German writers in holding the mirror up to the country in the early postwar years, in *The Smoking Mountain* (1951). In those stories, Kay Boyle used fiction to communicate what cold statistics, straight history, and the most thorough sociology can never quite convey —the affective shadings of the subject. Many subsequent books by Germans make a similar affective investigation of national guilt. Of course some books, for example Rudolf Walter Leonhardt's *X-mal Deutschland* (1962; translated as *This Germany: The Story since the Third Reich*), candidly admit blame but also defend German attitudes, in Leonhardt's case rather aggressively. In Iron Curtain countries, the local propaganda identifies West Germany with Nazism; but in East Germany more than three hundred former Nazis occupy leading government positions, once again happily serving a master state.

The attitude of East Germany in such matters may be judged by the career of the man appointed premier after the death of Otto Grotewohl in 1964: General Willi Stoph. He was in Hitler's time a fervent Nazi. Before the war he wrote articles for Fascist magazines in which he praised Hitler and, as suggested earlier, General Stoph is not the first former high-ranking member of the Nazi Party to be given an important post in East Germany, which has never had denazification trials. Another top-flight East German official, Alwin Schaper, was on the staff of Dr. Joseph Goebbels and wrote violently anti-Semitic articles for him. It is notable that the East Germans have harsh laws against Jews. At the time of Hitler's defeat in 1945, about 3,400 Jews had survived in what became East Germany; by 1964 their numbers had shrunk to 1,700. The East German government has refused to return to them the property confiscated by the Nazis; this is, to the Communists, "state property."

The people living in East Germany have not always taken kindly to the communist domination, and many thousands have slipped across the border. In June 1953 the workingclass in the Soviet section of Berlin and various other parts of East Germany staged revolts and strikes which were promptly crushed by Russian armed forces. In August 1961 the government of East Germany built a high wall to demarcate East Berlin from West—a wall that stands as the greatest subhuman obscenity since the Nazi concentration camps. Many people have tunneled under that wall to escape into West Germany; some who have tried to get away have been brutally murdered by the so-called Volkspolizei (People's Police). But although West Berliners are occasionally permitted to cross into the eastern sector to visit relatives, the Wall still stands as a reminder to the rest of the world that the Communists of the so-called German People's Republic have to keep their people captive behind a high stone barrier guarded by armed brutes.

The Postwar Novel: Winds from the East

One of the elder statesmen of the German novel, Arnold Zweig, settled in East Germany after the Second World War and remained there to become a kind of dean of literature. He has served as president of the Academy of Letters in East Germany. The author of *The Case of Sergeant Grischa* had lived in Israel (then called Palestine) during most of the Nazi years. His most spectacular postwar novel, *Das Beil von Wandsbeck* (1947; *The Axe of Wandsbeck*), was mainly written in London during the war. It is a rather overlong story of a butcher in the Hamburg area in 1938 who, in order to obtain money he needs to save his business, agrees to act as executioner of some prisoners condemned to death. Zweig subsequently published several collections of short stories, including *Der Elfenbeinfächer* (1953; *The Ivory Fan*) and *Der Regenbogen* (1955; *The Rainbow*). *Die Feuerpause* (1954; *The Cease-Fire*) and *Die Zeit ist reif* (1957; *The Time Is Ripe*); he continued *Der grosse Krieg der weissen Männer* (*The Great War of the White Races*), the series in which *Grischa* was one of the early volumes.

The considerably younger Anna Seghers—she was born in 1900, Arnold Zweig in 1887—is also one of the literary idols of East Germany. Anna Seghers is the pen name of the Jewish writer Netty Reiling, who married the Hungarian sociologist László Radványi. Anna Seghers earned her doctor's degree at Heidelberg in 1924 with a dissertation on the Jewish aspects of Rembrandt's paintings. She began writing stories for the *Frankfurter Zeitung* under the name of Seghers, and her work was at first thought to be that of a man. When she published *Aufstand der Fischer von St. Barbara* (1928; *Revolt of the Fishermen of St. Barbara*, translated as *The Revolt of the Fishermen*), she again signed herself simply as Seghers. *The Revolt*, which deals with the opposition of a village fisherman to a monopoly, is generally considered her finest story. Anna Seghers, who had become a Communist in 1929, fled from Germany to Paris in 1933 with her husband and two children. Her novel *Der Kopflohn* (1933; *The Ransom*) is the story of a young socialist escaping from the Gestapo; the book is among other things an idealization of the German peasantry, as *Die Rettung* (1934; *The Rescue*) is a glorification of the German miners.

Der Weg durch den Februar (1935; *The Road Through February*) tells the story of the brutal massacre of the Vienna socialists in 1934. When the Second World War broke out, the French government treated many refugees from fascism brutally; Anna Seghers' husband was pitched into the worst concentration camp in France, Le Vernet. She managed, however, to continue her writing, and completed the novel that was to become her best-known work: *Das siebte Kreuz* (1942; *The Seventh Cross*), which was made into a Hollywood film featuring Spencer Tracy, Hume Cronyn, and Jessica Tandy. The title refers to the crosses to which seven prisoners who escape from a Nazi concentration camp are to be nailed; six are caught and crucified, but the seventh, Georg Heisler, manages to slip through all nets. The Gestapo agents are desperate to recapture him, since he challenges the myth of their invincibility. Various people of no political persuasion help him to evade them. It is a story of tight suspense in which the character of the hero is by intention thinly sketched in: at the end, the Nazi who has been in charge of the case decides that he has been "pursuing not just a single human being, but a featureless and inexhaustible force."

Anna Seghers left Paris with her two children after the Nazis marched in. While she was living in unoccupied France, the Exiled Writers' Committee of the League of American Writers and Publishers Committee was successful in its attempts to get her husband out of Le Vernet, after which the family moved to Mexico City for the rest of the war. Before her return to East Germany, Anna Seghers helped found the magazine *Free Germany* and the Heinrich Heine Club for Free German Culture. While still in Mexico, she wrote *Transit* (1944), a panoramic novel about the German refugees trying to escape from Marseille after the fall of France. In *Die Toten bleiben jung* (1949; *The Dead Stay Young*), Anna Seghers wrote a story of Berlin from the revolution of 1918 to the arrival of the Russians in 1945, a tangled and impossible plot involving many members of various social classes.

Der Ausflug der toten Mädchen (1947; *The Picnic of Dead Girls*) was a collection of five Seghers stories about the fate of people who opposed the Nazis. Three other tales, *Die Linie* (1950; *The Line*), dedicated to Stalin on his birthday, are weighed down by propaganda, while *Friedensgeschichten* (1950; *Peace Stories*) have their tendential quality somewhat reduced by their value as pictures of daily life in East Germany.

Anna Seghers' collected short stories were published in two volumes as *Der Bienenstock* (1956; *The Beehive*). Her novel *Die Entscheidung* (1959; *The Decision*) is another propagandistic book, dealing with the supposedly good things that happened east of the Elbe in the years 1947–1951.

Some of the other leading East German novelists include Bruno Apitz, Willi Bredel, Eduard Claudius, Franz Fühmann, Bernhard Kellermann, Alfred Kurella, Hans Marwitza, Karl Mundstock, Erwin Strittmayer, and Bodo Uhse. Of these, the oldest was Bernhard Kellermann (1879–1951), well known before the war, who was particularly famous in Russia after 1927. He went to East Germany in 1945 and, before his death, wrote one novel about the Nazi epoch, *Totentanz* (1948; *Death Dance*). Hans Marwitza (born 1890), a Communist from the age of thirty, was a member of the workingclass who during the Second World War worked in a metal factory in the United States. A naïf and sentimental writer, he began in 1945 to publish partly autobiographical volumes, which he has followed with portraits of the idealized life of an East German family in the series *Die Kumiaks* (1948–1959; *The Kumiaks*). Bruno Apitz (born 1900), a Communist all his mature life, spent eight years in the Buchenwald concentration camp, which he wrote of in his novel *Nackt unter Wölfen* (1958; *Naked Among Wolves*). Another novel about the concentration camps is the popular paperback by Alfred Kurella, *Die Gronauer Akten* (1960; *The Gronau Documents*). Willi Bredel, born in 1901 and a Communist from the age of eighteen, was a loyalist officer in the Spanish civil war and spent the Second World War in Moscow. He has published abundantly, and is best known for his trilogy, *Die Väter* (1941; *The Fathers*), *Die Söhne* (1947; *The Sons*), and *Die Enkel* (1953; *The Grandsons*). This panel of portraits of a workingclass family goes from the beginning of the twentieth century to the middle of it; the books are highly regarded in East Germany, but their propagandistic distortions are hardly of the kind to make the novels interesting to readers in the Western world.

Bodo Uhse (born 1904), a man who was first a Nazi and then a Communist, spent the years 1940–1948 in Mexico, where he wrote his principal novel, *Leutnant Bertram* (1944; *Lieutenant Bertram*). From 1949 to 1958 he edited the East German magazine *Aufbau* (*Building*). A writer of some force, whose work is but slightly lessened in value by its devotion to social realism, Uhse was for the most part artistically successful in such novels as *Patrioten* (1954; *The Patriots*) and in the short stories of *Die Brücke* (1952; *The Bridge*). His *Gestalten und Probleme* (1959; *Forms and Problems*) contains essays and memoirs. Eduard

Claudius (born Schmidt in 1911) has been a Communist since adolescence. After spending the Second World War in Switzerland, he entered the East German diplomatic service. He has published several tendential novels, among them *Menschen an unserer Seite* (1951; *Men on Our Side*), in which an old worker by his sacrifices educates his colleagues to become better Communists, and *Von der Liebe soll Mann nicht nur sprechen* (1957; *One Should Not Only Speak of Love*), in which a naïve peasant girl develops into an aggressive Communist woman. Claudius' shorter tales are considerably less propagandistic.

Erwin Strittmayer (born 1912), a dramatist as well as a writer of fiction, has written some novels which in East Germany are considered to be among the finest examples of social realism, particularly *Katzgraben* (1954) and *Tinko* (1954). Karl Mundstock (born 1915) has written effective war tales and novels, among the former *Bis zum letzten Mann* (1957; *To the Last Man*). His novel *Die Stunde des Dietrich Conradi* (1958; *The Hour of Dietrich Conradi*) is about the inner conflicts of a Nazi officer. Franz Fühmann (born 1922) was a prisoner in Russia during the Second World War; after his release he became a resident of East Germany, where he has achieved fame as a poet and short-story writer. In 1955 his tale "Kameraden" ("Comrades") was one of the notable successes of the "thaw" that had come west from Russia; *Stürzende Schatten* (1959; *Plunging Shadows*) contains some excellent dreamlike stories.

The most promising recent novelist from East Germany is Manfred Bieler (born 1934), author of the satiric novel *Bonifaz oder Der Matrose in der Flasche* (1963; *Bonifaz, or the Sailor in the Bottle*, translated as *The Sailor in the Bottle*). Published almost simultaneously in East and West Germany and soon after elsewhere on the Continent and later in England and the United States, the book has been an international success. Bonifaz, a sailor who has been a war prisoner, is forbidden further combat—and he ardently wishes to be a neutral. The setting is Germany in the last days of the Second World War. As the Russians approach Bonifaz's home town he bids his wife farewell and goes wandering across the shattered country for a series of picaresque adventures, often highly amusing. Since the book makes fun of those who accept either communism or fascism, it is an oddball importation from behind the eastern-zone barriers; but although its satire is often funny it rarely bites deep. Bieler has been compared with the western-zone novelist Günter Grass, but so far (and Bieler has written numerous stories and radio plays) he has not indicated that his imagination, however mischievous, is of the scope of Grass's. But it is refreshing to find a book so comparatively good as *The Sailor in the Bottle* coming from behind the Wall.

Another surprising product of East Germany is the first novel of Fritz Rudolf Fries (born 1935), *Der Weg nach Oobliadooh* (*The Road to Oobliadooh*), published in West Germany in 1966. The outlandish word in the title comes from the Dizzy Gillespie song, "I Know a Wonderful Princess in the Land of Oobliadooh," which is a kind of Never-Never Land to Fries's characters, some of whom try living in West Germany but feel estranged there and return to Leipzig. The story takes place in the late 1950's; it is shrewdly witty, full of trenchant social observations, and it contains a gallery of convincing characters. The book has had the largest success of any novel since the first publications of Group 47, and Fries is now regarded as one of the most promising of the newer Germanic writers.

For the most part, the fiction of East Germany accurately reflects the life there, which was for many years mechanical and drab. The blossoming prosperity of the mid-1960's may change the tone of the literature, as it did earlier in West Germany. East German writers are not compelled to join the German Writers' Union, but for those who do not belong to it, chances for publication are slight. Censorship keeps a tight hold over writers; state commissions look over all publications, allocate paper supplies, and control the import and export of books. The government owns most bookstores and supervises the libraries. Stories of crime, adventure, or love must have favorable political implications, and the element of humor hardly exists in these writings. Most of the great modern authors of the outer world are ignored, and even Soviet writers who do not conform strictly to party principles are not published in East Germany. The reading public has German classics of the past at its disposal, in cheap editions, but most of these volumes contain prefaces telling the reader what to think about the book he is holding. The better early work of such authors as Brecht, Arnold Zweig, and Seghers is available, and occasionally a West German author is carefully permitted to be read by East Germans—for example, Heinrich Böll. But in the main East German writers and readers exist in a captivity symbolized by the Berlin Wall, which is patrolled by the armed "People's Police."

The Theater of East Germany

The theaters of Germany were reduced to rubble during the Second World War, particularly in the final bombardments. For a while after peace came, actors had to improvise playhouses, usually in back rooms

that had survived bombardment. Drama was given an impetus in the
Soviet zone long before the West German revival began: Soviet cultural-
affairs officers and the East German Kulturbund rustled up performers
and encouraged social-realist plays. As noted earlier, Bertolt Brecht was
given his own theater, but in the last years of his life seemed unable to
write plays to order. Yet his Theater am Schiffbauerdamm kept on presenting the older Brecht dramas, with continued réclame. But Brecht's
epic-theater disciples—such as the left-wing novelist and poet, Günter
Weisenborn, and Peter Hacks, who left Munich for East Germany—have
not been very successful in their attempts to imitate the master. Weisenborn, however, attracted some attention because in *Die Illegalen* (1948;
The Underground) he wrote the first anti-Nazi drama, dealing with a
subject Alfred Neumann had treated in his novel written in exile, *Es
waren ihrer sechs* (1945; *There Were Six of Them*, translated as *Six of
Them*)— the revolt and execution of some anti-Nazi students in Munich
during the war.

One of Brecht's followers, however, Helmut Baierl, has been fairly
successful, especially with his play *Die Feststellung* (1958; *The Test
Case*). This has been produced at the Theater am Schiffbauerdamm and,
throughout East Germany, in peasants' collective farms and before factory
groups. Although Brechtian in style, the little comedy often resembles
those written in the Soviet Union dealing with the problems of the
peasants' collectives. In the story a peasant who has left for West Germany
but has not been happy there goes back to his collective in the east zone.
He brings a problem home with him: shall he be punished as a deserter?
The local party leader and the peasant give quite different accounts as to
why he left in the first place, and then one of the other peasants suggests
a way of getting at the truth. In an episode which has a Brechtian in-
genuity, the peasant and the official re-enact the departure of the peasant,
reversing roles so that the party leader plays the stubborn peasant and
the peasant is the overbearing official. As they play this amusing scene,
each sees the other's point of view, and the party leader realizes that if
he had been in the peasant's place he would have left, too. So he permits
the fugitive to rejoin his collective. The play, written with colloquial
liveliness, has a wide appeal for East German audiences of all kinds.

In 1962 Baierl scored another success with *Frau Flinz* (*Mrs. Flinz*).
In recent years, other dramatic efforts that have met with approval include
Rainer Kerndl's *Schatten eines Mädchens* (*Shadow of a Young Woman*)
and Hedda Zinner's *Ravensbrücker Ballade* (1961; *Ballad of Ravens-
bruck*), plays that concern the recent past rather than the present. Other
dramatic successes that might be mentioned include Gustav von Wangen-

heim's *Studentenkomödie* (1959; *Student Comedy*) and *Die vertauschten Brüder* (1960; *The Exchanged Brothers*), Fritz Kuhn's *Venezianisches Glas* (1958; *Venetian Glass*), and Heiner Müller's *Die Umsiedlerin* (1960; *The Transplanted Woman*). Not all dramatic productions in East Germany are Tendenzstücke (message plays); indeed, only a minority of them are, and the theaters often revive classics of various countries.

Lyric Poetry since the Second World War

In both East and West Germany, lyric poetry, the poetry of intensely personal expression, recovered more quickly from the effects of the war than other literary forms did. Some of the older poets who had long been quiet reappeared, and important new writers of verse sprang up. The force of recent German poetry is almost that of a renaissance.

In outlook, much of this verse is sensitively personal. There is a nature-magic school deriving from the previously mentioned Oskar Loerke and from Wilhelm Lehmann (born 1882), whose *Sämtliche Werke (Complete Works)* came out in three volumes in 1962. Since the war his writings have had great influence. There are also various traditional poets, and in technique the newer verse is sometimes abstract. Often, too, it goes back to the dadaists and surrealists, as well as to the expressionists. The greatest single influence on the younger poets during these times was Gottfried Benn, who died in 1956. He brought out a collection of postwar poems in 1948 and published a number of influential essays, notably *Prosa ausserhalb von Raum und Zeit, ins imaginäre gebaut, ins momentane, flächige gelegt, ihr Gegenspiel ist Psychologie und Evolution* (1949; *Prose Beyond Space and Time, Built into the Imaginary, Set in the Temporary and the Superficial, Whose Opposite Is Psychology and Evolution*). Benn's approach was politically somewhat nihilistic, and in his poetry he concentrated on the moment non-historical, as in the first stanza of his poem "Chaos"

> Chaos—epochs and zones
> bluffing mimicry
> the long sequence of aeons
> into the moment of Never—
> the Miletus marbles, Travertines,
> of Hippocratic radiance.
> The columbine of the corpse:
> The doves fly in.

In contrast to such work and its influence, East Germany has often produced tendentious poetry, as propaganda not to be taken seriously, although the writers there have also turned out verse that has little to distinguish it from that of the West Germans, the Austrians, or even the Swiss.

A poet who might be considered highly representative of the age is Nelly Sachs, born in Berlin in 1891, who escaped from Germany in 1940. She has since lived in Stockholm, but is often celebrated in her native land. In 1960, the West German city of Dortmund established a Nelly Sachs Prize and two years later the world première of her play *Eli* took place there. Her postwar volumes of poetry include *In den Wohnungen des Todes* (1947; *The Habitations of Death*), *Und Niemand weiss weiter* (1957; *And No One Knows Further*), and *Flucht und Verwandlung* (1959; *Escape and Transformation*). Nelly Sachs often writes vividly of the horrors of the modern world and asks fundamental questions about it, as in the poem beginning "Aber vielleicht" ("Perhaps"), during the course of which the poet wonders whether, behind death, we are tilling the fields of creation:

> Perhaps the roundabout ways
> of man's fall
> like the stealthy desertion of meteors
> occur in the alphabet of thunderstorms
> along with rainbows?
>
> Who likewise knows
> the grace of fruitfulness
> and how the seed is turned
> in barren earth
> toward the sucking mouths of light?

Nelly Sachs revisited Germany in 1965 to receive the German Book Trade's Peace Prize at the Frankfurt International Book Fair. She said that she had made the journey because, despite the horrors of the past, she had faith in the newer generation of Germans. In 1966 Nelly Sachs was awarded the Nobel Prize for literature (with the Israeli author, Samuel J. Agnon).

Many of Nelly Sachs's fellow poets had been or have remained exiles. One of the most notable of these was Johannes R. Becher (1891–1958), previously discussed among the between-wars poets. After the Nazis came into power he moved to Moscow, where he stayed until the end of the war, at which time he went to East Berlin. Before his death Becher was president of the Kulturbund, the East German Cultural Union. Another East German poet, Peter Huchel (born 1903), was a prisoner of war in Russia. After his release he settled in the East Berlin area, where he edited the journal *Sinn und Form* (*Sense and Form*) from 1948 to 1962. His postwar volumes of verse include *Gedichte* (1948; *Poems*) and *Chausseen Chausseen* (1963; *Highways, Highways*). Huchel has often written nature poetry (he was once an agricultural worker) and sometimes deals with religious themes, as in his "Bericht des Pfarrers vom Untergang seiner Gemeinde" ("Report of the Minister on the Destruction of His Parish"), which carries a religious motif through its description of a town being ravaged by fire during an air raid. In the church, the burning figure of Christ falls from its cross, to the accompaniment of the cries of "brassy trumpets / Of angels, flying through the storm of fire." Huchel evokes moving images of horror and terror—women's hair blowing about like hay gleaming in fire, planes coming low to strafe the fleeing people: "It was not the ruin of Hell: / Bones and skull as if stoned / In fury, as the dust diminished / And in the shocked light Christ's head / Broke loose from the wood." The planes thundered away through a red sky, "As if severing the vein of midday." Even the graves had been torn up, lawlessness reigned, and "My day was too short to see God." Towns kept burning, lawlessness continued to thrive, and "children, old people / Walked with dusty feet across my prayer." As they all went along, weeping under their burdens, "There did not come down the long winter highway / A Simon of Cyrene." The unexpected allusion, going back to the beginnings of Christianity, gives force to the climax. It is not surprising that Huchel's poems, which often have a universal quality, are widely appreciated in the West.

Another East German poet also published in West Germany, Johannes Bobrowski (1917–1965), was also a writer of short stories; he brought out two collections of them in 1965, the year he died, *Mäusefest* (*Feast of Mice*) and *Boehlendorff und andere* (*Boehlendorff and Others*). His books of verse include *Schattenland Ströme* (1962; *Shadowland Streams*). A native of Tilsit, Bobrowski chose to live in East Berlin. His work is rich with the landscapes of East Prussia. He was not cut off from cultural contacts with West Germany and in 1964 attended a conference in Sweden with the advance-guard "47 Group" of West German writers.

Two Germanic poets living abroad in voluntary exile died of heart ailments in 1952: Jesse Thoor (born 1905) and Franz Baremann Steiner (born 1909). Thoor, whose real name was Peter Karl Höfler, was a workingclass poet, a former Communist, who spent a number of years in

England and died during a visit to Austria. A collection of his writings, *Sonette und Lieder* (*Sonnets and Songs*) was published in 1956. Steiner was a native of Prague who became an anthropologist at Oxford, where he died. His poetry, published in part in a volume called *Unruhe ohne Uhr* (1954; *Timeless Unrest*), is still little known but is gradually being recognized for its sensitivity of vision and expertness of phrasing.

Hans Egon Holthusen (born 1913), who has recently been living in New York City, was immediately after the war one of the most topical poets (Zeitdichter) in Germany, not only because he often dealt with the theses of destruction, but also because he embodied in his verse the influence of Eliot and Rilke. Yet he has a voice distinctly his own, particularly in such evocative poems as "Auch Variationen über Zeit und Tod" ("And Reflections on Love and Death"). "Tabula rasa" has an almost Rilkean opening: "To make an end. To make a beginning, / The unheard-of one which terrifies and weakens us. / Once more humanity will soak this earth in blood and tears"—but the poem goes on to somewhat post-Rilkean visions and images. Holthusen's books of verse include *Labyrinthische Jahre* (1952; *Labyrinthine Year*). In recent years he has written valuably perceptive essays on modern literature.

Hans Werner Cohn (born 1916), who left Germany after Hitler's takeover, has since lived in England, where he is secretary of a psychoanalytical association. He has continued to write poetry in his native language and has contributed verse to German anthologies such as *Transit* (1956) and *Expeditionen* (1959; *Expeditions*), as well as to the journal *Merkur*. He published *Gedichte* (*Poems*) in 1950 and 1964. His verse, which has become more disciplined with the years, has a haunting, imaginative quality that is somewhat reminiscent of the writings of Franz Kafka. Like Cohn, Erich Fried, born in Vienna in 1921, lives in London. He has translated T. S. Eliot and Dylan Thomas into German and has written several books of verse, including *Deutschland* (1944; *Germany*), *Österreich* (1945; *Austria*), *Gedichte* (1958; *Poems*), and *Reich der Steine* (1963; *Kingdom of Stones*). An admirer of such innovators as Gerard Manley Hopkins and e. e. cummings, Fried is an innovator with language and image, technically expert and often an exciting poet.

Paul Celan, a voluntary exile who has long lived in Paris, was born in 1920 in Czernowitz (Bucovina), Rumania, of Jewish parents. After studying medicine in Bucharest he went to Vienna in 1947, moving the next year to Paris. His collections of verse include *Der Sand aus den Urnen* (1948; *The Sand from the Urns*), *Mohn und Gedächtnis* (1952; *Poppy and Memory*), *Von Schwelle zu Schwelle* (1955; *From Step to*

Step), and *Die Niemandrose* (1963; *No Man's Rose)*. Celan has also translated a number of French and Russian authors into German, including Arthur Rimbaud, Paul Valéry, Sergei Esenin, Aleksandr Blok, and Osip Mandelshtam. Celan himself derives somewhat from the expressionists and the surrealists, and while his metaphors are often daring, he keeps them under control. Their associations may be splintered between different kinds of reality, stretched across vivid spaces of montage, but they are always fresh and suggestive of discipline working with imagination. Celan's best-known poem so far is "Die Todesfuge" ("The Death Fugue"), which he published in 1955; it is the most remarkable of all German poems dealing with the fate of the Jews in the time of Hitler. "The Death Fugue" begins:

> Black milk of dawn we drink it at nightfall
> We drink it at midday in the morning we drink it at nights
> we drink and drink it
> we will dig a grave in the sky where there is no crowd
> a man lives in the house who plays with snakes he writes
> he writes as night falls to Germany your golden hair Margarete
> he writes it and leaves the house and in the glitter of the stars he
>   whistles for his dogs
> he whistles for his Jews to come and dig a grave in the earth
> he commands us to play now for the dance. . . .

Through other stanzas the almost disembodied, choral voice repeats the word patterns with variations, until the end:

> Death is a master from Germany his eye is blue
> he hits you with a blue bullet he hits you exactly
> a man is in the house your golden hair Margarete
> he sets his dogs on us he gives us a grave in the sky
> he plays with snakes and dreams that death is a master from Germany
> your golden hair Margarete
> your ashen hair Shulamite.

A German woman-poet, Marie Luise Kaschnitz, was born in 1901 in Karlsruhe and has in recent years lived in Rome and Frankfurt-am-Main. She writes fiction as well as poetry; her recent volumes of verse include *Gedichte* (1947; *Poems)*, *Totentanz und Gedichte zur Zeit* (1947; *Death Dance and Poems for the Age)*, *Zukunftsmusik* (1950; *The Future's Music)*, *Ewige Stadt* (1952; *Eternal City)*, *Neue Gedichte* (1957; *New Poems)*, and *Dein Schweigen-meine Stimme* (1962; *Your Silence—My Voice)*. Marie Luise Kaschnitz is a traditional poet who is perhaps less

widely recognized than she should be because she does not practice the
verbal elaboration characteristic of so much recent German poetry. Her
themes are often religious, and she is a poet of lamentation. Few writers
have so vividly written of the ruins left by the Second World War. In
"Nichts und Alles" ("Nothing and Everything"), for example, she
begins, "Nothing is so sad as what half-remains / Rooms ripped open to
the sky, / and bed and cradle where once hope existed, / as lifeless as
stage sets. . . ." Light shines on the dust, and the beauty of a nearby
cloud seems as strange as it is unlovable:

> What became of the hands' tender touch,
> the tears' gleam, the moment's happiness?
> A storm comes and seizes us before the end
> Of our fated fellow travelers.
>
> So we know ourselves as fugitives
> And from now on know everything and nothing as our own.

Among contemporary Austrian poets, three women have attained high
rank: Christine Lavant, Christine Busta, and Ingeborg Bachmann. The
first two were born in 1915, the last in 1926. Christine Lavant is a native
of Carinthia, where she lives permanently, now nearly blind and deaf.
Christine Busta is a librarian in her native Vienna, while Ingeborg
Bachmann, who was born in Klagenfurt, Austria, has lived in Berlin,
Rome, and Zürich. Lavant and Busta frequently deal with religious
themes; Bachmann often writes in an existentialist vein, the poetry of
"engagement."

Christine Lavant's books of verse include *Die Bettlerschale* (1956;
The Beggar's Cup), *Spindel im Mond* (1959; *Spindle in the Moon*), and
Der Pfauenschrei (1962; *The Peacock's Cry*). She is often personal
("My eyesight has become so feeble / in the last bitter weeks.") Her
religious strain appears in such poems as "Jesus Christus, ich bete und
bete" ("Jesus Christ, I Pray and Pray"), in which she tells Christ that
he will have to wait for her until she is healed: poison is in her blood,
her heart is a set trap, and her thoughts, when she stops praying, are
sly and horrible snares. Even her mother might hesitate to stay the night
in this house. The poet doubts that she can purify herself; her heart
yearns for love, for simple human love that warms, that can cleanse and
prepare one for heaven:

> Therefore, Lord Christ, my prayer is
> perhaps merely a lure, not meant for you,

though I have faith in your splendor,
which every day grows greater
in my unworthy eyes.

The poetry collections of Christine Busta include *Lampe und Delphin* (1955; *Lamp and Dolphin*), *Die Scheune der Vögel* (1958; *The Birds' Barn*), and *Die Sternenmühle* (1959; *The Mill of Stars*). This librarian frequently writes verses for children. And, as noted earlier, she also produces religious poetry. Sometimes she writes of love, as in "Jahreszeiten" ("Seasons"), in which the snow comes down night after night "as quietly as secret sadness." And: "I know not where you sleep"; in other gardens it is now spring, all is in bloom; love lives not by right, but by magic: "For every hour when you were far away, I have / Saved a snowflake. I cannot find them now. / And snow will be falling on strange windows."

Like Christine Lavant, Ingeborg Bachmann has often composed radio plays of the kind so popular in Germanic countries. And in 1960 she wrote the libretto for the opera *Prinz Friedrich von Homburg*, by Hans Werner Henze, the best known among recent German composers. Ingebord Bachmann's books include *Die gestundete Zeit* (1953; *Borrowed Time*) and *Anrufung des grossen Bären* (1956; *Invocation of the Big Dipper*). She often expresses the apprehension of the age, as in the title poem of *Borrowed Time*, beginning:

Harder days are coming.
The termination of our borrowed time
Is apparent on the horizon.
Soon you must lace your shoe
And drive the dogs back to the swampland farms.

The wind makes the fishes' entrails cold; the lupins' light burns faintly. Your gaze searches through the fog. Your beloved sinks in the sand, which rises to her wandering hair, choking her into silence and finding her mortal, willing to part after each embrace. Then:

Do not look back.
Lace your shoe,
Drive the dogs back.
Throw the fish into the sea.
Light of lupins!

Harder days are coming.

Ingeborg Bachmann often draws forcefully upon nature in her work, as in the poems "Das erstgeborene Land" ("The Firstborn Land") and "Nebelland" ("Fog Land"), which take their symbols and images intensely from nature, often in its chill and bleak aspects. But there is sometimes a metaphysical strain in her verse as well as the existential involvement. Bachmann's poetic ancestors have been enumerated as Goethe and Hölderlin among writers of the past, Rilke and von Hofmannstahl among the earlier moderns, with Benn, Brecht, Trakl, and Ivan Goll (who also wrote in French) among the more recent innovators, and Eliot and Auden among foreign authors. But, whatever the echoes, Ingeborg Bachmann writes out of her own intensity, and of her own place and time, always with a fiercely personal pressure. In 1964 she published *Gedichte, Erzählungen, Hörspiel, Essays* (*Poems, Narrations, Radio Play, Essays*), a rewarding miscellaneous volume.

Outstanding German-Swiss poets of the time include Werner Zemp (1906–1959), Rainer Brambach (born 1917), Kuno Raeber (born 1922), and Hans Rudolf Hilty (born 1925). Zemp is best known for his pastoral poetry; a passage from his "Vorosterliche Landschaft" ("Landscape Before Easter") reads:

> When at last from darkness and grave
> We were bewildered like Lazarus in open air,
> See, for there the day had darkened.
> Wind fled from the hill, emerald green
> Before the tower of cloud, and with it a scent
> Of young buds, and in a stall
> A raging black horse stamped and whinnied....

A second and augmented edition of Zemp's *Gedichte* (*Poems*) was published in 1954. Raeber, who after various residences in Switzerland, France, and Germany, settled in Munich, has written several volumes of poetry, including *Flussufer* (1963; *Riverbank*). Hilty brought out a book of verse, *Eingebrannt in den Schnee* (*Burned into the Snow*), in 1960, and a novel, *Parzifal*, in 1962. Brambach, who has worked as a gardener, farmhand, and peat-cutter, first wrote poetry for the annual collection published in Munich, *Junge Lyrik*. His first volume was *Tagwerk* (1959; *Day Work*). Most of his writing is nature poetry, as in "Der Baum" ("The Tree"—"Foliage hangs flag-like") and "Granit" ("Granite"—"You taste the dust of stone forests"), but he can be epigrammatically ironic, as in "Paul":

Nineteen hundred and seventeen
on a day below zero he was born,

he ran wild across the playground,
fell, and kept running,

he threw the ball across the schoolyard,
fell, and kept running,

with his gun in his arm across the training ground,
fell, and kept running,

on a subzero day
into Russian barrage-fire

and fell.

Among today's best-known poets who have elected to live in West Germany, Günter Eich and Albrecht Goes have seniority. Eich was born in 1907, Goes in 1908. Their work is of different caliber though each of them writes with a religious sense.

Eich brought out his first verses in 1930, but it was not until after the Second World War that he attained wide recognition. A native of Silesia, he now lives in Bavaria. He studied law and Sinology; the influence of Oriental culture upon his verse gives him, at least on one level, a trait in common with Ezra Pound. Eich's "Japanischer Holzschnitt" ("Japanese Woodcut"), for instance, is technically and spiritually evocative of Eastern life and poetry:

A pink horse,
with bridle and saddle—
for whom?

However close the rider is,
he stays hidden.

You come instead,
step into the picture
and seize the reins!

Eich's postwar volumes include *Abgelegene Gehöfte* (1948; *Remote Farms*), *Untergrundbahn* (1949; *Underground Railway*), *Botschaften des Regens* (1955; *Messages of the Rain*), *Ausgewählte Gedichte* (1960; *Selected Poems*), and *Zu den Akten* (1964; *Into the Files*). Eich has been one of Germany's most popular authors of radio dramas, employing an economical, unrhetorical style. In *Träume: Vier Spiele* (1953; *Dreams: Four Plays*), Eich wrote a forceful passage that sums up the felt but often unexpressed terror of modern man; counseling his listeners to "Consider this," Eich says that "man is man's enemy," thinking of destruction:

As you taste wine in the Randersacker cellars
Or pick oranges in the Alicante gardens,
As you drift into sleep at the Miramar hotel near the Taormina beach,
Or light an All Souls' Day candle in the Feuchtwangen churchyard,
While as a fisherman you draw in the net over the Dogger Bank,
Or in Detroit remove a screw from the conveyor belt,
As you set plants in the Setzuan rice terraces,
Or ride a mule over the Andes,
Consider this!

Consider it when a hand tenderly touches you,
Consider this in your wife's embrace,
Consider this when you hear your child laugh!

Consider this, that after the enormous destructions
Every man will demonstrate that he was innocent.

Consider this:
No place on the map are Korea and Bikini,
But in your own heart.
Consider this, that you are guilty of every atrocity
However far from you occurring—

Eich, who often expresses pessimism, is nevertheless a poet of religious enthusiasm when he writes of nature, as he frequently does. He has said that he composes his poems in order to adjust himself to reality.

Albrecht Goes is a clergyman in the German Evangelical Church who, besides his war poetry, has written a gripping novella, *Unruhige Nacht* (1949; *Unquiet Night*), about his experiences in the Second World War, when he was a hospital and prison chaplain and knew a deserter facing execution. The first important collection of verse by Goes was in his *Gedichte: 1930–1950* (1950; *Poems: 1930–1950*); in 1964 he brought out a volume of poems, essays, and stories, under the title *Aber im Winde das Wort* (*But the Word in the Wind*).

Another poet with a strong religious strain, Rudolf Hagelstange, was born in 1912 at Nordhausen in the Harz Mountains. While serving as a soldier in the German army in the Second World War he wrote a sonnet sequence, *Das Venezianische Credo* (*The Venetian Creed*), which was first passed around secretly as an anti-Nazi document and then published after the war. Hagelstange has also written such volumes of poetry as

Es spannt sich der Bogen (1943; *The Bow Tightens Itself*), *Strom der Zeit* (1948; *Stream of Time*), *Zwischen Stern und Staub* (1953; *Between Star and Dust*), and *Lied der Jahre* (1961; *Song of the Years*), as well as a travel book, *How Do You Like America?* (1957). His most notable poetry is found in *Ballade vom verschütteten Leben* (1952; *Ballad of the Buried Life*). One of his typical poems, vividly presenting and at the same time investigating experience, is the Heraclitean "Der Gletscher" ("The Glacier"), which begins:

> Abruptly, in the middle of the night,
> which around the sparkling axis of the moon
> strikes her peacock-blue wheel, you understand:
> time is all and nothing. And place is
> great and small, for both
> are hollowed and diminished
> by the only certitude:
> the grand motion.

The glacier moves in silence, breathing; it fills time and place and the expectant valleys. Who made the great flanks where light calculates its day? A falling of thunder answers this, along with the myriad melting drops mixed in a second's atom:

> All is flow. The living
> ripens with death itself, and death
> carries
> upon its spinning corpse
> glowing life.

Of the resident West German poets born since Hagelstange, the best known both in and out of Germany are Karl Krolow, Heinz Piontek, and Günter Grass, who will be discussed after several writers almost as well known though not necessarily any less competent in their verse than that trio. The eldest of the poets to be considered now is Hilde Domin, Hagelstange's contemporary; she was born in Cologne in 1912. After studying in Italy she taught school in England and Latin America; she has also translated numerous works from the Spanish. Since returning to Germany in 1954, she has brought out three volumes of poetry—*Nur eine Rose als Stütze* (1959; *Only a Rose as Support*), *Rückkehr der Schiffe* (1962; *Return of the Ships*), and *Hier* (1964; *Here*). Dispensing with meter and rhyme, Hilde Domin writes with a compressed intensity, often in a form resembling the little Japanese type of poem known as haiku.

Hans Bender, born in Mülhausen in 1919, served with the German army in the Second World War, and after it was kept as a prisoner in Russia until 1949. Upon his return to Germany he settled in Cologne. He has written poetry and fiction and edits *Junge Lyrik*, an annual anthology. He is co-editor of the literary magazine *Akzente* (*Accents*), with Walter Höllerer, who teaches at the Technical University of Berlin. Höllerer, born in Bavaria in 1925, writes in a language of comparative simplicity in an age characterized by verbal intricacy. His books of poetry include *Der andere Gast* (1952; *The Other Guest*) and *Wie entsteht ein Gedicht?* (1964; *How Does a Poem Originate?*). The poet Helmut Heissenbüttel is an experimenter with language in a way that Höllerer is not. Heissenbüttel, born in Wilhelmshaven in 1921, moved to Stuttgart after the Second World War. His books include *Kombinationen* (1954; *Combinations*) and *Topographien* (1956; *Topographies*), as well as several volumes named *Textbuch 1* and so forth, beginning in 1961. Heissenbüttel is a kind of neo-dadaist, a poet always in the process of becoming, filling his pages with experimental work. Much of it is striking, somewhat in the manner of the imagists and of the short, sharp poems of Ezra Pound's early period, such as "In a Station of the Métro." Yet Heissenbüttel is more daring, particularly in his telescoping of words, with which he strains even the German language, accustomed as it is to multiple compounds. In presenting a view from a window, for example, he can write of Waschleinenphysiognomie, clotheslinephysiognomy. But he often brings modern cities or riverside landscapes startlingly to life, as in "Kombination XI," which begins:

Night is a design of arclamps and autocarrearlights.
On the surface of the Alster the white flags of night stand.
Under the trees the shadows walk.
It's myself.

—and ends:

And the questions are the sentences I cannot utter.
And the thoughts are the birds that fly away and do not come back.

Another poet who uses words in an arresting way is Dagmar Nick, born in 1926, author of volumes of poetry entitled *Märtyrer* (1947; *Martyr*), *Das Buch Holofernes* (1955; *The Holofernes Book*), and *In den Ellipsen des Mondes* (1959; *In the Ellipses of the Moon*). The poem "Liebeslied" ("Love Song") gives a suggestion of the force of Dagmar

Nick's writing. Having killed the she-wolf whose heartbeat she was, she drank her wolf's blood, making her throat bitter and filling her voice with pain. To forget, she opened the sluices of dreams, which bore her to the shore of other eyes:

> I have slept
> in the flaming feathers of the phoenix.
> Fire burst out of the ash.
> And I was not burned.

A poet startling in a different way, Hans Magnus Enzensberger was born at Kaufbeuren, Bavaria, on November 11, 1929, the eleventh anniversary of the armistice. There are no truces in his poetry, which uses ideas as weapons of attack. Some of his poems, such as "schaum" ("foam"), have a kinship with the violent protest of the American beatnik verses, particularly Allen Ginsberg's "Howl."

Enzensberger grew up in Nuremberg in the days of the Nazis' black parades. At the age of sixteen he was conscripted into the German army and, after brief service, went on walking tours of Europe and the United States. He has subsequently lived in both Norway and Germany and has been a columnist for the lively journal *Der Spiegel*. His books of poetry include *verteidigung der wölfe* (1957; *vindication of the wolves*), *landessprache* (1960; *national tongue*), and *Gedichte* (1962; *Poems*). He has also published essays and compiled a *museum der modernen poesie* (1960; *museum of modern poetry*) in fourteen languages. In his own work, Enzensberger seems to have been influenced mostly by the Germans Bertolt Brecht, Erich Kästner, and Gottfried Benn, by the Chilean Pablo Neruda, and the American e. e. cummings, with whom he generally shares an aversion for capital letters.

In his terse, tense lines, Enzensberger often praises the natural at the expense of the civilized. In "ehre sei der sellerie" ("in honor of celery"), for example, he eulogizes herbs, owls, rock, egg yolk, even the whale and the lightning: "they deserve an ode." He does not glorify cigar ashes or the dough-faced human beings who have filled "the bloody sky" with "these surgical stitches of smoke." But:

> the tender heart of earth, celery,
> more human than the human,
> does not eat its fellows,
> and lightning, let us praise lightning,
> or, for all I care, egg yolk.

The poem "an alle fernsprechteilnehmer" ("to all telephone subscribers") cries out its warning against the smugness of civilization, into
which a subtly destructive "something" is seeping. The poem "ins lesebuch
für die oberstufe" ("for an upper school textbook") warns a boy to
read timetables because they are more exact than odes. Be careful and do
not sing. The day will come when they will put up new blacklists on
the door and brand those who say no. The thing to do is learn to go
unrecognized; change neighborhood, identity, face. "Become adept at the
small betrayal." You, the fastidious, must learn an angry patience and
to grind fine the deadly powder to be blown into the lungs of power. In
"konjunktur" ("inflated market"), the poet turns his bitter satire against
the boom, telling the people it is not meat they are eating but bait. It
is not biscuit the hook tastes of but blood: "you sink your fangs into
one another's throats. / frightened by hunger, / your battle is for the
deadly bait."

This is almost the world the artist George Grosz saw in the Germany of
the years after the First World War. But Enzensberger dwells in the
world of Albert Camus, who wrote at length about the myth of Sisyphus,
who pushed uphill a stone that grew larger and larger until, near the top,
it rolled over Sisyphus' shoulder and bounded back down the hill, growing smaller as it went. Sisyphus patiently descended to recover it and
again began his upward journey, always with the same cruel result. Enzensberger's poem, "anweisung an sisyphos" ("instructions to sisyphos"),
tells Sisyphus it is good that he understands what he is doing, but he
should not be contented with it; he will not be thanked for what he is
doing: "hopelessness / is not a career. with their own / tragic condition
only changelings, / scarecrows, augurs are on good terms." Sisyphus
must not take comfort in his own importance, but should increase the
anger of the world, at least by a grain. For:

> there are too few men
> quietly going about the hopeless,
> uprooting hope like grass, rolling
> their laughter, the future,
> rolling their wrath up the mountains.

Hans Magnus Enzensberger has been associated with Gruppe 47 (Group
47), whose members are often satiric in outlook. Their work in general
belongs with a discussion of the recent German novel, although one of
the principal fiction writers of the circle is also a well-known poet:
Günter Grass.

Grass (born in 1927) is one of the poets who draws upon dadaism and surrealism for his striking verbal effects. His books of verse include *Vorzüge der Windhühner* (1956; *The Merits of the Wind Chicken*) and *Gleisdreieck* (1960). The latter takes its title from the name of the frontier station on the Berlin elevated when trains used to run between the sections of the divided city.

> Gleisdreieck, where with hot glands
> the spider who spins tracks
> makes his home and spins tracks. . . .

In "Brandmauern," Grass again writes of the divided city, taking his central symbol from the Brandmauern, or fireproof walls, which often outlasted the houses in the heavy bombings of the Second World War and therefore suggest a city in ruin. In this poem Grass also uses the fireproof wall as an emblem of the division of the city. He begins:

> I greet Berlin as I
> three times bump my head against one
> of the walls, three times.

He sees the wall projecting its shadow "where once your house stood." The blue of a sign advertising a cleaning fluid—"this means nothing"— now it is snowing—persists on a nearby blackened wall.

> Black and with no inscription
> the wall marches toward me,
> casts its glance over my shoulder.

The ending of Grass's poem "Saturn" shows him at his most dadaistic:

> I reclined,
> smoking a cigarette
> and knew in the darkness
> that someone held up his hand,
> as I crushed out the ashes
> of my cigarette.
>
> Saturn comes at night
> and holds his hand up.
> With my ashes
> Saturn cleans his teeth.
> Into his jaws
> we shall climb up.

A younger poet (born 1935), Christoph Meckel also makes use of startling dadaist and surrealist images, as in his poem "Goldfisch" ("Goldfish"), which opens with a shock:

> Since I love the moon and the water,
> A goldfish lives in my hair,
> Which bewilders me, and I notice
> That with others this is not the case.

He has gone swimming in rivers, but his goldfish has not liked the water, and when he offered it as a gift to the man in the moon, it would not swim in the starlight. It would not even go into the Red Sea; it intends to age in the dusk of the poet's heart.

> I must go on wearing it
> Until its scales fall off,
> And it turns black
> And, dead, falls into a gray puddle.

Besides being a poet, Meckel is a graphic artist who has published several volumes of his etchings. His books of verse include *Nebelhörner* (1959; *Foghorns*), *Tarnkappe* (1961; *Invisibility Cap*), *Wildnisse* (1961; *Wildernesses*), and *Land der Umbramauten* (1961; *Land of the Brown Tollhouses*).

A somewhat older poet who also was influenced by the surrealists, Karl Krolow in his first and more recent phases wrote along somewhat more traditional lines. Born in Hannover in 1915 and now a resident of Darmstadt, Krolow began his career as one of the modern German nature poets. He translated a good deal of modern Spanish and French verse, and in the latter was probably influenced by Guillaume Apollinaire, Paul Éluard, Max Jacob, Henri Michaux (the Belgian), and René Char, among others. He undoubtedly learned much from these writers and incorporated their discoveries into his own range of utterance, and now he has turned again toward his earliest manner.

Krolow's volumes of poetry include *Hochgelobtes gutes Leben* (1943; *Praise Be to the Good Life*), *Heimsuchung* (1948; *Affliction*), *Auf Erden* (1949; *On Earth*), *Wind und Zeit* (1954; *Wind and Time*), *Tage und Nächte* (1956; *Days and Nights*), *Fremde Körper* (1959; *Foreign Bodies*), *Unsichtbare Hände* (1962; *Invisible Hands*), and *Gesammelte Gedichte* (1965; *Collected Poems*). Among other books, he has written *Aspekte deutscher Lyrik* (1961; *Aspects of German Lyrical Poetry*), a volume of critical essays which indicate his familiarity not only with German but with foreign literatures.

One of Krolow's best-known and most highly praised sequences of verse is his "Gedichte gegen den Tod" ("Poems against Death"), of which the sixth and last begins:

> In a face the flicker of joy,
> Quiet ship, journeying forth, never to return:
>
> So evening comes.

Golden clouds in his arms, he does not weigh down the shoulders, "And once more death is patient," a seer hated by his own body, while the water aloes bloom and dusk is light of weight. The lips of darkness are as beautiful as women who never existed and, amid whispering, death holds back. So evening arrives, lying but lightly on one's shoulder:

> And the night has the color of Jenny's eyebrows.
> She is not like the friend who changes her perfumes.
> She is like the friend whose eyes flash with St. Elmo's fires.
> She has little gleaming teeth.
> She has a mouth of exaltation and calm.
>
> And once more death is patient. . . .

And here the poem ends. This fragment has indicated some of the metaphorical daring of Krolow; while the language is fairly simple, the surrealist touches show through, as when the night is found to have "color of Jenny's eyebrows"; Jenny has not been introduced in the earlier poems of the series, and she makes a startling intrusion here, in the best manner of Apollinaire or Éluard. But only the German original can project the sensual quality of Krolow's poetry. The passage about the lips of darkness (for example), the beautiful woman, death, and the whispering, reads as follows:

> Das Dunkel bewegt seine Lippen.
> Es ist schön, wie die Frau, die es nicht gibt.
> Unsicher macht es den Tod, den sein Flüstern eine Zeitlang abwendet.

Then the evening, whose life weighs light on the shoulder:

> So kommt der Abend.
> Sein Leben liegt leicht auf der Schulter.

And the last line, about the patience of death:

> Und der Tod hat noch einmal Geduld. . . .

Heinz Piontek, born in 1925, rarely uses shock effects in his verse. Born in Kreuzberg, Upper Silesia, in 1925, he has since the Second World War lived in West Germany, recently at Dullingen on the Danube. His books of verse include *Die Furt* (1952; *The Ford*), *Die Rauchfahne* (1956; *The Wisp of Smoke*), *Wassermarken* (1957; *Watermarks*), and *Mit einer Kranichfeder* (1962; *With a Crane Feather*). Starting as a poet of the school of Naturmagie (nature-magic) of Oskar Loerke and Wilhelm Lehmann, Piontek (who for a while was a construction worker) then wrote a special type of urban poetry and eventually turned to rather traditional verse, often with religious themes. His "Vergängliche Psalmen" ("Short-Lived Psalms") contain such passages as: "Where Thou permittest the earth between the burnt walls of sorrow / and over the stones of ruined bridges, / there Thy mercy is always with me."

One of Piontek's most striking poems, "Krähen" ("Crows") begins:

> They scrape with greedy wings
> snow-fences and dusk.
> In my winter dreams
> their black profile intrudes.
>
> I think through their shrieks
> of the misery of the desolate world,
> when out of the frosty hollowness
> their sorrow overwhelms me.

Their dusty wings move his heart, and he looks up and listens anxiously, and although the birds disappear behind the hills in the distance, "their black distress haunts me in another form."

Such stirring poems attest to the vitality of the German lyric of today, of whatever school: the nature-magic, the expressionist-dadaist-surrealist, or the plainly traditional which, as illustrated, has maintained a vigor. Like the novel and the drama, poetry has flourished among German-speaking writers since the Second World War and, as mentioned before, German verse of today has a force that virtually suggests a renaissance.

The West German Theater—a Curtain Slowly Rising

In the postwar confusion of West Germany, the theater recovered slowly. The condition was different from that of the eastern zone, whose officials encouraged drama as propaganda. But gradually the West German theater revived. One of its first notable successes was a play imported from Switzerland. This was written by Carl Zuckmayer, whose earlier plays such as *The Happy Vineyard* have already been discussed. In 1946,

Zuckmayer put on the stage in Zürich a drama he had written during his wartime residence in the United States, and there was an immediate demand for it in West Germany, where it repeated its popular success. This play is *Des Teufels General* (*The Devil's General*), and it is essentially anti-Nazi.

It attempts to show, however, that all Nazis were not necessarily devils —if Hitler was a demonic figure, the general who appears in this play certainly is not. He represents the people in Germany and in the armed forces who privately opposed Hitler. There has been some harsh criticism of the play because it tends to treat General Harras, of the Luftwaffe, sympathetically; he dislikes Hitler and Nazism, yet as a military man he obeys orders. For relief, he makes outrageous anti-Nazi witticisms (here is a reflection of Freud's *Wit and Its Relation to the Unconscious*) which the Minister of Culture, Dr. Schmidt-Lausitz, hastily translates—"What the General is really saying is"—into remarks favorable to the Third Reich. But Harras's witticisms do not purge his conscience. There is sabotage in the aircraft production which Harras is in charge of, and the Gestapo suspects him; but Harras discovers that the culprit is his old flying comrade the chief engineer, who has a secret group working with him. Confronted by Harras, the chief engineer explains that he carries on the sabotage not because he has relatives in a concentration camp, or because he has loved a Jewish girl, none of which applies, but rather because of his shame at being a German in Hitler's time. Having told the chief engineer that he is right and having urged him to keep up his sabotage, Harras says that the devil's general will fly one last advance mission to hell. Harras goes out to the flight line and pilots one of the defective Messerschmidts to his own suicide.

Even those who disliked this drama because of its sympathetic portrait of a man who could play along with the Nazis for years had to admit its theatrical force. Harras is a complicated character who represents a segment of the German people who were caught on the horns of the Nazi dilemma, and he is also distinctly individualized as a dramatic personage. The play contains a number of excellent scenes, including one in a restaurant, in the course of which Harras tries to disillusion a young Luftwaffe officer. There is a large gallery of characters, representing a wide variety of German types.

During the five years Zuckmayer lived in Austria (1933–1938), he tried his hand at historical dramas with *Der Schelm von Bergen* (1934; *The Rogue of Bergen*) and *Bellman* (1938). In *The Rogue of Bergen*, based on a story of the Rhineland in the Middle Ages (a tale preserved in one of Heinrich Heine's poems), Zuckmayer tells of an executioner's son who is knighted for providing a sterile emperor with an heir—the executioner's son had fallen in love with the empress. Zuckmayer, essentially a realist, often fails in this romance in trying to create poetic language and situations; he is most successful in the play when he uses the flavorful Rhenish dialect. *Bellman*, which has some of the quality of *The Happy Vineyard*, is artistically sounder: here, Zuckmayer portrays a wine-loving Swedish poet of the eighteenth century, many of whose lyrics are used in the text. Originally staged in Zürich in 1938, *Bellman* was revived in Germany in 1953 as *Ulla Winblad*, taking its new title from the name of Bellman's mistress.

Another of Zuckmayer's historical plays, one written after the war, *Barbara Blomberg* (1949) deals with the mistress of Charles V who became the mother of Don John of Austria. After a strongly dramatic beginning, the play falls apart toward the end. Zuckmayer returned to the modern scene in *Der Gesang im Feuerofen* (1950; *The Song in the Furnace*), the story of a French Resistance group burned to death by the Germans in a French château. As in *The Devil's General*, Zuckmayer presents a wide range of characters, but *The Song* lacks the dramatic concentration of the earlier play. The author touches upon a Christian theme—the action takes place at Christmas—when he shows the Maquis forgiving the men who murder them.

In *Das kalte Licht* (1956; *The Cold Light*), Zuckmayer draws upon the Klaus Fuchs case to project the story of a scientist who betrays the secrets of the atomic bomb to the Communists. Zuckmayer shows Kristof Wolters as a misguided idealist who realizes that he has not helped all humanity, as he had hoped to do when he gave the nuclear secrets to Soviet agents; he regrets his act and confesses to a sympathetic British agent, to whom he says he has always been filled inwardly with frost by a cold light from the outside—but there can be a single blazing moment that transfigures everything. In such quick revelations of character, Zuckmayer is at his finest; unfortunately, too much of *The Cold Light* is weighed down by attempts at intellectual formulation: Zuckmayer is best at the instinctual. In *Die Stunde schlägt eins* (1962; *The Hour Strikes One*, translated as *The Stroke of One*), he scored something less than a hit with a play that is a rhetorical appeal in behalf of the youngest generation. Yet Zuckmayer has been the most popular postwar dramatist in West Germany. He helped to bring the theater alive again, and it has become extremely active. The newer playwrights of West Germany will be considered in a later section.

Some Austrian and Swiss Playwrights

Like Zuckmayer in West Germany, another elder dramatist has continued to have his works produced; although he has never attained the popularity of Zuckmayer, Max Mell has many admirers, particularly among those who like traditional and religious plays. Mell (born 1882) brought his work to the stage as early as 1921, with *Das Wiener Kripperl von 1919* (*The Vienna Manger of 1919*), whose setting is a tramcar terminal on a foggy winter night where a mixed group of Viennese citizens are transfigured by a vision of the terminus' waiting room as the manger of Bethlehem. Mell's *Das Apostelspiel* (1923; *The Apostle Play*) has been performed often; the setting is again a winter night, and when two evil creatures break into a hut in the bleak mountains, the faith of two children there transfigures the intruders into apostles.

A similar religious theme pervades Mell's *Das Nachfolge-Christi-Spiel* (1927; *The Imitation-of-Christ Play*), which takes place at the time of the wars between the Turks and the forces of the Holy Roman Empire. The lord of a castle in Styria is nailed to a cross by marauding deserters. He is still alive when rescued by imperial troops and, having seen life "from above," forgives those who crucified him.

Mell, while an anti-modernist in technique, is concerned with presenting biblical as well as historical themes in modern terms. He writes in a strictly disciplined classical mode, as in his version of *Die Sieben gegen Theben* (1931; *The Seven against Thebes*). The two-part *Die Nibelungen Not* (1944-1951; *The Nibelung Necessity*), produced at Vienna's Burgtheater, is a prophetic play which indicates that the hero, Siegfried, should become a Christian. *Jeanne d'Arc* (1956) deals with the last phases of Joan of Arc's trial, her recantation and then her withdrawal of it. Mell's *Paracelsus* reopened the Schauspielhaus at Graz in 1965. Like his other plays it is written in verse, and it presents a newly humanized view of the famous physician.

Austrian contributions to the current Germanic theater have been varied. One of the older playwrights, Franz Theodor Csokor (born 1885), wrote expressionist drama in such productions as *Die rote Strasse* (1918; *The Red Street*). His *Gesellschaft der Menschenrechte* (1929; *Society of the Rights of Man*) was based on the life of the revolutionary playwright Georg Büchner, who died in 1837 at the age of twenty-three. Csokor has continued his own work as a dramatist with *Treibholz* (1959; *Driftwood*) and *Das Zeichen an der Wand* (1963; *The Mark on the Wall*). Another older playwright, Theodor Tagger (1891–1958), wrote his mature work under the pseudonym of Ferdinand Bruckner. When he was director of the Renaissance Theater in Berlin in 1928, he staged his first great success, *Krankheit der Jugend* (*Sickness of Youth*). The following year Max Reinhardt produced another Bruckner play that created a sensation: *Die verbrecher* (*The Criminals*). On a worldwide basis his most famous drama is *Elisabeth von England* (1930; *Elizabeth of England*). Bruckner, who often made use of the multilevel stage and of a chorus, was heavily influenced by Freudian theory. After the Second World War he adapted the famous Indian play, *The Little Clay Cart*, as *Das irdene Wägelchen* (1957), and wrote two dramas in verse—*Tod einer Puppe* (1956; *Death of a Puppet*) and *Der Kampf mit dem Engel* (1956; *The Battle with the Angel*).

Still another elder dramatist, Friedrich Schreyvogel (born 1899), who wrote a play about Columbus as long ago as 1926, in 1960 brought out *Ton und Licht* (*Sound and Light*), a drama about Maximilian and Carlotta. He followed this with *Ich liebe eine Göttin* (1961; *I Love a Goddess*). Franz Hrastnik (born 1904) is a painter who wrote *Vincent* (1954), a play about Van Gogh and, among other dramas, *Das Fräulein vom Kahlenberg* (1958; *The Girl from Kahlenberg*). Hans Holt (born 1909), who has achieved success with several plays, including his comedy *Der Herzspezialist* (1957; *The Heart Specialist*), is an actor as well as an author. Kurt Klinger (born 1925) wrote *Hans Christian Andersen* (1925), adapted a play from Carlo Goldoni, *Die neue Wohnung* (1960; *The New Lodging*), and turned out *Wer die Wahl hat?* (1960; *Who Can Choose?*), a successful comedy.

The best-known Austrian dramatist of this time is Fritz Hochwälder, born in Vienna in 1911. He often draws upon the tradition of the greatest Austrian dramatist, Franz Grillparzer (1791–1872), as well as upon the tradition of the Wiener Volksstück, or Viennese popular play. The latter in turn is somewhat indebted to the grotesque and often impromptu comedy which characterizes the Italian commedia dell'arte. Hochwälder in 1938 moved from Vienna to Switzerland, where his first internationally successful play was originally produced—*Das Heilige Experiment* (1943; *The Holy Experiment*). In 1952 it had a triumphant run in Paris as *Sur la Terre comme au ciel* (*On Earth as in Heaven*), followed by an equal réclame in London as *The Strong Are Lonely*. This is the story of a group of Jesuit fathers in South America in the eighteenth century who are creating a kingdom of God on earth. Orders from high authority (the Spanish king and the Pope's emissary arrive) tell them to cease their efforts, and thus their belief in these comes into conflict with their sense of duty. One of them persists in his belief until he is brought before a firing squad; then he abandons his moral position and receives absolution. The conflict of interests, tensely dramatized, is not resolved, but it compels the audience to examine a moral issue.

Hochwälder's next play, *Der Flüchtling* (1945; *The Fugitive*), was based on a sketch Georg Kaiser had prepared just before his death in Switzerland in 1945. It is a story of three people in a country occupied by the Nazi armies; this theme took Hochwälder away from the historic settings he usually draws upon, and in it his writing was less forceful than in some of his other dramas. *Meier Helmbrecht* (1946), for example, gave him the opportunity to exploit a medieval background and introduce elements of the Volksstück. The play is based upon a tale by the thirteenth-century Bruder Wernher the Gardener: in it a young peasant copies the arrogant criminality of the marauding barons until he is brought to retribution. Here Hochwälder was obviously pointing out a moral to the Nazis.

In *Der öffentliche Ankläger* (1949; *The Public Prosecutor*), Hochwälder deals with the French Revolution and with Robespierre's successor as prosecutor who discovers himself prosecuting the people's enemy hence accidentally putting an end to the Reign of Terror. *Donadieu* (1953), based on a poem by the Swiss writer Conrad Ferdinand Meyer, has as its setting the Huguenot wars in France. The story of a man who refrains from vengeance in order to let divine justice take its course is a dramatization of the problems of conscience, again the theme in *Die Herberge* (1956; *The Inn*), in which the investigation of one crime uncovers a far more serious one. *Der Unschuldige* (1958; *The Innocent One*), somewhat in the comic vein, tells the story of the discovery of a skeleton in the garden of an innocent man. He is eventually cleared—the skeleton proves to be that of a soldier of Napoleon—but it awakens him to the knowledge that he is capable of committing a crime. Hochwälder's other dramatic efforts include *Schicksalkömodie* (1960; *Fate Comedy*) and *Der verschwundene Mond* (1960; *The Vanished Moon*). Hochwälder also wrote a modern miracle play in *Donnerstag* (1959; *Thursday*), a story with overtones of *Faust* (the devil, and an architect willing to consider selling his soul), presented at the Salzburg Festival. Hochwälder had apparently tried to write a replacement for Hugo von Hofmannsthal's *Jedermann* (*Everyman*), regularly offered at Salzburg, but he failed to do so. Nevertheless he remains one of the more interesting Germanic playwrights.

Two Swiss authors are generally regarded as being at the top of the modern Germanic theater; Max Frisch (born 1911) and Friedrich Dürrenmatt (born 1921). Both these men are also novelists, but their achievement in the theater has been more impressive.

Frisch is a native and permanent resident of Zürich where, during the Second World War, Brecht had a great influence on the theater. Two of his greatest plays, *Mother Courage* and *The Good Woman of Setzuan*, had their world premières at the Zürich Schauspielhaus. Furthermore, the very kind of cabarets which had helped Brecht's own dramatic growth flourished in that city, and these cabarets produced witty and grotesque skits, all of which made an impression on Frisch as well as on the younger Dürrenmatt. In his youth, after an incomplete university career, Frisch became a journalist for a while and in the 1930's traveled widely in Europe. At sixteen he had written a play, *Stahl* (*Steel*), which he had sent to Max Reinhardt, who did not produce it. Frisch attempted a number of other dramas, all of which he destroyed when he was twenty-six; he then resumed his studies. After completing his university work in 1940, he became an architect, but was increasingly disappointed over the stodgily bureaucratic attitude of the Swiss toward modern building. In 1951–1952, a grant from the Rockefeller Institute (on the basis of Frisch's accomplishments as both architect and author) brought him to the United States; he also visited Mexico.

Frisch's *Santa Cruz* (written in 1944, produced in 1946) is a dream romance, the story of a woman in drab circumstances reliving an old love. But rather than actually revive this past love she chooses the present drabness. *Nun singen sie wieder* (1945; *Now They Are Singing Again*) shows first the war, with its air raids and murder of hostages, and then the hunger, greed, and racketeers in postwar Germany. Here Frisch stresses the futility of combat: the dead have sacrificed themselves for nothing, and the living have not learned. With a theatrical effectiveness reminiscent of Thornton Wilder's *Our Town*, the dead and the living mingle, with the living unaware of them and the dead singing futile choruses of hope.

Frisch's first international success was *Die chinesische Mauer* (1947; *The Chinese Wall*), an investigation of the dangers of the atomic bomb. It is a play which defies time, for although its action takes place essentially during the years when the Great Wall of China was being built, characters from various periods of history keep intruding—Napoleon, Cleopatra, Columbus, Pilate, Philip of Spain, Don Juan, and Romeo and Juliet are among those who appear—and the play makes frequent use of masks and dancing. A man called simply Der Heutige—The Contemporary (he is one of our twentieth-century contemporaries)—acts as commentator and chorus. Although the tone of the play is farcical, there is a serious undercurrent, particularly when the emperor of China utters Hitler-like boasts about his indestructible army; and the contemporary grimly realizes that history is a grim fact which will inevitably work out its grim events.

The setting of *Als der Krieg zu Ende war* (1949; *As the War Came to an End*) is Berlin—the cellar of a ruined house in which a German woman is hiding her officer-husband, wanted by the Russians for war crimes in Poland. In order to save her husband, she lets a Russian officer make love to her, and the husband comes out of hiding. The wife, who has fallen in love with the Russian, kills herself—but not until after the central characters discuss at length the problems of war guilt and war crimes. The woman, who addresses the audience in the style of the Stage Manager in *Our Town*, is pitched into despair when she learns that her husband actually is a war criminal.

Graf Öderland (*Count Öderland*, written in 1951, revised in 1956), originally a prose sketch in one of Frisch's journals, deals with the problem of an intellectual confronted by the dull routine of existence. The very name Öderland means Wasteland. The hero of the play is a legal official who runs amuck and almost accidentally becomes head of a revolutionary terrorist movement; but at the moment of success, rather than become a successful leader—which would involve more convention and banality—he commits suicide.

Frisch, even at his most grotesque, deals with the profoundest questions confronting humanity, particularly as they relate to the people of today. Just after the Second World War, Frisch was hotly concerned with the problems of the country neighboring his own, Germany, whose people speak the language in which he writes. Plays such as *Now They Are Singing Again* and *As the War Came to an End* displayed various aspects of recent German activity; *The Chinese Wall* concerned itself with the future of mankind seen against the terms of its past, while *Count Öderland* again dealt with contemporary anxieties, in this case again examining power, here contrasted with bovaryste dullness. The last of these is in part existential because it involves a choice, and Frisch in his plays is as acutely concerned with exploring present-day problems as any of the French existentialists are. Technically, he is often more experimental than they are: there is the Zürich-café and Brecht background, and the influence of plays by Thornton Wilder, particularly *Our Town* and *The Skin of Our Teeth,* is often discernible. Frisch has, however, assimilated his influences usefully, and has a distinctly forcible personality of his own in the theater.

In *Don Juan oder die Liebe zur Geometrie* (1953; *Don Juan, Or the Love of Geometry*), Frisch reintroduces a character who had been one of the visitors to the emperor in *The Chinese Wall.* But this Don Juan is no Don Juan, endlessly pursuing women for the sake of pursuit; he has a pure love of geometry, and geometry contrasts with the lack of precision that characterizes love. He tries to escape from women through the trick of his descent to hell, and when this doesn't work he is seen trapped in a miserable marriage, the victim of the dullness Frisch writes of with a kind of terror, as in *Santa Cruz* and *Count Öderland.* In *Don Juan* he gives the theme a bright originality of treatment, permeated with irony.

Biedermann und die Brandstifter (1958; *Biedermann and the Firebugs*) is a parable of responsibility. *Die grosse Wut des Phillip Hotz* (1958; *Phillip Hotz's Great Rage*) is a one-act comedy about an infuriated, furniture-smashing husband who in his anger rushes away from his marriage to join the Foreign Legion, which rejects him because of his poor eyesight. *Andorra* (1961) is a harsh indictment of humanity because of the existence of anti-Semitism, here concentrated in the story of a boy who is not Jewish but comes to think he is because his fellow townsmen treat him as if he were—treat him cruelly. These are three dramatically effective plays, and of them *Biedermann* has the greatest force in the theater. The two full-length dramas were emphatic successes in Europe, but both failed in New York during the 1963 season. In Los Angeles, however, in 1964, *Biedermann* had a sensational success when staged by the noted scene designer Mordecai Gorelik, who also translated the play (as *The Firebug*). It has a message for American as well as for European audiences, although Frisch has called it "ein Lehrstück ohne Lehre"—a lesson-play without a lesson.

Originally a radio play first heard over the Bayrischer Rundfunk (Bavarian Radio) in Munich in 1953, *Biedermann* was considerably rewritten for stage presentation five years later. With a chorus of firemen, soliloquies, and a rapid shuttling of the action from scene to scene, it has somewhat the flavor of a Brecht or Wilder drama, and it has been claimed for the Theater of the Absurd. The play ends with fire and explosion, managed so skillfully in the Los Angeles production that audiences were frightened.

The fire and the firebugs themselves are symbolic, and because they have the ambiguity that often characterizes symbolism at its most effective, they are probably a bit too much for many American audiences, more accustomed to straight and easily comprehensible realism. Furthermore, the characterization of Biedermann perhaps holds the mirror up to nature a bit too cruelly. For Biedermann is Everyman, as the play at one point suggests—the name is close to the German Jedermann, and at the same time it suggests the dull, the ordinary, the humdrum. While he is plainly Germanic, he often resembles the business-as-usual type of American businessman.

The actions of Biedermann—really his non-action—are the motivating force of the story. Biedermann is worried by the outbreak of fires in his town, fires obviously caused by arsonists. He is even furious that firebugs exist. Yet when Schmitz, an athletic young tramp, invades his house and wheedles food and shelter from him, Biedermann refuses at first to consider that Schmitz might be a firebug even though he is following the pattern of the arsonists who have moved into and eventually burned other houses in the town. Biedermann even lets Schmitz bring in his friend Eisenring, who rolls barrels of gasoline into the attic. The more conciliatory Biedermann gets, the less the intruders are appeased; it might be said that they burn for action.

Schmitz and Eisenring are joined by a character designated only as The Ph.D. or the Professor. He is an unambiguous caricature of the modern intellectual, confused between theory and action. This Ph.D. is at first on the side of the incendiaries, but before they start their fires he turns against them. Then, instead of taking action, he reads a paper of protest until his voice is at last beaten down by the crackling of flames and the shriek of sirens. The Professor then hands the paper to Biedermann, who reasonably asks what he is to do with it; but the Professor climbs down from the stage and takes a seat in the audience, now the pure onlooker.

Biedermann too is unambiguous, easily recognizable, the heartless businessman, the Babbitt who lets the world catch on fire, who even supplies the arsonists with their matches. At one point he asks the audience what it would have done—he can always rationalize his position —but the play has already shown what he could have done. Obviously he could have thrown the incendiaries out, even preferred charges against them. But there is in Biedermann, for all his terror of fire, a self-destructive urge. Frisch makes that plain at the opening of the play, as Biedermann appears onstage lighting a cigar and saying that it is disgusting that one cannot even light a cigar anymore without thinking of burning houses—and then as he walks out, he throws away his lighted cigar, in his own parlor.

The ambiguity that has occasioned some of the criticism of the play lies not in its characters but in its theme. But this ambiguity is ultimately part of the play's strength, along with the characterizations and the development of the odd relationship between Biedermann and the firebugs. Some commentators believe that the play represents the failure of the democracies to act against Hitler before he acted against them after warning them so plainly, in *Mein Kampf*, of his intentions. Hans Bänzinger, in his book *Frisch und Dürrenmatt*, traces the origins of the play to entries in Frisch's diary for 1948, when President Eduard Beneš of Czechoslovakia made the mistake of accepting Communists in his cabinet, enabling them to take over the government. Still other interpreters see Frisch's play as emblemizing the atomic age; Mordecai Gorelik, for example, writes of "the spectacle of middle-class behavior in countries which threaten each other with nuclear incineration. Faced with this terror the bourgeois citizen resolutely shuts his eyes in the hope that it will go away; or else puts himself in the hands of fire-happy incendiaries—with results that are not surprising." With so many possible interpretations, the theme of the play is truly a rich one, and the author has worked it out with dramatic dexterity.

Friedrich Dürrenmatt, ten years younger than Frisch, is better known outside Switzerland, chiefly because of his play *Der Besuch der alten Dame* (1956; *The Visit of the Old Lady*, performed in England as *Time and Again*). Considerably toned down for American audiences and staged under the title of *The Visit*, this play was highly successful in New York in 1958, in a production starring Alfred Lunt and Lynn Fontanne—two actors who, after performing brilliantly in Shakespeare, Shaw, and Chekhov, devoted the rest of their career to theatrical trash, making anything they appeared in look suspect to those interested in quality. But, whatever the merits of the bowdlerized American version of *The Visit of the Old Lady*, it was extensively popular.

The author of the play is the son of a Swiss Protestant minister and the grandson of Ulric Dürrenmatt, a rather spectacular politician who wrote satirical verse. Friedrich Dürrenmatt was born in the village of Konolfingen and was educated in Berne and Zürich. For a while he was a painter, and he has illustrated some of his published plays. The first of these, *Es steht geschreiben* (1947; *It Is Written*), is set in Münster during the Thirty Years' War; this story of the Anabaptists there, and of their attempts to establish heaven on earth, takes many mischievous liberties with history. *Der Blinde* (1948; *The Blind Man*) is an ironic parable of a blind nobleman who believes that his ruined castle is intact. Dürrenmatt in his essay "Theaterprobleme" ("Problems of the Theater") indicates that he truly discovered himself as a writer while working on *The Blind Man*: "The joy of being able all of a sudden to write, of possessing language, as it came over me, for instance, while I was writing *The Blind Man*, can make an author talk too much, can make him escape from his subject into language." Despite the highly rhythmical style of *The Blind Man*, Dürrenmatt did not lose control of his subject, and the play is a grand moral parable, with irony in its grandeur.

Dürrenmatt turned to history again in *Romulus der Grosse* (1949; *Romulus the Great*), a wry comedy somewhat in the manner of George Bernard Shaw's treatment of historical themes. The setting is an estate near Rome on the Ides of March in A.D. 476, the day the Roman Empire "fell." Actually, the emperor, Romulus Augustus (who in history was a boy, Romulus Augustulus), is more interested in raising chickens than in ruling Rome. Ironically named for the city's founder and the most famous of the Roman emperors, he sees the record of Rome as a series of crimes, and he is only too glad to cease being their heir. On the other hand, the barbarian conqueror, Odoaker, has no desire to rule either, but feels greatness thrust upon him, and he establishes a pension for Romulus. Revised in 1957, this play is aptly subtitled "A Historical Comedy without Historical Basis."

Die Ehe des Herrn Mississippi (1952; *The Marriage of Mr. Mississippi*, also translated as *Fools Are Passing Through*) is partly an expressionist play and partly a parody of the old-fashioned melodramatic theater. Floristan Mississippi is a public prosecutor with an impressive number of convictions who wants to restore the strict Mosaic law. The former friend of his youth, Frédéric René Saint-Claude, is a Communist who, however, finds little good to say about Soviet Russia; but he appreciates Mississippi's Draconian point of view and would like to make use of it. Mississippi, who has poisoned his wife—it was a matter of justice to him because she was unfaithful—marries a woman whom he unmasks as the poisoner of her husband (who was of course the lover of Mississippi's wife). The new wife of Mississippi, Anastasia by name, is pursued by several other men, and she finally poisons her new husband. There is also a political murder: the play opens with the execution of Saint-Claude, who after he is killed steps forward and addresses the audience to tell them about the plot, which is then unreeled in flashbacks. It is easy to see in this play the influence of Bertolt Brecht, Frank Wedekind, Thornton Wilder, and others, as well as that of the Zürich cabarets. Dürrenmatt has skillfully threatened an essentially serious story with a sense of burlesque that heightens the effect of the main theme—the mad ideals of Mississippi and Saint-Claude.

In *Ein Engel kommt nach Babylon* (1953; *An Angel Comes to Babylon*) Dürrenmatt wrote another of his historical comedies with modern overtones, this one concerning an angel who arrives in Babylon accompanied by a radiant girl who is to be given as a prize to the most miserable creature among men. This would seem to be Akki, the last remaining beggar, but King Nebuchadnezzar of Babylon, temporarily disguised as a beggar in order to work out some intricate aspects of policy, seems even more wretched; he pretends to be the outstanding beggar of Nineveh. In a "begging contest" with Akki, the king wins the girl and, when she is unveiled, he is smitten with her; but he turns back to his kingdom: "I betrayed the maiden for the sake of my power." Akki, who has been Nebuchadnezzar's hangman, takes Kurrubi into the desert with him. She grieves for the beggar she has lost, and Nebuchadnezzar decides to defy the forces beyond him by building the Tower of Babel. All this is worked out craftily on the stage; and Akki is a comic triumph.

Dürrenmatt, apparently sensitive to criticism to the effect that his plays were ultimately "light," provides an explanation and an answer in the preface to the American edition of his *Four Plays* (the preface is adapted from a lecture, "Problems of the Theater," which he delivered in Switzerland and Germany in 1954–1959). In it he discusses the work of Wilder and authors to whom his own writing is somewhat analogous; and he contrasts the classical repertory of theaters (to him "the museum") with the new plays which he thinks they all too seldom produce. The fault, he implies, lies with the application of too severe standards: "What is wanted is the perfection which is read into the classics. And let the artist even be suspected of having taken one step backwards, of having made a mistake, just watch how quickly he is dropped." Dürrenmatt further says that "literature can be studied but not made" in such a climate:

How can the artist exist in a world of educated and literate people? The question oppresses me, and I know no answer. Perhaps the writer can best exist by writing detective stories, by creating art where it is least suspected. Literature must become so light that it will weigh nothing upon the scale of today's literary criticism: only in this way will it regain its true worth.

Putting some of these ideas into practice, Dürrenmatt has written detective novels; and some of his plays have the properties of the mystery story. This applies to the play Dürrenmatt brought out not long after his "Problems of the Theater" lecture—*The Visit of the Old Lady,* first staged in 1956.

The setting is Güllen, a town "somewhere in Europe," a place whose contact with the outside world is largely through the great trains that rush through, without stopping, on their way from Hamburg to Naples or from Venice to Stockholm. But one day the great Flying Dutchman Express does the unprecedented: it halts at the Güllen station to let off a former resident of the town, Mme. Claire Zachanassian. As a girl she had been seduced by one of the citizens of Güllen, Anton Ill (Schill in the American production), and had been cast out; she had become a prostitute for a while and then married a millionaire, and upon his death she became the richest woman in the world. She has returned for revenge upon Anton. Part of her baggage is his coffin: she will make the townspeople wealthy if they kill Anton.

Those who saw the New York performance of the play may always consider it only a series of tricks displayed by two experimental technicians in the leading roles, and certainly *The Visit* never quite makes a satisfying adjustment between its grim and its comic elements. It is an extended anecdote with a climax coming too early in the play. This occurs when the citizens, who had first bristled with righteous anger when Claire Zachanassian made her outrageous proposition, suddenly begin to go in heavily for credit-buying—even the family of the now-respectable Anton begins to speculate. This is the high comic moment of *The Visit*, and the town meeting followed by the death of Anton is all an anticlimax, made interesting, however, by Anton, who had increased in stature as he went from despair to stoicism. But most of the characters are stereotypes, and even Claire is nothing more than a caricature, with her cigar smoking, her pet panther, and her macabre coffin. She has the single rigid motif of the "flat" character: "The world made me into a whore; now I make it into a whorehouse."

The play is full of ironic ambiguities—even the death of Anton. As the townsmen close around him, he sinks to his knees; they cut him off from view, then draw back, and he is seen dead on the stage. The doctor, after a stethoscopic examination, diagnoses heart failure; when the Bürgermeister says Anton died of joy, the crowd takes up the cry. Then the scene changes, with the town looking elegant and Claire departing, two men carrying the coffin as she boards the glittering express, which now makes regular stops at Güllen.

After the first production of the play, Dürrenmatt wrote an epilogue showing the corruption of Güllen into a place of mechanized existence. A chorus of citizens chants an appeal for divine help against their new-found wealth. But this epilogue is unnecessary: the corruption of the town and its miserable future were apparent in the play itself. Dürrenmatt has said that his intention in *The Visit* was not didactic, but ideas certainly dominate the play. It seems more of an allegory than the kind of story that could at any level be called realistic, or even humanistic.

In an even more broadly exaggerated play, *Die Physiker* (1962; *The Physicists*), Dürrenmatt presents another mixture of the grotesque and the grim. The title alerts one: physicists, at once so respected and so dreaded, play a controlling part in our world. Yet it soon becomes apparent that the scientists in this play are chained to something more than their laboratories. They are in an insane asylum.

This comedy-drama is a moral parable and a detective mystery as well as a spy story. The curtain goes up with a police inspector at the asylum looking at the corpse of a murdered nurse. One of the physicists has killed her, and before the two acts of the play are over, the other two physicists referred to in the title will have each slain a nurse also.

One of the physicists, Johann Wilhelm Möbius, describes the visions in which King Solomon appears to him. Another of them, Herbert Georg Beutler, wears an eighteenth-century costume, with a full-bottomed curly wig, and claims to be Sir Isaac Newton. The third physicist, Ernst Heinrich Ernesti, says he is Albert Einstein; he has long white hair and a mustache, he smokes a pipe, and he plays a violin. This Luigi Pirandello world has further complications; the Newton man, for example, tells the police inspector that Ernesti is sick, imagining himself to be Einstein; actually it is Beutler who is Einstein; he only pretends to be Newton, and he tells the police inspector to call him Albert.

As the play proceeds, the true identity of the three central characters becomes apparent: Beutler, whose real name is Kilton, is a secret agent for one of the Western powers, while Ernesti is really a man named Eisler, a spy for an Eastern country. Möbius, the most brilliant physicist imaginable, is not mad either but is merely seeking refuge from his own discoveries, which could destroy mankind. The two secret agents have killed their nurses because the women were about to spoil their plans; Möbius murdered his attendant because she believed in him, as an unrecognized genius, and Möbius wished to remain unrecognized.

The three men discuss all this candidly and are overheard by the woman doctor who has made her late father's villa into the main building of the asylum: Fräulein Doktor Mathilde von Zahnd is herself mad, power-drunk, and she has plans for controlling the world. She does not have to pretend to hear Solomon—she does hear him. She locks up the three physicists and, as the play ends, they turn to the audience: with brief biographical sketches they introduce themselves as Newton, Einstein, and Solomon.

The action of the play is at times effective, but often it is no more than a projection of the world of spy thrillers, the world menaced by a paranoid figure grasping for power and threatening large-scale annihilation. With the madhouse as a symbol of the entire world of today, the play has a certain force; but since it is not developed in the area of serious ideas but rather in that of a grand-guignol shocker, it remains more in the realm of chilling entertainment than in that of comedy-drama to be taken thoughtfully.

The same applies to some extent to *Herkules und der Stall des Augius* (1963; *Hercules and the Augean Stable*), a radio play which Dürrenmatt lengthened for stage production. This comedy makes no advance over Dürrenmatt's earlier works. It deals with the fifth labor of Hercules, the cleaning of the stalls, not swept for thirty years, where three thousand cattle are kept. The situation gave Dürrenmatt plenty of chance for ridiculous parallels with contemporary situations.

Like Frisch, Dürrenmatt has taken over much from earlier modern theater, from that of Wedekind, Pirandello, and Wilder; like Frisch, he has used the techniques of these men for different purposes, following Brecht in dramatizing contemporary ideas. Neither Frisch nor Dürrenmatt has as yet demonstrated that he is on Brecht's level of expressional ability, but each of these Swiss playwrights has in turn helped to make the current West German theater into a theater of ideas.

9

THE RECENT
WEST GERMAN
THEATER

A number of elder playwrights followed Carl Zuckmayer in his return to the West German theater, and groups of new dramatists also appeared. While the postwar theater has not attained the quality of the novel and poetry in West Germany, the drama has nevertheless been excitingly revived, with full and enthusiastic audiences for both classical and new plays.

The postwar playwrights of West Germany will be considered largely in chronological order, by age, with some exceptions: the three most spectacular recent playwrights (Heinar Kipphardt, Rolf Hochhuth, and Peter Weiss) will be discussed last.

A contemporary of Zuckmayer's, Hanns Henny Jahnn (1894–1959), a native of Hamburg, was a novelist as well as a playwright. Early in his career he went through a phase of expressionism, in such plays as *Der Arzt, sein Weib, sein Sohn* (1923; *The Doctor, His Wife, His Son*), but he eventually developed his own kind of nonrealist writing, tinged with mysticism. In 1925, Jahnn's *Medea* raised a clamorous protest when staged at the Berlin State Theater, and it was taken out of the repertory. He had presented Medea as a Negro woman, and her two sons by Jason as half-castes. But in 1964 the play was produced with acclaim at the State Theater in Wiesbaden, in a new version prepared by Jahnn in the year of his death. While he was still living, Jahnn had an outstanding success with *Thomas Chatterton* (1956), which dramatized the experiences of the brilliant eighteenth-century poet-forger who killed himself at eighteen. Jahnn toward the end of his own life became one of the dramatists concerned with projecting current ideas in the theater, as shown in several Denkspiele (idea plays) published after his death: *Hier ist ein Neger zu lynchen* (*Here Is a Negro to Be Lynched*), *Der staubige Regenbogen* (1961; *The Dusty Rainbow*), and *Die Trümmer des Gewissens* (1962; *The Ruins of Conscience*). *The Dusty Rainbow* is the tangled story of the fate of an atomic scientist; *The Ruins of Conscience* strongly dramatizes a plea for banning the atomic bomb.

A playwright who died young, Wolfgang Borchert (1921–1947), is known for one dramatic work which immediately caught the postwar mood—*Draussen von der Tür* (1947; *Outside the Door*, translated as *The Man Outside*). Although timely in the extreme, the drama was in the mode of the kind of play called Heimkehrer after the First World War: the return-home play about a former soldier. Borchert began the play with his hero, Beckmann, making an unsuccessful attempt to kill himself. A former prisoner in Siberia (as the author himself was), Beckmann cannot readjust to civilian life and is continually defeated, always the outsider. Borchert used expressionistic techniques and symbolic figures, but his play had a fundamentally realistic quality. Borchert, ill in Switzerland after his experiences as a prisoner of war, died in Basel the day before the play was first performed in his native Hamburg. The bitter mood of the drama caused it to be shown extensively in Germany, but as the war receded into the past and the new prosperity came, *Outside the Door* was no longer performed regularly.

Born a year before Borchert (1920), Hans Günter Michelson, also a native of Hamburg, has written several plays, including *Helm* (1965). The character Helm is a former army cook who is now operating a tavern. He invites some officers to have a drink, among them his former general, Klenkmann, who suggests that his own feelings about his failure in the field are only a part of the guilt of everyone. Dialogue rather than action is the moving force of this play, which brings various modern types into sharp contrast. *Helm* is virtually a continuation of Michelson's earlier drama *Steinz*, in which a high-ranking officer also tried to justify unsuccessful military action. Among Michelson's other plays, *Drei Akte* (1965; *Three Acts*) stands out. It concerns the confusions (physical injuries, a helter-skelter love affair) that attend the birthday party of an old man who does not want to face the fact of a birthday. Michelson, neither expressionistic nor actually realistic, is perhaps more philosophical than most contemporary German dramatists.

One of the writers of comedies among the newer group is Karl Wittlinger (born 1922), author of a two-character play in cabaret style, *Kennen Sie die Milchstrasse?* (1955; *Do You Know the Milky Way?*), and of *Kinder des Schattens* (1957; *Children of the Shadow*), and *Seelenwanderung* (1963; *Transmigration of Souls*). Klaus Hubalek (born 1926) has written several war plays, including *Der Hauptmann und sein Held* (1954; *The Captain and His Hero*) and *Die Festung* (1958; *The Fortress*), the latter dealing with the experiences of an officer in the German army between 1934 and 1945. Hubalek's *Keine Fallen für die Füchse* (1957; *No Traps for Foxes*) is about Berlin in its divided condition. *Die Stunde der Antigone* (1960; *The Hour of Antigone*) adapts the classical myth to the last days of the Nazis. Consistently concerned with the war, Hubalek in 1961 dramatized Theodor Plievier's novel *Stalingrad*.

Another of the outstanding writers of the postwar generation is Gerd Oelschlegel (born 1926), who advocates objective reality in such plays as *Die tödliche Lüge* (1956; *The Deadly Lie*) and *Staub auf dem Paradies* (1957; *Dust upon Paradise*). Leopold Ahlsen (born 1927), still another of the newer realists, sometimes mingles objective reality with parables. In 1960 he made a free translation of Dostoevsky's *Crime and Punishment*, as *Raskolnikov*. Ahlsen's *Philemon und Baukis* (1955) is about an old couple in the mountains of Greece who meet their death because, for humanitarian reasons, they have given shelter to a Greek partisan fighter and a wounded Nazi. This has been one of the most popular plays by newer West German dramatists.

The poet and novelist Günter Grass, one of the leaders of Group 47, also writes plays. Indeed, Grass (born 1927) began as a dramatist, with *Hochwasser* (1957; *High Tide*). His other plays include *Onkel, Onkel* (1957; *Uncle, Uncle*), *Die bösen Köche* (1959; *The Wicked Cooks*), and *Zweiunddreissig Zähne* (1961; *Thirty-two Teeth*, translated as *Demisemiquaver Teeth*). Of these, *The Wicked Cooks* is the best known, an allegory in favor of individualism. The cooks of the play symbolize the tycoons of modern bourgeois society, in this case in quest of a recipe possessed by a man known as The Count. The cooks—capitalistic gangsters—force him to agree to reveal it, but he loses his recollection of it while recognizing that the recipe is more than a commodity which these entrepreneurs wish to market: it is a credo. With The Count failing to supply the recipe, he and the woman he loves are killed; but one of the cooks, who apparently has guessed what the recipe is, runs away from the others. The central idea here is fairly simple, and what might have been more effective in a short play Grass extends to five acts. Another play by Grass was first performed in Berlin in January 1966, *Die Plebejer Proben den Aufstand* (*The Plebeians Rehearse the Uprising*), a play about the East Berlin uprising of 1953. A group of workers come to a character apparently based on Bertolt Brecht, who is directing rehearsals of his version of Shakespeare's *Coriolanus* (into which he interpolated a proletarian revolt), and ask him to help in their rebellion against tyranny; but instead he uses them as characters in his play. Although the theme of the intellectual unwilling to take part in politics is a popular one in Germany today, the critics did not take to Grass's drama and suggested that he stick to writing novels.

A close contemporary of Oelschlegel, Ahlsen, and Grass, Konrad Wünsche was born in 1928. He scored a success with his first full-length play, *Der Unbelehrbare* (1964; *The Unteachable*), which has a somewhat Hamlet-like situation. A professor is poisoned by his jealous wife; his son, "the unteachable," wants to rise above his criminal surroundings but finds himself too weak to avenge his father's death. A suggestion of the Hamlet theme occurs in Martin Walser's play *Der schwarz Schwan* (1964; *The Black Swan*). Walser had earlier written a farce about a ménage à trois, *Der Abstecher* (1961; *The Detour*), and a fierce satire on those who were fellow travelers during the Nazi years: *Eiche und Angora* (1962; translated as *The Rabbit Race*). *The Black Swan* also deals with those who had traffic with the Nazis, in this case a doctor who attempts to destroy all connections between his sanatorium and the Nazis; he finally convinces himself that he was not even in Germany between 1933 and 1945. He has a colleague who has served a prison sentence for being involved with the Nazis; this man's son has a Hamlet-like obsession to root out the truth and, like that truth-seeker Gregors Werle in Henrik Ibsen's *The Wild Duck,* this son-turned-detective brings about catastrophe. The play, by a man who in the past had been known for his realistic treatment of events, baffled many who saw it; it is one of the most complicated of dramatic investigations of German guilt.

Hermann Moers (born 1930) scored his first success with *Zeit der Distelblüte* (1959; *Time of the Thistle Bloom*), a one-act play about prison life, containing both social criticism and a fantastic aspect reminiscent of Franz Kafka. In *Der kleine Herr Nagel* (1965; *Little Mr. Nagel*), Moers projects a totalitarian state in which Nagel, owner of a printing company, is denounced by a printer named Gülden and given six years' imprisonment. On his release he finds that Gülden now owns the printing company. Nagel seeks him out—with a pistol that is not loaded. The plays of Moers have been extremely popular in West Ger-

many, and like so many authors there he has often turned out *Hörspiele,*
or radio plays, including the collection *Liebesläufe (Love's Course),* published in 1963.

In recent years, the three West German playwrights who have attracted the most attention, in their own country and beyond its borders,
are Heinar Kipphardt, Rolf Hochhuth, and Peter Weiss. Hochhuth and
Kipphardt base their work on careful documentation; Weiss gets beyond
this, however luridly, into the realm of imagination.

Heinar Kipphardt (born 1922) saw his father taken away to spend
five years at Buchenwald. The younger Kipphardt was conscripted into
the Wehrmacht and sent to the Russian front. He wrote several comedies
early in his writing career, including *Shakespeare dringend gesucht*
(1953; *Shakespeare Urgently Sought*), *Der staunenswerte Aufstieg und
Fall des Alois Piontek* (1958; *The Astonishing Rise and Fall of Alois
Piontek*), *Esel schreien im Dunkeln* (1958; *Donkeys Bray in the Dark*),
and *Die Stühle des Herrn Szmil* (1961; *The Chairs of Mr. Szmil,*
adapted from a Russian novel). *Der Hund des Generals* (1961; *The
General's Dog*) is the story of an officer who is kind to animals but
vicious to human beings. *Joel Brand* (1965) is another West German
play exploring the guilt of National Socialist Germany. This one focuses
on the year 1944. Kipphardt gives the events a distinct air of reality by
using actual documents, and although the play is expertly done it is not,
just as a play, in any way first rate.

In der Sache J. Robert Oppenheimer (1964; *In the Matter of J. Robert
Oppenheimer*), Kipphardt revised one of his radio plays for stage production and it soon appeared, with spectacular success, in theaters in Berlin
(produced by Erwin Piscator) and Munich and throughout West Germany. Other European capitals came up with productions of the play,
whose true-life hero, Dr. Oppenheimer, threatened to sue the playwright.

The drama is based on the 1954 hearings of the Atomic Energy Commission, after which its members dismissed Oppenheimer as a security
risk. The dialogue is timely and stirring. At one point in the play, Oppenheimer, not eager to develop the hydrogen bomb, dramatically explains
that Russia has only two targets of value, Moscow and Leningrad, while
the United States has fifty.

During the action, the Commission's counsel and several hostile witnesses fight fiercely against Oppenheimer. Dr. Edward Teller appears in a
somewhat friendly light, if occasionally grouchy, as a middleman between
the extremes. Senator Joseph McCarthy broods demonically over the play,
prompting the thought that no dramatist as yet has presented a full and

convincing picture of McCarthy in all his evil aspects. In relation to Kipphardt's play, the actual Dr. Oppenheimer has objected to what he speaks of as "improvisations which were contrary to history and to the nature of the people involved," particularly referring to Kipphardt's representation of the late Dr. Niels Bohr as being opposed to the creation of the bomb at Los Alamos. And Oppenheimer says that he himself was not, as the play states, opposed to the making of the original bomb. In a letter to Kipphardt, he has recalled the atmosphere of the time: "You may have forgotten Guernica, Dachau, Coventry, Belsen, Warsaw, Dresden and Tokyo. I have not."

The play has gone on, a raging success on the Continent.

Its controversial aspect is fairly limited, since it involves only one man. But Rolf Hochhuth's somewhat earlier play, *Der Stellvertreter* (1963; *The Deputy*) has far greater potentialities (which were realized) because it apparently attacked not only a recently dead Pope, who could not answer back, but also many of his associates and other members of his faith. The play has so far inspired two books, one in Switzerland, *Der Streit um Hochhuths "Stellvertreter"* (1963; *The Dispute over Hochhuth's "Deputy"*), and one in America, *The Storm over the Deputy* (1964). The latter was edited by the noted drama critic Eric Bentley, who pointed out that he included only thirty commentators "out of some thousands." In his foreword, Bentley states (italics his) that the storm aroused by this drama *"is almost certainly the largest storm ever raised by a play in the whole history of the drama."*

There is really more storm than play. *The Deputy* is theatrically exciting because of its topicality and because it speaks out boldly, but as a play it is mediocre. Yet it is an interesting matter to discuss because it shows how effective ideas can be when dramatized with at least a moderate amount of skill.

Rolf Hochhuth was born in 1931 in Eschwege/Werra, in what is now part of West Germany. He came from a Protestant family. In 1959 he left his editorial position with a German publishing house in order to travel to Rome to begin work on his first draft for *The Deputy*. It was first produced by Erwin Piscator at the Freie Volksbühne in West Berlin, in a shortened version, on February 23, 1963, the same day on which the full text was published as a book.

The controversy over the play rages chiefly around the principal questions it asks: Why did God's deputy on earth, Pius XII (Pope from 1934–1958), not speak out in behalf of the Jews during the Hitler terror?

This question had been raised before Hochhuth gave it so great a public airing in his first play. The play, incidentally, can hardly be called anti-Catholic since the hero—an imaginary priest—is a devout Jesuit. This is Father Ricardo Fontana, a young Italian who while in Germany during the war discovers the truth about the Nazi corpse camps. He goes back to Rome to ask the Pope to protest. When the Pope refuses to do this, Ricardo pins onto his cassock one of the yellow stars the Jews were required to wear in Germany and Nazi-occupied countries. Ricardo then returns to Germany, where he insists on being sent to Auschwitz. During a scuffle there, Ricardo is shot by a guard and killed.

The play is really a projected sermon, written in verse, with a few dramatically exciting scenes and enormous stretches of dialogue. Piscator's introduction to the German text compares *The Deputy* to Schiller's dramas. But whereas Schiller, like Shakespeare and other earlier writers of historical plays, took liberties with fact, Hochhuth follows the records as closely as possible. In order to encourage belief in his reliability, he appended to the published text a long essay on historical sidelights.

Some churchmen have criticized Hochhuth for inaccuracy, but the plain fact remains that Pius XII did not raise his voice against the anti-Jewish violence, even when it occurred (as the play shows) under the very windows of the Vatican. But it must be repeated that the play is not essentially anti-Catholic. The Pope appears in it as a representative figure, emblemizing the many who did not raise their voices against the atrocities (admittedly he was in an especially high moral position). As Albert Schweitzer noted in the preface to the English-language version of the play, "the failure was not that of the Catholic Church alone, but of the Protestant Church as well." Nevertheless the Catholic Church was somewhat more guilty because "it was an organized, supra-national power in a position to do something, whereas the Protestant Church was an unorganized, impotent, national power."

Albert Schweitzer is not the only prominent figure who has discussed *The Deputy* publicly: Karl Jaspers and other noted European writers and thinkers joined in the controversy, along with Cardinals of the church, Jewish spokesmen, and literary and drama critics in all countries. Sometimes mobs gathered outside the playhouses; at the New York opening, the American Nazi Party picketed the theater. The management shocked the audience by suggesting that no one stroll out of the building between the acts.

There was little aesthetic controversy among critics, most of whom found *The Deputy*, particularly in its reduced stage version, not a great play, though often a stimulating one. Perhaps Hochhuth should not have written the concentration-camp scenes, which are both cliché and distraction, and should have intensified the sections providing the reasons for Ricardo's martyrdom. The characters are not profound; they do not measure up to the scope the play attempts. Yet they are not mere mouthpieces either, since some of the scenes have an effective intensity. The ideas predominate, however, and the play seems to be one of the auguries of a new kind of dialectical theater. Ideas have of course often appeared in drama, but rarely has a play, put forth as a play, been so emphatically documentary.

Hochhuth's fellow dramatist Martin Walser paid *The Deputy* a high compliment when he said it combined the theater of ideas of Jean-Paul Sartre with the epic theater of Bertolt Brecht. Perhaps this praise is too great; but it cannot be denied that *The Deputy* has provided rare theatrical as well as extra-theatrical excitement.

Peter Weiss's play, called *Marat/Sade* for short, is not devoid of ideas, but it generates an almost entirely theatrical response. Weiss, born near Berlin in 1916, left Germany in 1934 to escape persecution by the Nazis, and lived for some years in Sweden. He has been called by Manfred Delling (in *Die Welt* of Hamburg) "one of the most interesting authors writing in German at the present time." He has written fiction and, besides *Marat/Sade,* a famous one-act play—*Nacht mit Gästen* (1963; *Guest Night*)—in which, amid a Punch-and-Judy atmosphere, murders occur as marionette-like figures move about the stage.

The full title of *Marat/Sade,* first produced in Berlin in 1964 (and later in France, Austria, Sweden, Poland, England, and the United States as well as in other countries and throughout Germany) is a long one: *Die Verfolgung und Ermordung des Jean Paul Marat aufgeführt von den Insassen des Irrenhauses von Charenton unter der Leitung des Marquis de Sade (The Persecution and Assassination of Jean Paul Marat as Performed by the Inmates of the Asylum of Charenton under the Direction of the Marquis de Sade).*

The longer title summarizes the main action of the story. De Sade, himself an inmate of Charenton, is permitted to write a play, direct it, and act in it. With the other inhabitants of the asylum, he projects the murder of Marat by Charlotte Corday. During most of the drama, Marat sits in the tub in which he is to be assassinated (he continually soaked himself because of a skin disease), and he talks at length with de Sade. The madmen dance around them, moaning and grimacing and howling as the protagonists argue, de Sade insisting on the futility of revolution, Marat saying that it must occur to rid society of social injustice.

There is almost no theatrical technique that the author does not draw upon, from the realist to the expressionist, while the tone ranges from the hysteric to the ironic. The setting of the action in the communal bathhouse of the asylum gives a gigantic symbolic emphasis to Marat's bathtub, which itself looks like a black coffin. Various individual episodes have an unforgettable horror, as when Charlotte Corday uses her long hair to whip de Sade, stripped to the waist and enjoying himself immensely. In another scene, one of the inmates sticks his bare backside out at the audience. Throughout, shock and violence recur regularly, and blood is spattered about. Music composed by Hans-Martin Majewski blares through the play, trumpets and drums, along with lute, flute, and harmonium. The total effect of the production has left audiences nerve-shattered.

Marat/Sade, however, is not really new theater. It derives first of all from Georg Büchner and then, quite obviously, from Bertolt Brecht, along with Franz Kafka, Jean-Paul Sartre, and Samuel Beckett. The shock effects are hardly more striking than those which characterize the plays of Jean Genet. Beneath the tumult of *Marat/Sade* no genuine tragedy exists, nor does the intellectual content of the play, chiefly the dialogue of de Sade and Marat, offer anything philosophically new. But *Marat/Sade* is, at its hideous best, effective theater.

Weiss has followed this drama with *Die Ermittlung* (1965; *The Investigation*), which he calls an oratorio in eleven songs. It deals with the 1964–1965 trials, at Frankfurt-am-Main, of those who were in charge of the corpse camp at Auschwitz. The play, unlike some of the recent more strictly documentary dramas, does not follow the trial exactly, but makes a psychological-emotional explanation of the activities at Auschwitz. It is a part of those continuing examinations-from-within of German guilt which keep occurring even with the new prosperity and the passing of time. *The Investigation* aroused hot controversy as it was played throughout Germany, produced not only in the West but also in the East.

In general, the recent West German theater had not come up with any plays that can reasonably be labeled as great, but it has turned out some exciting drama of diverse kinds. And the theater is extremely popular. In West Germany the 1963–1964 season attendance reached a figure of twenty-five million. Twenty million of these playgoers witnessed performances in the theaters sponsored by local and regional governments, and the other five million went to private playhouses, many of which are fairly small. The public theaters collected at their box offices 125 million marks (nearly 32 million dollars), and were given twice that amount in subsidies. More than eight million marks went to the private playhouses for subsidies. With such enthusiasm, and so many actors being given experience and so many playwrights encouraged, the West German theater may in the next few years be in a condition of renaissance, although so far the quality of the postwar plays has not been anywhere near the level of that of postwar West German poetry and fiction.

10

THE POSTWAR
WEST GERMAN
NOVEL

As in East Germany, older novelists dominated the literary scene in the years immediately following the war. One of these was Alfred Döblin whose prewar work has been discussed earlier. His final novel was published in 1956, after his return to Germany to live in the western sector. This book was *Hamlet oder die lange Nacht nimmt ein Ende* (*Hamlet, or the Long Night Comes to an End*). Published the year before Döblin's death, *Hamlet* is set in England and France after the war. There are no German characters in the story.

Its central figure is a young Englishman, wounded in battle, who sees himself as a Hamlet, and in this spirit he deals with his parents' problems as well as his own. With its interstitial short novels, its flashback to the Second World War—concentrating on an English battleship under Japanese air attack—and with its probing of human complexities, *Hamlet* is one of Döblin's strongest works. Though tragic in tone, it at least mildly suggests a hopeful future for Europe.

A somewhat younger writer than Döblin, Theodor Plievier (1892–1955), died a year earlier. He has been mentioned previously as one of the German writers who (like the philosopher Karl Jaspers) early in the postwar years faced up to the problems of guilt and readjustment. Drawing upon his own experiences and documenting his work thoroughly,

Plievier wrote of the Germans under arms. Kay Boyle quotes one of his famous passages at the beginning of *The Smoking Mountain,* a paragraph in which Plievier speaks of the "wretched" Germans, who had shown genius as builders of cities and cathedrals, as renowned artists and scientists, whose military organization could be regarded as only one aspect of social complexity. But the militarism flourished, and tillers were drawn away from the soil, priests from their parishes, husbands from wives. "The people ceased to exist as a people and became nothing but fuel for the monstrous, smoking mountain, the individual became nothing but wood, peat, fuel oil, and finally a black flake spewed up out of the flames." Plievier wrote about those flames in novels about both world wars.

The son of a Berlin workman, Plievier earned his own living from the age of twelve. In the First World War he served in the German navy, taking part in the 1918 mutiny. He wrote of his experiences in a novel, *Des Kaisers Kulis* (1930; *The Kaiser's Coolies*), following this with *Der Kaiser ging, die Generäle blieben* (1932; *The Kaiser Went, the Generals Remained*). These were books hardly calculated to please the Nazis. When they came into power in 1933, Plievier—who as a member of the Berlin League of Proletarian Writers had spoken out against Hitler and his followers—left Germany. In the following year, the Nazis took away Plievier's citizenship in the same set of orders that deprived Albert Einstein of his membership in the German community. Einstein had gone to the West, Plievier to Moscow.

Plievier was apparently happy there, but he could not leave Soviet-controlled territory until after the Second World War, when in 1947 he slipped out of the Russian zone of Germany into American-occupied Bavaria. He had by this time written the first volume of his Second World War trilogy, *Stalingrad* (1946); the other two units of the story are *Moskau* (1952; *Moscow*) and *Berlin* (1954). The development of these books reflects Plievier's changes of mind and heart.

These three novels deal with the war on the Eastern Front. *Stalingrad* (translated as *The Death of an Army*) is a thoroughly documented account of the siege by the German Sixth Army which resulted in the most terrible disaster in German military history. At the beginning of the retreat Colonel Vilshofen ironically hears on the radio that, in the name of the glorious fatherland, he has been made a brigadier general. Now he walks over the frozen ground accompanied by Corporal Gnotke, with whom he feels on equal terms—Gnotke, whose assignment as a gravedigger no longer has meaning because there are so many corpses lying stiff and grotesque in the vast acreage of snow. When Vilshofen says that the wars of the future gleam beyond these icy battlefields, Gnotke announces that he has "had enough of that," and Vilshofen admits that he has also. Gnotke says he doesn't know how the two of them can team up, and Vilshofen tells him this is what they have to learn, this is what matters.

Although Plievier's *Moscow* begins in June 1941, when the Germans attacked Russia, it too is full of the devastating snows of an Eastern winter as the German army eventually besieges Moscow. Since the book is set a year ahead of this author's *Stalingrad,* though published several years later, Plievier's residence in West Germany enabled him to make criticisms of the Soviet conduct of the war which he could not make at the time he wrote the earlier book. The Russians are shown as winning despite military ineptness and logistic bungling: the weather and the spaciousness of the country were simply too much for the German army, inhumanly driven toward disaster.

In *Moscow,* Plievier is also able to present the earlier experiences of Vilshofen and Gnotke, showing the latter being court-martialed for criticizing Hitler. Vilshofen, captured by a group of Russian partisans, wonders what the rulers of both armies had wanted for them all: Charles XII and Napoleon had been defeated in Russia, and now the frozen corpses of the modern German army lie across the snows of Russia. Before the partisans release Vilshofen and send him homeward, the old peasant Shulga, who criticizes Stalin's contempt for human lives, says that man had been given the earth by God, without frontiers, and all the earth belongs to every man.

In *Berlin,* Plievier again writes with naturalistic detail, projecting a vividly horrible picture of the destruction of the city, a blazing Wagnerian ruin as the wild-eyed Hitler still screams orders from his underground headquarters. The story goes beyond these events and on to the uprising of 1953, with a disillusioning view of life in the eastern zone, particularly as seen through the failures of those who attempt to administer justice in the Soviet orbit.

Plievier's trilogy presents some of the most remarkable fiction to come out of the Second World War. The novels are naturalistically graphic, as in the case of General Bomelbuerg in *Moscow.* This fiercely courageous Prussian thought he was invincible because a bullet had passed through his head without killing him, although it left him deaf and partly blind. Bomelbuerg, refusing to retreat, freezes to death against a pillar and becomes "a macabre signpost for the retreating Germans and the leaders of the Russian advance." The three books contain the unceasing and detailed documentation that goes with naturalism, making them wearying at times despite their shocks of interest. Ultimately, despite all their horror and disillusion, however, these novels strike a note of hopefulness. Written out of a despair with mankind, they try to show mankind a way out of despair.

War is frequently the theme of West German novels since 1945, as the following discussion will show. Many of the writers also deal trenchantly with the nation's guilt because of the Third Reich. Still another favorite subject is the willingness of some to forget or ignore that guilt, particularly in the Wirtschaftswunder (economic miracle) of these postwar years; these books are predominantly of the social type. Still other writers deal with fantasy, often after the manner of Franz Kafka.

These trends will be illustrated in the rest of this section, which will deal with a number of representative books of each kind. But the three most important among the newer novelists—Heinrich Böll, Uwe Johnson, and Günter Grass—will be discussed separately at the end of the book, following a section on recent Swiss and Austrian novelists.

And now, before taking up the younger West German writers, let us look at three older authors—Hanns Henny Jahnn, Hermann Kasack, and J. Klein-Haparasch—all born in the 1890's.

Hanns Henny Jahnn (1894–1959) may be included among postwar novelists because some of his most important writings were published in this era: indeed, his series of books, *Fluss ohne Ufer* (*River Without Banks*), was left incomplete at the time of his death. In such novels as *Pastor Ephraim Magnus* (1919) and *Perrudja* (1929), Jahnn had written of the power of sex and the unconscious, in a style that mixed the realistic with the fantastic. He began *River Without Banks* after his exile from Germany in 1933, when he removed to Denmark. The three volumes of the series are: *Das Holzschiff* (1937; *The Wooden Ship*, translated as *The Ship*), *Die Niederschrift des Gustav Anias Horn* (1949–1950; *The Notes of Gustav Anias Horn*, in two sections), and *Epilog: Fluss ohne Ufer, dritter Teil* (1962; *Epilogue: River Without Banks, Third Part;* this last is a fragment of more than four hundred pages). In these books, Gustav Anias Horn, who has lost his fiancée, Ellena, when a ship carrying a mysterious cargo sinks, identifies himself with human outcasts in various parts of the world. In mid-life, he becomes a composer of music. And he falls in love with the young sailor responsible for the death of Ellena. As in the other works of this author, realism and fantasy mingle;

one macabre touch is Horn's preservation of the body of his dead friend, whose coffin he keeps with him. Jahnn (also discussed as a playwright) was an expressionist in the 1920's and essentially remained one—his work is highly poetical and musical, frequently obscure.

As in the novels of Hanns Henny Jahnn, so realism and fantasy blend in those of Hermann Kasack (born 1896). Kasack, who often writes in the manner of Franz Kafka, was less successful with *Das gross Netz* (1952; *The Big Net*), an antimaterialist satire, than in his earlier novel, *Die Stadt hinter dem Strom* (1947; *The City beyond the River*). That book is a surrealist projection of the imaginary life of the hereafter, in which a man who finds himself in a bewildering city discovers that he is the only living person among all the dead. This is an allegory of the state of Western civilization, an effective story but one lacking the tension and suspense of a Kafka novel. Kasack is intensely concerned with Chinese civilization, as evidenced in his volumes of poetry, *Aus dem chinesischen Bilderbuch* (1955; *From the Chinese Picture Book*) and *Wasserzeichen* (1964; *Watermarks*).

J. Klein-Haparasch, a native of Rumania who writes in German, is an altogether different kind of novelist from Jahnn and Kasack. Born in 1897, brought up in Vienna, Klein-Haparasch fought in the Austrian army in the First World War. During the Second, for a while he was in a concentration camp and later in the anti-Nazi underground; his entire life has been full of adventures. A journalist for many years, in 1961 he brought out a large-scale novel, *Der vor dem Löwen flieht* (*He Who Flees the Lion*), which became a bestseller across the Continent. The setting of the novel flicks the reader's interest at once: East Europe in the early months of the Second World War. Flashbacks bring in Vienna, Zürich, and other places, but the main action occurs in the Russian-occupied part of Poland and in a Rumania which Hitler's agents are wooing. The story bristles with intrigue as the people who are caught between the magnetic forces of the Soviet Union and Nazi Germany engage in smuggling, love affairs, and assassinations.

Out of the jangle of events two principal characters emerge. One of them is a Rumanian landowner, horseman, and citizen of the world, Ludovic (Lutz) Alda, a firm-nerved man even when going through the most harrowing experiences. The other central figure is Mira Rosen, an auburn-haired Jewish beauty from the Vienna slums, who marries into a Rothschild-like family. After its members arrange for her to have a Liza Doolittle-like polishing (in London, too!), she proves herself to be a financial wizard who commandingly devises family policy. The story of the clan of international financiers is given an interesting new fillip when Mira finds a way to meet the threat of impending war. Lutz meanwhile moves through Rumanian upper-class circles in the kind of life now lost. He and Mira meet at a collective farm in occupied Poland, both with disguised identities, and there they have a temporary love affair. Mira is merely a refugee using the kolkhoz as a hiding place; Lutz is there as a spy harvesting information.

Ironically enough, though both are opposed to the Soviet system, they are the ones who keep the collective operating despite the politicians, who are not agricultural experts and who have an "I'll-denounce-you-if-you-don't-denounce-me-first" obsession. The author is at his most creative in bringing this community, with all its weird contrasts, dynamically to life. And his irony functions neatly because the sympathetic characters virtually prompt the reader to cheer on their attempts to make the kolkhoz work despite Soviet obstructions. Throughout, the most important element in the book is espionage, that product which thrives so lustily in East Europe. A native of that area, Joseph Conrad, showed in *The Secret Agent* and *Under Western Eyes* that spy stories can have psychological depth; and *He Who Flees the Lion* has this at times, although the author too often sacrifices depth as well as character to keep his intrigues going.

Yet this novel is more than an elongated spy thriller, however greatly it depends upon the mechanisms of suspense and coincidence. The author does not handle all the structural problems of the story adequately, and he fails to resolve the problems of many of the situations he has devised. The book cries out for a coda of some kind, if only a Victorian-style epilogue. But *He Who Flees the Lion* is often successful as an event-crowded story of a place and time, written with a comprehensive humanism. If anti-Semitism appears, so does its opposite, with non-Jews undertaking strenuous risks to save Jews; and in the light of recent history most readers will find this gratifying. The authoritative knowledge of European affairs which the book displays illuminates not only the six months the narrative covers but also much that has happened since that time and will continue to happen. More than most books of its kind, this one is a tale for our time, with its lessons writ large across generally effective dramatizations.

He Who Flees the Lion is one of the novels dealing with the backstage side of war rather than with its combat phases. A satirical non-combat view of the war from inside the military machine itself, a novel by Erich Kuby, scored an international success because of its incisive satiric qualities. This was *Sieg! Sieg!* (1960; *Victory! Victory!*, translated as *The Sitzkrieg of Private Stefan*). Kuby, who had in 1957 brought out the novel *Rosemarie*, also a bestseller in several countries, was born in Baden-Baden in 1910. After the Second World War he was one of the founders of the Group 47 journal *Der Skorpion*, which became one of the rallying points for younger German writers.

The Sitzkrieg of Private Stefan starts in 1939, when the French and German armies face each other in a war of no moves, and the story ends after the collapse of France. Private Stefan Wolgozen, a bookseller in "real life," is a conscript who strongly dislikes the military life. His continual war against stiff regulations becomes a war against the entire army, and the book concludes with his court-martial. The commanding general reduces by one year Stefan's sentence of two years and five months' imprisonment. There are serious notes in this satire, but most of the story moves on the comic plane. If it is not so consistently hilarious as that comic classic of the First World War, the Czech writer Jaroslav Hašek's *The Good Soldier Schweik*, nevertheless *The Sitzkrieg of Private Stefan* provides some amusing pictures of various German-army types.

Another indictment of the German army, done without overtones of comedy, is found in Stefan Olivier's *Jedem das seine* (1961; *To Every Man His Due*, translated as *Rise up in Anger*). Herbert Boysen, a much-decorated lieutenant from the Russian front, reports for duty in Athens shocked because in Greece he has seen a trainload of Jews which has been stranded for three days in more than hundred-degree weather, without water for the men, women, and children. When Boysen had complained to the Schutzstaffel officer in charge, the officer had threatened to turn his shepherd dog loose against him. When Boysen files a complaint with his new commanding officer in Athens, Major Bredenhoff, the major tells him to forget it ("They're only Jews"). Boysen manifests a stubbornness in insisting that the report be forwarded, just as later he makes a similar demand in relation to his discovery that the palatial residence of a Greek count and countess is a high-class brothel.

Since Bredenhoff is involved in this, as one of the heads of the local black market, he and his associates—Dr. Christian Schippers, Theo Grimm, and the brutal Dr. Anton Resch—conspire to have Boysen sent to a concentration camp in Germany. From there he returns to the Russian front as a volunteer in a labor battalion and, after being captured, serves five years in the Siberian mines. He is finally freed and arrives in West Germany just in time to become a quick millionaire in the new prosperity. Then he has the means to track down his enemies, which he does ruthlessly; one of them (Bredenhoff) he causes to have a stroke, another (Resch) to commit suicide.

The story, for all its flaws, contains interesting pictures of wartime and postwar Germans, in Athens, in concentration camps, on the Russian front, and in the inflation period. There is even a vivid episode built around the East Berlin riots of 1953. Psychologically, however, the book is rather shallow, with Boysen changing in an unconvincing manner; and the element of *The Count of Monte Cristo* in his pursuit of those who conspired against him makes the story a shade melodramatic.

A novelist of quite a different kind, Willi Heinrich, wrote at first of the war in Russia in such novels as *Das geduldige Fleisch* (1955; *The Willing Flesh*); as in the books of Theodor Plievier and Heinrich Gerlach, a realistic horror dominates Willi Heinrich's writing of this kind, based on his own experiences in Russia. Heinrich produced an altogether different kind of novel in *Gottes zweite Garnitur* (1960; *God's Second Best*, translated as *The Lonely Conqueror*). Its hero is a Negro in the postwar American army in Germany, but a Negro who is not a native American, although he has spent some years in the United States; he was born in Rhodesia (then Southern Rhodesia). He is a light-colored Negro, part Egyptian, with the upright walk of the African. A German family that has invited an American to dinner is shocked when Sergeant John Baako appears. He meets the fiancée of the son of the family, with whom he falls in love. Claire Heggelbacher, who had a French mother, is about to take her medical degree at Marburg and about to marry, without enthusiasm, Alfred Fahrenbach, with whom she has been having a love affair, without enthusiasm.

From the first, she and John Baako have troubles to overcome. Everyone is against them, the American army no less than the German townspeople, with Alfred quite expectedly doing all he can to stir up trouble. And when John and Claire take an airplane to Rhodesia to meet his family—semi-primitive owners of a profitable cotton factory—the white citizens and police there impose obstacles. Back in Germany, hounded by two privates from the American South and by a martinet of an officer, John goes absent without leave and makes deeper trouble for himself by striking a military policeman. Both he and Claire have learned much from their experiences; she will wait as he serves out his year of imprisonment, and from the events John emerges as a kind of hero, with dignity and pride. In this story, Willi Heinrich shows not only how well he knows his own countrymen, but also that he can convincingly deal with African settings and people. His knowledge of the inner workings of the American army verges on the uncanny. Heinrich was somewhat less successful, artistically, in *Ferien im Jenseits* (1964; *Holidays in the World to Come*, translated as *The Devil's Bed*), a melodrama about a wealthy American woman and Sicilian bandits.

In connection with Willi Heinrich's novels about the war on the Russian front, Heinrich Gerlach was mentioned. In 1957 he published *Die verratene Armee* (*The Forsaken Army*), another story of the retreat from Stalingrad. The horror of this experience has haunted the minds of various Germanic writers. Another of them is Ignor Sentjurc, born in Yugoslavia in 1927, but now a West German author who writes in German. He shows, in the retreat from Stalingrad, the conflict between two men in *Der unstillbare Strom* (1960; *The Unceasing Stream*). In this book, the ferociously brutal antagonists are Sergeant Fink, representing "the killers," and the humanely idealistic Dr. Braun, representing "the healers." Sentjurc, at sixteen, saw action on the Eastern Front; another, later author of a book about the Battle of Stalingrad, Alexander Kluge, was too young at eleven to have been in combat, but he dramatizes the Stalingrad agony with objective realism and a penetrating irony in *Schlachtbeschreibung* (1964; *Battle Description*).

The novelist who has written most about the German army is Hans Hellmut Kirst, born in Osterode (East Prussia) in the famous war year of 1914. At twenty he became a soldier, eventually an officer. After the Second World War he was for a while a film critic and then began devoting all his time to writing plays and novels. His latest play, *Aufstand* (*Rebellion*), first produced in 1966, dramatizes the 1944 plot to assassinate Hitler.

Kirst is probably best known for his novel *Die Nacht der Generale* (1962; *The Night of the Generals*) and for his series of books about the soldier he calls Herbert Asch.

The Night of the Generals was made into a motion picture in 1966, partly filmed in Warsaw. The Germans had smashed that city to rubble, but the Poles rebuilt it, for the most part after its original plan, and the moving-picture company wished to acquire authenticity by shooting the opening scenes there. Citizens of Warsaw stood just outside the range of the cameras and glared angrily at the Nazi uniforms and swastika flags. But there was some consolation for these citizens of Warsaw who were having ugly memories churned up: the city was being paid half a million dollars by the film company.

Only the early episodes of *The Night of the Generals* occur in Warsaw. One night in 1942 the local police call in the Gestapo to investigate a murder. A woman who sometimes worked for the German Secret Service has been brutally killed, obviously by a psychopath. A witness has seen a man leave the dead woman's room, a man with a wide red stripe down his trousers which might be blood or might be the markings on a German general's uniform. The Germans have seven generals in Warsaw that night. The activities of three of them cannot be accounted for on that fatal evening: General von Seydlitz-Gabler (fat), Lieutenant General Tanz (athletic), Major General Kahlenberge (bald). It is not until fourteen years later that the culprit is officially discovered, and then only through the efforts of a French detective.

For there had been another murder in Paris, two years after the first one. The same three generals were in the city. By this time the reader knows who the killer is. He strikes again in 1956, when he is a general in East Germany; confronted by the Sûreté inspector at a West Berlin party, the guilty man goes into a side room and, in the best European-officer tradition, blows his brains out.

The outline of the story is grim, but Kirst throughout employs the satire for which he is famous. Yet beyond the satire there is real horror.

Between the narrative sections, reports and testimonials carry the story. It is possible to see a Javert type of detective tracking down his criminal across time and space. Yet Inspector General Prévert is less like Victor Hugo's Javert than he is like Georges Simenon's Inspector Maigret or even Agatha Christie's Hercule Poirot. For all its psychological interest, the book is essentially a tour de force, full of crime-story clichés and lacking in depth, essentially just a superior detective story. The American reviewer who in discussing *The Night of the Generals* evoked Dostoevsky's *Crime and Punishment* was being fatuous. That Kirst's novel is readable, however, and even crowded with interesting scenes and characters cannot be denied.

Kirst's finest achievement so far is the Gunner Asch trilogy, whose general title is *Null-Acht Fünfzehn* (1954–1955; *Zero Eight–Fifteen*). The three separate volumes are: *08/15 in der Kaserne. Die abenteuerliche Revolte des Gefreiten Asch* (*08/15 in the Barracks. The Adventurous Revolt of Lance-Corporal Asch,* translated in America as *The Revolt of Gunner Asch* and in England as *The Strange Mutiny of Gunner Asch*), *08/15 im Kriege. Die seltsamen Kriegserlebnisse des Soldaten Asch* (*08/15 in the War. The Strange War Experiences of Soldier Asch,* translated as *Forward, Gunner Asch*), and *08/15 bis zum Ende. Der gefährliche Endsieg des Soldaten Asch* (*08/15 to the Last. The Dangerous Ending of Soldier Asch,* translated as *The Return of Gunner Asch*). The titles suggest the content of these stories of life in the German army before, during, and at the end of the Second World War. But the character of Asch is something which can be experienced only in the reading, for he is the humanized soldier in conflict with the machine, and the burr under the saddle of bullying sergeants. The term "08/15" derives from a type of German machine gun and corresponds to the American locution "G.I." Altogether, the Gunner Asch series presents one of the most mischievous and sardonic pictures of the last big war.

Among Kirst's recent novels, one is partly (but only partly) a sequel to the Gunner Asch books: *Null-Acht Fünfzehn Heute* (1963; *Zero Eight–Fifteen Today*, translated as *What Became of Gunner Asch*). In this novel, Asch plays a secondary role, displaced in centerstage by one Corporal Karl Kamnitzer, another of Kirst's attractive military rogues. The story is set in a West German town of which Herbert Asch, now a retired officer, is mayor as well as an innkeeper. But he is only at the edge of the central conflict of the story.

This conflict rages between two military groups stationed in the town. One is a Luftwaffe unit, the other a proud part of the new German army, the Bundeswehr. The latter has for its commander a martinet who would go well in the old army whom Kaiser Wilhelm II was the first to call the modern Huns; and this officer has the fanatic support of various subordinates, particularly Sergeant Major Rammler, the villain of the story. And it is a story in which the villain succeeds in bringing the good men down. Told with bitter humor and compelling irony, *Zero Eight–Fifteen Today* contains a warning not only about the Prussian-sadist elements who might turn up in the Bundeswehr, but about all fanatic militarists everywhere.

Turning to fiction about war guilt and the new society, we find one of the most remarkable first novels of the postwar period, Christian Geissler's *Anfrage* (1960; *Inquiry*, translated as *The Sins of the Fathers*). This was the cause of furious debate in West Germany because it is an examination of national guilt. Geissler points out, in a preface to the English translation, that influential groups within his own country had insisted that he be convicted of treason for writing the book, which he indicates has also been widely defended. Geissler, born in Hamburg in 1928, grew up in an ideologically divided household, for his father was a Nazi and his mother, who was Polish, opposed fascism. Christian Geissler, after serving in the war in an anti-aircraft battalion, worked as a clerk, forester, youth leader, surveyor, hotel porter, and journalist. He wrote several radio plays before his first novel, which shows that the sins of the fathers—in this case including the murders of the Jews—are disaffirmed by the fathers and not recognized for what they are by the sons.

In Geissler's story, Klaus Köhler, a young scientist in the postwar era, tries to find out the truth about the murder of a Jew, Dr. Simon Valentin, and attempts to trace Valentin's son, who supposedly escaped

Nazi persecution. Helped by the former gardener of the Valentins, Anton Mollwitz, Köhler carries on his private investigation, which leads him down labyrinthine ways, his progress continually hampered by evasions. He locates Dr. Valentin's murderer, who is living in Köhler's own house, where the younger Valentin, who has just died, has also been staying, under the name of Meyer. But throughout, Köhler is really motivated by the transference of guilt from his own father, a former storm-troop officer: Köhler's obsessive quest is that of many Germans of his generation, a searching out of the roots of guilt. The book, scattered and ambiguous as it is, projects with force the problems which still haunt the country which once surrendered itself to the Nazis.

Another novel which, like Geissler's, made trouble for its author was Wilfrid Schilling's *Der Angstmacher* (*The Fear Maker*, translated as *The Fear Makers*). It is difficult to ascribe an exact date for this book whose English edition seems to have appeared in 1959, the German in 1960. The English and Dutch editions were anonymous, the German and the American (which was also 1960) acknowledged by the author. In West Germany, Schilling was severely scolded for his book and called both a Nazi and one who was unfair to the Nazis. He finally took refuge in Belgium. Actually, his story deplored the success of former Nazis in the newer Germany, and their ability to pay off old grudges. The narrative concerns a journalist who had operated in the anti-Fascist underground and who, eleven years after the war, finds himself in a police station charged with assault and robbery. Alfred Link had helped French officials take in some Nazis as war criminals in 1945, but he had not struck them or taken their watches or typewriters, which the Frenchmen actually did. In 1956, however, the police imprison Link.

An appeals board frees him temporarily, but he realizes that he will still be tried. He learns that the prosecutor is a former Nazi military judge. No lawyers want to take Link's case; he considers fleeing to Switzerland. He is haunted by dreams, in one of which he visits a new German city called Sodom; in another, at the end of the book, he has an apocalyptic vision in which he sees robot-like storm troopers on the march. All this is gruesomely effective, though like so many thesis-novels the characters lack the dimension that makes them live in the medium of the novel. To say this is not to belittle the author's serious intention but merely to point out that, however cogently he expresses his ideas, the result is not necessarily art. This applies to a number of these newer German novels that attempt to deal with contemporary situations. Some of them are indeed forcible, but are books only of the moment. It is the artistic quality in the novels of Günter Grass, Uwe Johnson, and Heinrich Böll which give them a special value. Yet the lesser books dealing with topical themes are often exciting to read, and through the medium of fiction they make statements which would be less moving if rendered statistically or in other coldly factual ways.

A more artistically contrived novel is by a man who belongs to West German literature by a technicality: Joseph Breitbach. His novel *Bericht über Bruno* (*Report on Bruno*) was written in German and first published in Frankfurt-am-Main in 1960. But Breitbach is a French citizen, born in Lorraine, who has written a play in French, *Le Jubilaire* (1960; *The Celebrator*), successfully produced on the Paris stage. Breitbach after many years' work had in 1937 completed a novel, *Clemens*, whose manuscript he lost during the Second World War. Thomas Mann, who had read the first chapter, printed that chapter in his journal *Mass und Wert* (*Measure and Worth*), from which this surviving part of the book was recently republished in both German and French. The novelist and essayist Jean Schlumberger (another native of Alsace-Lorraine), who had read the entire manuscript of *Clemens*, has said it is the kind of book a writer could produce only once in a lifetime. Distressed over the loss of his novel, Breitbach did not for many years attempt imaginative writing again, but finally turned out *Report on Bruno*. It is set in the postwar period in a Graustark-Ruritania country governed by a parliamentary monarchy. The situation is obviously patterned after that of several nations in which either fascism or communism grew; there are some striking parallels with Germany. The events of the story are viewed from the other end of the telescope than those in Geissler's *The Sins of the Fathers*—in *Report on Bruno*, a grandfather watches his clever grandson grow up to become a potential dictator.

The grandfather, leader of the liberal party in this Benelux-like land, notices how, in adolescence, his grandson Bruno Collignon is already craftily demagogic. And he is cruel. The same cruelty impels him, some years later when he is a precocious politician, to drive his former tutor Stijn Rysselgeert—also now a politician—to his death. Bruno in the process ruins the political career of his grandfather, who realizes that before Bruno is thirty he may destroy the constitution and set up a totalitarian state. At the end, the grandfather wonders what Bruno really feels when he now sees him: "It is not necessary, in order to have a conscience, to believe in the Christian God." Joseph Breitbach has, in one of the most gripping postwar Germanic political novels, a subtly woven book, stated the situation of today's world.

One of the most effective German writers to come along since the war is Gerd Gaiser, born in 1908, a combat veteran of the Luftwaffe, about which he wrote in his novel *Die sterbende Jagd* (1953; *The Dying Pursuit*, translated as *The Falling Leaf*). A group novel, with a confusing array of characters, its story is set in one grim week in Norway when the pilots there realize they are outnumbered by their attackers from Great Britain, and also at that time they come to see that they are fighting for a worthless cause. This is written in a more straightforward style than Gaiser's earlier novel, *Eine Stimme hebt an* (1950; *A Voice Is Raised*), which in often obscure and ambiguous language, crowded with symbols, tells of the hardships of a returned soldier in the chaos of the early postwar years. Gaiser again draws upon such a style, suggesting the manner of the expressionists, in *Schlussball* (1958; *The Final Ball*). In theme, this book is reminiscent of some of the German novels of the inflation period that followed the First World War, such as Heinz Liepmann's *Der Friede brach aus* (1932; *Peace Broke Out*). *The Final Ball* deals with the prosperity that began to fatten West Germany in the 1950's. As one of the characters says to her daughter, "Ditta, we shouldn't say a single word. But the Lord has after all let us win the war"—a point evident to visitors as long ago as 1950, particularly those who had just come from an England pinched by rationing and who found Germany a well-stocked larder.

In Gaiser's book, a young schoolmaster named Soldner helplessly watches the decline of morals as greed rises among the people of Neu-Spuhl, an ugly industrial town. The greed is emphasized by the materialistic outlook of his students. Soldner's existence is complicated because he falls in love with one of the decent people in the book, Herse Andernoth, a Penelope who insists that her missing-in-action husband will one day return. The horror of the materialist rapacity of the town is intensified by the presence of a maniac with an eye for Herse Andernoth's young daughter: this helps to give the novel a suspense-story climax. Soldner, who cannot break through Herse's faith in the ultimate return of her husband, tells himself that this generation lost everything it reached for. Yet he is still waiting, not knowing what he is, or why, or what he is awaiting: "Nevertheless I'm waiting."

An author who rivals Gaiser in attacks upon the new prosperity, Martin Walser, is particularly noted for his huge novel *Halbzeit* (1960; *Half Time*). Walser, born in Wasserburg, Bodensee, in 1927, is also a dramatist, best known for his play *Eiche und Angora* (1962; translated as *The Rabbit Race*), a satire on those who perpetuate the spirit of

Nazism. In *Half Time,* narrated in a parody of the conversational style, Walser attacks the upper world of society and industrial magnates. And he tells the story of a traveling salesman surrounded by prostitutes, perverts, and crooks, a man with a dull wife and come children destined for a hollow existence. Walser is not saying anything new, but he is often trenchant, and he effectively satirizes advertising, the mechanical outlook, and the mistaken values of a materialistic time. He is sometimes compared to Sinclair Lewis, but Walser's shafts are cruelly sharper.

The familiar modern theme of the search for the father occurs in Herbert Heckmann's *Benjamin und seine Väter* (1962; *Benjamin and His Fathers*), which is in large part a social novel. Heckmann, born in Frankfurt in 1930, is of the generation that in childhood saw the Nazis staging their black parades; a member of the scientific faculty at Heidelberg, Heckmann in 1958 brought out a volume of short stories, *Das Porträt* (*The Portrait*). In *Benjamin and His Fathers* he tells of a boy born illegitimately in March 1919, while the Versailles Treaty was also being born. The narrative continues until 1934, when the Nazis are in power; Benjamin has never succeeded in finding more than traces of the father he has never seen. But in a final chapter, in 1941, he at last locates the man in Paris, a clown out of employment because of wartime conditions. As Benjamin leaves the futile man he realizes that at last he has found his father, and that he has also recognized himself.

These are the grim features of the story, emphasized by the death of Benjamin's mother, in his childhood, after she is run over by an automobile. Most of the book, however, is robustly comic, dealing with the repeated adventures of self-discovery by the boy Benjamin as he grows up in a flat in Frankfurt. For a while he thinks that his father is a man who lives in the same building. This is his mother's lawyer, who has befriended them: Dr. Fritz Bernouilli, known as Jonah. Jonah's motives are altruistic, not erotic; he is a neatly delineated character who plays his important part in the comedy. Against those who protest that Benjamin is a Jewish name, Jonah answers that he has insisted that the boy be named this because of the great Benjamin Franklin.

Most of the story belongs to Benjamin, who is actually brought up as a Catholic. He continually gets into scrapes, largely because he is dominated by fantasy, like one of his heroes, Don Quixote. There is at times a comedic vigor in this story, but too much of it is diffused, unfocused, and the lively characterizations of Jonah and Benjamin do not quite carry the narrative, which because of its length needs somewhat better shaping. The symbolic aspects of the book, because of their obvious relation to the Germany of the time, are fairly easy to discern. When the father of Benjamin's schoolfriend Max kills himself, Benjamin's exclamation is one that echoes through many German novels of this time: "Damn all fathers who put us in a life like this!"

Luise Rinser (born 1911) is a novelist who generally portrays the social scene, but often with strains of the psychological and the religious. Her short novel, *Jan Lobel aus Warschau* (1948; *Jan Lobel from Warsaw*) shows the reactions of Bavarian villagers to a Jewish refugee from Poland who, later in the Second World War, arrives in their midst and asks for shelter. This fine story was reprinted in the collection, *Ein Bündel weisser Narzissen* (1956; *A Bundle of White Narcissi*). Luise Rinser's *Mitte des Lebens* (1950; *Middle of Life*) is the story of a woman whose fierce respect for truth brings suffering to herself and those who know her. This woman, who has worked in the German anti-Nazi underground, achieves some success as a writer in the postwar world, but does not find sexual satisfaction. In *Daniela* (1953), the heroine from whom the book takes its name gives up her comfortable Bürger existence in order to engage in social work among the poor in a desolate countryside. *Der Sündenbock* (1955; *The Scapegoat*) presents a young woman who has complex motivations for murdering an elderly relative. In *Die vollkommene Freude* (1962; *The Perfect Joy*), Luise Rinser attempts to uplift her readers and help them build barriers against temptation. As always in her work, the forces of passion and restraint collide.

One of the leading postwar short-story writers of Germany, Klaus Roehler is somewhat reminiscent of Thomas Mann in his use of humorous irony. And Roehler, as an observer of manners, has a special value as a social commentator. His collection, *Die Würde der Nacht* (1958; *The Dignity of Night*), is notable particularly for "Der 18te Geburtstag" ("Eighteenth Birthday"), made into a film in 1961. It is a witty survey of the postwar generation. Roehler, who was born at Königsee, Thuringia, in 1929, was called into military service at the age of sixteen. After the war he settled in West Germany, and now lives in Frankfurt. The title story of his book, "The Dignity of Night," tells of the experiences of a young American Negro studying in Germany. For a while a German girl keeps company with Nicholas, but her friends shame her out of the relationship, and the abandoned Nicholas fades into "the dignity of night," where the color of his skin is not noticeable. Other students appear in the story "Bubul," the diary of a young man who records his love affairs in physical detail: the one with a fellow student, Istrid, and the momentary renewal of an old one with Alexandra, now married and living in Spain, who passes through. Bubul regularly notes down his intention (perhaps an echo of Rilke's "Archaic Torso of Apollo") to change his way of life. "New Year's Every Day" has as its setting a party at which the attitudes of the elder and younger generations are compared. But most of Roehler's work deals with the latter in the years of inflation, postwar boredom, and creative excitement. The prose is youthfully lively, with a swift-moving rat-ta-tat quality.

Comedy and satire often form the basis for social novels. Comic satire of the between-wars period in which fascism was bred occurs in Gregor von Rezzori's *Ein Hermelin in Tschernopol* (1958; *An Ermine in Tschernopol*, translated as *The Hussar*). Von Rezzori (born 1914), who has lived in Germany since 1938, is a Rumanian by birth. He has been prominent in broadcasting and film production, and several of his books have had an international success, including *The Hussar*. It is the story of a man who, though a major in a stiff-jointed army, is a kind of last, lone individualist. He is quartered in a town in southeast Europe, Tschernopol, whose mean-spirited inhabitants gossip endlessly about one another's only too common misdeeds. There is, for example, a vulgarly anti-Semitic editor, and the willowy and beautiful wife of the hussar goes to live with this editor. At the end of the story the hussar himself is killed in a grotesque accident: a tramcar goes out of control and plunges down a hill; the major tries to save the life of the drunken old Professor Ljubanarov and is himself hit by the car and killed. In a paragraph of epilogue, the author indicates that life continued much as usual in Tschernopol—the kind of life that led the world toward 1939.

Satire is sometimes not too great a step from fantasy, though fantasy in itself is usually more intensive; satire draws upon the imagination, and exaggerates the believable, while fantasy brings the incredible within the range of the believable. Fantasy has been a constant among the Germanic peoples, from the earliest fairy tales to the ancestor of most contemporary writers of qualitative fantasy—Franz Kafka.

One of the striking fantasies of recent years is *Teddy Flesh oder die Belagerung von Sagunt* (1964; *Teddy Flesh or the Siege of Sagunto*), by Klaus Nonnenmann (born at Pforzheim in 1922). This is the story of a man living in a Swiss farmhouse and indulging in daydreams of the fabulous Teddy Flesh who, with the help of Hannibal's elephants, takes possession of a Spanish town. But this is more than a children's story, for it projects a man's quest of self-discovery, and it contrasts everyday life with the world of dreams which is the basis of myth and of all human aspirations.

Hans Keilson's *Der Tod des Widersachers* (1960; *The Death of the*

Adversary) has an even more serious intention, and it is the work of an author, an exile from Germany since 1933, who is a psychiatrist in Holland. Obviously influenced by Kafka, the book projects its own nameless world, and most of the characters appear only in the form of initials. On the contrary, Nonnenmann's *Teddy Flesh* had a protagonist distinctly named Martin Schünemann, and it carefully evokes the scenery around the Lake of Constance.

The Death of the Adversary is, as a prologue suggests, supposedly a manuscript given to an unnamed "I" in Holland, and it purports to be the account of the experiences of an anti-Fascist underground fighter; in the prologue, the "I"—possibly a psychiatrist—is told that the author of the manuscript is dead because of betrayal by a Nazi agent. None of this has an organic connection (except possibly to a profound student of the manifestations of the unconscious) with the body of the book, in which another "I" tells the story of his relationship with the man known, in Kafka fashion, only as B., or sometimes as "my friend" or "my enemy." They were friends at first, as boys, and then their friendship was broken off. Later, when B. is a rising politician, obviously on the way to a dictatorship, he is "the enemy." The narrator talks of killing him.

Yet when B. is dead, the "I" misses him, however much he had hated the grown-up B. The clue to the emotional relationship is contained in a fable B. told the narrator when they were boys: when the Kaiser was visiting his cousin the Tsar, the Tsar gave him some elks to take home; but the elks slowly died in Germany. No reason could be found for this, so the Kaiser wrote to the Tsar, who asked his forester about the matter. He said that the elks were dying because they missed the wolves. Not the steppes, the Russian sky or trees, but just the wolves. When B. had told the narrator this story, the narrator had not liked it; because of this, their friendship was sundered. And so the narrator missed B. after his death, as the elks had missed the wolves. This is an interesting idea, but Keilson worked it out at too-great length, more than two hundred pages; it would have held up better as a short story. The idea has to be too elaborately decorated to be stretched out into a novel.

On the other hand, Gisela Elsner in some three hundred pages has managed to write a sustained fantasy in *Die Riesenzwerge* (1964; *The Giant Dwarfs*), which won the international Formentor Prize. The author of the book was born in Nuremberg in 1937 and grew up watching the Nazi rallies there, which were in themselves a mad fantasy. Gisela Elsner, after education in Vienna as well as in Munich and several other West German cities, lived for a while in Rome and then moved to London with her German-artist husband. In *The Giant Dwarfs* she wrote a first novel of imaginative force.

It is at once fantasy and satire, distorting the adult world into a monstrous universe. Seen from the eyes of the child Lothar Leinlein, the adults (the giant dwarfs) are comically macabre, particularly Lothar's father, a schoolmaster with a mechanized soul who represents the totalitarian personality at its worst extreme. The very act of his eating at dinner is suggestive of cannibalism, and everything he does is exaggerated into a kind of hideous lunacy. Herr Leinlein is the survival of the Nazi spirit, never pointed out as such except in the symbolic overtones of the book, whose meaning cannot be missed. The story is often surrealist in tone, yet it has an underlying gruesome reality in which horror comes recognizably through all the grotesqueness. And, without being pedantic, the book is a story with a lesson.

Another young writer of outstanding achievement, Peter Faecke, was born in Silesia in 1940. At the end of the war, when Faecke was five, his family transferred to Hanover. His first novel appeared when he was only twenty-three—*Der Brandstifter* (1963; *The Firebug*). The title is reminiscent of a play by Max Frisch and, like Frisch, Faecke uses nonrealist techniques. *The Firebug* of Peter Faecke is not so much fantastic as symbolic, the story of a German Pole from Silesia who wants to produce a son above reproach. Glonski leaves his wife when he discovers she is Jewish, and Hitler's racial pronouncements also make Glonski abandon his French mistress and even their illegitimate son Pnip; but Glonski keeps trying, meanwhile burning down the sawmills of rival millowners.

There is an idiot son—in subject matter as in technique, the book is often reminiscent of William Faulkner. The story continually shifts its narrative focus: Pnip tells the story part of the time, and later another son of Glonski's rather miraculously appears: the book is full of such surprises.

Faecke goes into the mode of symbolic fantasy with *Der rote Milan* (1965; *The Red Kite*), whose dominating image is a kite which appears one day and drives all the sparrows into silence. A boy who is terrified by the piercing glance of the kite is stirred to recollections of his earlier years, during the Second World War. He remembers above all a cruel incident that occurred in his town, and this moment of recognition, of awareness, becomes one of the rites de passage, in this case the maturing of the boy through sudden knowledge. Again Faecke has written an important book, and he is already becoming established, in comparatively early youth, as a significant German writer.

How many Germans of today are haunted by that red kite is problematical; but it is certain that many German writers have seen it and have felt its truth-breeding stare.

THE NEWER
SWISS AND
AUSTRIAN NOVEL

Austria and German-speaking Switzerland have recently produced only a few writers of fiction known outside the Germanic world. The Austrian Heimito von Doderer has been gathering fame in English-speaking countries, in which the Swiss writers Friedrich Dürrenmatt and Max Frisch are better known for their plays than their novels.

Among the somewhat older generation of Swiss writers, Alfred Kübler is best known for *Öppi*, a trilogy published between 1943 and 1951. The story of Öppi's boyhood and youth takes place in the first quarter of the twentieth century. Appropriately, since Switzerland is supposed to be full of innkeepers, Öppi is the son of one. Öppi studies at a Swiss university and, after abandoning geology, takes up sculpture, later becoming an actor. From his village boyhood to his life in academic and artistic circles (there is a stimulating visit to Italy), Öppi goes through a wide range of experiences, including the erotic; and the novel is an enlivened picture of Swiss society of its time.

A Swiss by adoption, Edzard Schaper is a native of Ostrowo, Posen Province, where he was born in 1908. After living in Finland and Estonia, he settled in Switzerland in 1947. He has written several historical novels, including two set in the France of Napoleon: *Die Freiheit der Gefangenen*

(1949; *The Freedom of the Captives*) and *Die Macht der Ohnmächtigen* (1951; *The Power of the Powerless*). In two connected novels, *Die sterbende Kirche* (1935; *The Dying Church*) and *Der letzte Advent* (1949; *The Last Advent*), Schaper drew upon his Baltic background for stories of an attempt to keep the Orthodox faith alive after the First World War. In *Das Tier* (1958; *The Animal*, translated as *The Dancing Bear*), Schaper set his scene in Lithuania, in Germany, and in Switzerland. It is the first-person narrative of Oscar Stepunat, member of a refugee family; after the war drives them out of Lithuania, Oscar goes to Switzerland, where he is engaged to dress up as a bear to amuse the tourists. Gradually he assumes the characteristics of the bear and, in a moment of crisis, attacks and claws his employer, who dies from loss of blood. The lawyer defending Oscar suggests that he write an account of his life while awaiting trial; this might turn up facts about Oscar's rootless existence that could be used in his defense. The symbolism of the story is easy to discern and is effectively worked out; Oscar has the benefit of Edzard Schaper's considerable narrative skill.

Kurt Guggenheim, a native Swiss (born 1896), in his novel *Der Friede des Herzens* (1956; *Peace of Heart*) shows the failure of a middle-aged man to break out of the routine of his commonplace existence. The choking effect of small-town existence is also seen in Hans Walter's three short novels, collected in *Im Verborgenen* (1950; *On the Quiet*), while Carl J. Burckhardt's *Drei Erzählungen* (1952; *Three Narratives*) deals largely with the effect of the Second World War on Switzerland. Essentially an optimist, Burckhardt believes that Christian and humanistic civilization will survive all onslaughts.

One of the newer Swiss writers who has had an international success is Otto F. Walter (born in 1928). He is by coincidence a publisher, head of the firm which bears his name. His work has sold well across Europe, and he won the international Charles Veillon Prize for *Der Stumme* (1959; *The Mute*), a tense story of the conflict of a father and son at a roadbuilding site in the heights of the Jura region. The son, who has been mute ever since in early childhood he saw his mother strike his father, seeks out the father at the roadbuilding camp. The fatal drama which is then played out would probably be more effective if the author had not switched his comparatively simple story around to so many different points of view. But Otto Walter, who has also written a number of short stories, remains one of the highly promising authors of the Germanic world.

Other younger Swiss fiction writers of distinction include Peter Bichsel,

Louis Jent, and Jürg Federspiel. In 1965, Bichsel (born 1936) received the Group 47 prize of 5,000 marks; he had the year before brought out a distinctive collection of stories, *Eigentlich mochte Frau Blum den Milchmann kennenlernen* (*Actually, Mrs. Blum Would Like to Make the Acquaintance of the Milkman*). Louis Jent (born 1936) is the author of the novel *Ausflüchte* (1965; *Evasions*), the story of a cinema critic in Zürich who feels he is leading a life of desperation and flees to Seville. There he relives the past by writing of his childhood and youth, and rediscovers himself. Jürg Federspiel, author of the volume of short stories *Orangen und Tode* (1962; *Oranges and Deaths*), has written a novel, *Massaker im Mond* (1964; *Massacre on the Moon*), which is a shrewdly told story of the gradual psychological deterioration of an aging woman.

Friedrich Dürrenmatt, discussed elsewhere as one of the leading Germanic playwrights, is best known as a fiction writer for detective-style novels, such as *Der Richter und sein Henker* (1952; *The Judge and His Hangman*). In *Grieche sucht Griechin* (1955; *Greek Seeks Female Greek*, translated as *Once a Greek*), Dürrenmatt writes a fable with a modern setting, as he often does in his plays. This novel deals with an obscure bookkeeper, Arnolf Archilochos, who advertises for a wife who must be Greek like himself. A glowing beauty named Chloé appears and agrees to marry him. Suddenly he finds himself a man of distinction and wealth, and it is only after the wedding that he discovers his bride is a famous and popular prostitute. Archilochos survives the irony of this revelation, and does so believably only because the author keeps the story strictly in the realm of the fabulous.

Another of Dürrenmatt's stories in the mystery-novel genre is *Die Panne* (1956; *The Breakdown*, translated in America as *Traps*, after the name of its leading character). The breakdown of the original title referred only to the car driven by Alfred Traps, a salesman. The breakdown of the automobile forces him to spend the night in a village in which Traps, an outward-going vulgarian, immediately plans erotic adventures. But first he looks for quarters and can find none; the inns are all full. At one place where he asks for lodging he finds himself among some brilliant old men who have devised a game to help them overcome the boredom of provincial existence. They are retired judges and lawyers, and one of them is an innkeeper who was once an executioner. Their game is to stage mock trials; they particularly appreciate having an actual defendant, so Traps soon finds himself fighting desperately against them in a trial which has become altogether too real, and whose ending is a grisly surprise. This novel was dramatized by James Yaffe as *The Deadly Game* and staged unsuccessfully in New York in 1960 with Traps changed into an American.

Another novel of Dürrenmatt's was made into a film: *Das Versprechen: Requiem auf den Kriminalroman* (1958; *The Promise: Requiem for the Crime Novel*, translated as *The Pledge*). This story of the murder of a young girl is also the story of a police inspector, and it raises moral questions as to how far police can go in setting traps for criminals. By giving the detective story a depth it does not usually have, Dürrenmatt in this genre somewhat resembles the notable French writer of the roman policier, Georges Simenon.

Dürrenmatt's fellow dramatist from Switzerland, Max Frisch, has written several novels in which the protagonist investigates his own identity, including *Stiller* (1954; translated as *I'm Not Stiller*), *Homo Faber* (1957), and *Mein Name sei Gantenbein* (1964; *Let My Name Be Gantenbein*, translated as *A Wilderness of Mirrors*). Stiller, in the first of these, is a Swiss sculptor of no great ability who tries to escape from bourgeois society by pretending he is someone else. He lives in America for a time and returns to Switzerland with a false passport. The authorities assert he is Stiller, and he firmly denies this, whereupon they methodically prove his true identity and then methodically fine him for the trouble he has caused.

In Frisch's *A Wilderness of Mirrors*, Theo Gantenbein builds a special identity by pretending to be blind—he buys dark glasses, a white stick, and receives official permission to wear a yellow armband. Supposedly blind, Gantenbein does not have to see anything he does not want to see —his wife's lover, for example. On the other hand, he can pretend to the special clairvoyance of the afflicted and can utter uncomfortable truths. The story, for all its detailed presentation of Gantenbein's mechanisms for keeping up his pose of the blind man, is not naturalistic, but is rather almost spasmodically expressionistic as it leaps from one consciousness to another, and from paradox to paradox. Gantenbein's ruse ultimately gets him nowhere, and after he gives it up he lapses back into a life of the commonplace and the futile.

Switzerland's famous neutrality protected the country in the two world wars, but indirectly their impact was felt even in the quietest valleys, and Swiss literature reflects this in its frequent portraits of the nervously upset. Another constant, however, is the bovaryste theme, the reaction against the commonplaceness of ordinary provincial life, often also resulting in nervous upsets. But the drama, particularly with Frisch and

Dürrenmatt, has proved to be a more effective vehicle for expressing these matters than the novel; and in their plays, Frisch and Dürrenmatt have not limited themselves to matters of concern only to the Swiss, but—as in Frisch's *The Firebugs* and Dürrenmatt's *The Physicists*—have dealt with questions important to all mankind.

Austria, the scene of great changes in a comparatively short space of time, often expresses in its literature the sense of differences brought on by time. This is nowhere more evident than in the novels of Albert Paris Gütersloh, particularly in his long book *Sonne und Mond* (1962; *Sun and Moon*). This deals with the decline of the old Austria and throws a dramatic light on the conflicts among those trying to discover a way of life for themselves in the newer Austria. In *Der Lügner unter Bürgern* (1964; *The Liar among Citizens*), Gütersloh continued with these themes.

Among other Austrian novelists, several who stand out noticeably are Ilse Aichinger, Herbert Eisenreich, Franz Tumler, Peter von Tramin, Elias Canetti, Denis Bernard, Jakov Lind, and the previously mentioned Heimito von Doderer.

Ilse Aichinger has lately published *Eliza, Eliza* (1965), some two dozen prose sketches of a highly poetical nature. Similarly, Herbert Eisenreich in 1965 brought out an important collection of tales, *Sozusagen Liebesgeschichten* (*Love Stories, So to Speak*). They are utterly distinctive and comically objective, bordering on the absurd. Franz Tumler's first novel, *Aufschreibung aus Trient* (1965; *Writing About Trent*), is a quietly paced novel about a young Austrian couple, delayed in the Italian Tyrol when their car is wrecked. They recall that Austria once held this territory and discuss its problems with the people there. Peter von Tramin's *Die Herren Söhne* (1964; *Our Sons, the Gentlemen*) is the story of a quartet of young people in postwar Vienna and the fierce mutual hatred of two of them. It is an exceptionally fine first novel, marked by humor as well as intense drama, and underscored by subtlety.

A native of Bulgaria (born 1905) who resided some years in Vienna and now lives in London, Elias Canetti is generally considered an Austrian author; he has written both drama and fiction. Internationally he is best known for his novel *Auto da Fe* (1946; translated for its 1963–1964 English and American editions by C. V. Wedgwood under the author's supervision). Alternately frightening and comic, full of perverse and ghoulish nightmares, *Auto da Fe* tells the story of a Faust-like scholar whose Mephistopheles is a dwarf that leads him away from his books into the dreamlike underworld of an unnamed city. The self-destruction of the scholar Peter Kien is accomplished amid such grotesquerie that it is hardly tragic, but it is effectively horrifying and shocking; the author has a Brueghel-like vision.

Denis Bernard, born in Vienna in 1915 and now living in Uruguay, in *Mensch ohne Gegenwart* (1958; *The Suspended Man*) deals with the unrest of the generation dispossessed by war. Written as a prison journal, it looks back over the experiences of a young Frenchman, his involvement in postwar rackets and, eventually, in murder. More than the experiences of a single man, the story has a representative quality, and it is full of bitter wisdom. Another Viennese-born writer (1927), Jakov Lind, now lives in London. His *Eine Seele aus Holz* (1962; *Soul of Wood*) is a collection of stories, mostly fantastic. The title story concerns a man left in charge of a paralyzed Jewish boy whose parents (the father is a doctor) are deported from Vienna. Abandoned on a nearby mountain, the boy undergoes a strange transformation. In this and the other stories in the book, Lind shows great ability at blending the fantastic and the grotesque with the realistic; and presents a horrifying vision of modern life, but one relieved by an intense humanity. Lind's novel, *Landschaft in Beton* (1964; *Landscape in Concrete*), is characterized by the bizarre qualities of the earlier stories. Europe in war-madness is emblemized by a German army sergeant, Gauthier Bachmann, pronounced insane and therefore unfit for military service. He refuses to accept this judgment and, in the later phases of the war, wanders across most of German-occupied Europe seeking a regiment that will allow him to serve with it. The surrealist story has a fitting Götterdämmerung climax. For his symbolic inventiveness, Lind has sometimes been compared to Günter Grass.

Although Heimito von Doderer was born as long ago as 1896, he has achieved his international fame only since the Second World War. He is now generally recognized by critics and hosts of other readers as one of the most important of recent European novelists.

In the First World War, Doderer was a lieutenant in the Dragoons. After being captured on the Eastern Front he spent several years in Siberia; following his release as a prisoner of war he stayed on as a lumberjack. Returning to Vienna, he published his first volume of poems in 1923. Two years later he took his doctor's degree in history at the University of Vienna. During the Second World War he served as an officer in the Luftwaffe. He died in December 1966.

Doderer's first important novel was *Ein Mord den Jeder begeht* (1938; *A Murder That Everyone Commits*, translated as *Every Man a Murderer*). Here Doderer shows how dexterously he can weave a story in and out of everyday, apparently commonplace happenings. In point of time, he deals with the first quarter of the twentieth century, the years he treats in most of his books. His central figure, his "everyman," is Conrad Castilitz, known as Kokosch, who after an untroubled childhood and a somewhat lonely adolescence becomes a younger executive in the textile industry. He marries the daughter of one of the owners of the firm, a woman several years older than he is. And then he sees a painting that captivates him—it is of his wife's radiant younger sister, Louison. She had died eight years earlier, under mysterious circumstances, in a locked railway compartment in which she was alone. The police had investigated the matter, but had come to no conclusions.

Kokosch Castilitz is so obsessed by the picture of the beautiful Louison that he turns detective in order to find her murderer. The book then becomes another story of the investigator bringing about a resolution that is unexpected, though perhaps always dimly suspected in the nebulous chambers of the unconscious; this is the central plot of a play as old as Sophocles' *Oedipus the King* and as of a novel as new as Günter Grass's *Dog Years*. Kokosch finally discovers that as a boy of fifteen he was aboard that very express, roaring toward Stuttgart, on which Louison was found dead without explanation. Kokosch had been in the same compartment with a group of prankish medical students. They enlisted him in their expressions of fun, explaining that a girl was traveling alone in the next compartment. They had a skull and thought it would be great fun to scare her with it. They put it on a cane to be held out of a window the next time the train went through a tunnel so that she would see the skull balefully beside her in a semi-darkness. The prank apparently did not come off; they had no sign that the girl had seen the skull. But Kokosch, the investigator, is smitten by recognition and awareness.

Reduced to its simplest elements, the story might seem to have little subtlety; but as Doderer wrote it in a full-length novel, it has a network of delicate interrelationships. Indeed, in giving the book its intensive complications as well as its physical density, Doderer often goes too far; the reader, tracing Kokosch's quest through his childhood and through later events, frequently wishes that the author were less digressive. But as a picture of a place and time—an elaborate and many-mirrored picture —*Every Man a Murderer* has a reality projected at times so believably that the reader feels he can virtually step into the pages of the story.

Doderer has written three important novels since the Second World War. *Die Strudlhofstiege* (1951; *The Strudlhof Steps*) takes its name from a famous winding staircase in Vienna. The story itself winds between two periods, 1910–1913 and 1925. And various plots wind around the career of Major Melzer, a former army officer who has Hamlet-like hesitations about taking up a new career but finally finds himself a comfortable place in the network of Austrian bureaucracies. There are also twins whose close resemblance creates many confusions, perhaps suggesting that people of modern times have lost the ability to distinguish between truth and falsity. In *Die Dämonen* (1956; *The Demons*), Doderer takes several of the characters from *The Strudlhof Steps* and adds many more for a multilevel story of Vienna in the mid-1920's, dealing with events leading up to the general strike of 1927 and the burning, by the workers, of the Palace of Justice. The first volume of Doderer's projected long work, *Roman No. 7* (*Novel No. 7*), is *Die Wasserfälle von Slunj* (1963; *The Waterfalls of Slunj*), a story set in the late nineteenth century and the early twentieth. It concerns Robert and Harriet Clayton, an Englishman and his wife who have established a prospering business in Vienna. Although the book depicts Vienna as a smoothly ordered society, the rather grim ending of the story suggests that all is not well beneath the surface.

Novel No. 7 might have turned out to be Doderer's masterpiece; the *Rheinischer Merkur* of Cologne has said that, in *The Waterfalls of Slunj*, Doderer had reached "a high point of his writing." But, as a complete and rounded work, his finest achievement has proved to be *The Demons*. It took Doderer more than a quarter-century to compose it.

The book is supremely Viennese, full of searching analysis, rococo elegance, and crafty surprises. Most of it is supposedly the journal of a civil servant, Georg von Geyrenhoff, whom a windfall has enabled to retire before his time is up. But occasionally the narrative is taken over by the novelist Katejan von Schlaggenberg, and there are several other interpolations, so the story sometimes has a change of pace. One wit has called the book "the Ninth Symphony of Viennese gossip."

Certainly it is, among other things, a chorale of chitchat, but no full-scale presentation of life anywhere could avoid such an effect. Beneath the surface twitter there are resonant depths. As in his other books, Doderer, trained as a historian, includes a great deal of surface detail, and while this sometimes seems distracting it adds firmness and coherence to the story underneath, which often depends upon stock devices—mistaken identity, a hidden inheritance, an unsolved murder. All these complications are framed by the tangled city of Vienna, from the mountain heights of Kahlenberg, down through the myriad byways of the wine suburbs and on into the city itself, with its hoop of the Ring branching off into intricate little streets. Doderer's story and the lives of his characters thread in and out of this labyrinthine design.

Besides Geyrenhoff and Schlaggenberg, the narrators, the principal male character is René von Stangeler, like Doderer a doctor of philosophy in history. Stangeler is a holdover from *The Strudlhof Steps*, in which he appeared as a somewhat dissolute character. He has become a serious historian in the later book and, when invited to inspect the library of a castle in Carinthia, he finds there a late-medieval manuscript which forms a story-within-the-story and has the added function of providing a commentary on the novel which includes it. The narrative, reproduced in full, is in Early New High German; Richard and Clara Winston, who translated *The Demons* into English, neatly rendered this interpolation "into the English of Caxton." The narrative concerns the captivity of two respectable women, accused of witchcraft, who are subjected to the basest sexual indignities, most carefully and quaintly described. It is partly from this manuscript that Stangeler forms his theory of "the second reality" of illusion, an area in which the demons fester; one of the main points of this book—which is after all a philosophical novel—is that one must come to terms with his own second reality and master the demon in it.

Some of the characters don't—for example, the murderer Meisgeier, known as The Claw. He is a cat burglar who kills a prostitute and gets away with it; but he is burned to death in the Palace of Justice fire, a properly demonic ending which he shares with a friend of the murdered girl.

These are figures out of the Vienna underworld and bespotted back streets, but most of the characters are from the middle-higher ranges of society—not the top aristocrats, but the upper bourgeoisie and minor nobility. They are all rather sad, for with the passing of the Habsburgs the city has lost its gaiety. Bad as the Habsburg regime may have been, with its topheavy structure of empire and its acid of anti-Semitism, Vienna had a sparkle when the Habsburgs were there. The people in *The Demons* do not grieve over the past, and live intensely in the present (even Stangeler applies his medieval manuscript to the modern age), but they have the melancholy of those who have lost something. They care nothing about the empire and its faded glories, but one feels that with them a little Johann Strauss would go a long way. The story is essentially a macabre comedy, with an air of resignation about it—if the characters do not live in the past, the author himself (a profound conservative) probably does so, with a sadness that infects the story.

The characters, as noted earlier, find their second realities in different directions. The novelist Schlaggenberg for a while becomes obsessed with fat women. He introduces his observations on them into the book, but

Geyrenhoff excises much of what Schlaggenberg has written, which is an offbeat eroticism. Another of the characters, the beautiful, middle-aged woman known only as Mary K., who at the end of *The Strudlhof Steps* had lost a leg in a street accident, reappears in this story, outfacing her second reality and recovering her contagious charm. Jan Herzka, head of a webbing company, to whom a distant relative leaves the manuscript Stangeler interprets, annotates, and publishes, has already indulged himself in visions of sadism which gave him a second reality to share with some of his castle-owning ancestors. Leonhard Kakabsa is a worker in Herzka's factory who educates himself, persists in learning Latin, and finally achieves a position of intellectual distinction. And so it goes, throughout the more than thirteen hundred pages of *The Demons:* the people either overcome the demons of their second reality, assimilating them, or they let the demons possess them as demons possessed the Gadarene swine.

Doderer's vision of the modern world is, then, a special one. Aside from the murder by the roof climber, another somewhat melodramatic element in the story is the suppression of a will. But the persistence of Geyrenhoff brings this will to light, and it benefits a girl born out of wedlock who has been brought up as the sister of Schlaggenberg, a rather gawky, wide-mouthed but completely charming girl named Charlotte, known familiarly as Quapp or Quappchen. As the story ends, she is leaving Vienna and has not yet adjusted herself to the idea of being an heiress. Schlaggenberg has made dire predictions about her future, but it is possible she will overcome the demon existing in her second reality.

It is an evil time, however, with the burning of the Palace of Justice—symbolic deed—and with the workers and the police, who should be friends and allies, fighting one another.

Geyrenhoff sadly records the departure of Quapp and of the breaking up of the group he had always referred to as "our crowd," most of them characters in the story. He has cunningly caught them in his journal, relieved here and there by Schlaggenberg and others, and reinforced by that medieval story that throws a lurid glare across the experiences of modern man. New readers of *The Demons,* if they are patient enough to stay with its qualifications and digressions, will be rewarded by an unusually rich story of compelling people in a fascinating city and will understand the reasons why Doderer's reputation, however slowly it spread, is now firmly established on an international scale.

12

THREE GROUP 47 NOVELISTS: BÖLL, JOHNSON, GRASS

The most remarkable recent West German novels are the work of three men usually associated with the previously mentioned Gruppe 47 (Group 47): Heinrich Böll, the eldest of them; Uwe Johnson, who did not come over to West Germany until Group 47 had been meeting for some years; and Günter Grass, the most versatile and, internationally, the best known of the circle.

The actual leader of the 47ers is the journalist and novelist Hans Werner Richter, who issues the invitations for their meetings. He first assembled a number of young writers in 1947 to launch the literary periodical *Der Ruf* (*The Call*). The occupation authorities suppressed this journal, but the writers who attended Richter's conference so greatly enjoyed talking over their common problems that they decided to meet annually.

Sometimes they convene in countries other than West Germany. The first time this happened was in 1964, when they went to the small Swedish town of Sigtuna for ten days. Those attending included Peter Bichsel, Hans Magnus Enzensberger, Günter Grass, Walter Höllerer, Walter Jens, Uwe Johnson, Joachim Kaiser, Alexander Kluge, and Erich Kuby, among others. Johannes Bobrowski, who has since died, was allowed to leave East Germany to take part. Two years earlier he had been awarded the Group's prize. At the 1965 gathering in Berlin, this award went to the Swiss writer Peter Bichsel, who in Sweden the year before had read from the manuscript of a novel-in-progress, *Zusammenhänge (Connections)*. The prize is sometimes worth 5,000 DM (about £550). In 1966, Group 47 met in the United States, at Princeton University. Several East German authors were invited and this created difficulty for the State Department, which was hard pressed to find entrance permission for them, but their government would not let them attend. A number of West German authors appeared, however, including Ingeborg Bachmann, Hans Enzensberger, Günter Grass, Uwe Johnson, and Jakov Lind.

Heinrich Böll has been mentioned as the oldest member of Group 47 —he was born in 1917 in Cologne. In the Second World War he was drafted into the German army, was wounded several times, and was taken prisoner. His first novel, *Der Zug war püntlich* (1949; *The Train Was on Time*), reveals the stupidity of the war on the Russian front. Similarly, *Wo warst du, Adam?* (1950; *Adam, Where Wert Thou?*), is a story of the retreating German army and also an indictment of war. *Und sagte kein einziges Wort* (1953; *And Never Said a Word,* translated as *Acquainted with the Night*) concerns the hardships of a married couple who were separated during the war and are now unable to find a home because of the housing shortage brought on by peace. *Haus ohne Hüter* (1954; *The Unguarded House*) again deals with postwar miseries, this time with a war-shattered family whose father is missing. *Das Brot der frühen Jahre* (1955; *The Bread of Early Years*) tells the story of a young man with a good job in the new prosperity who cannot forget his hunger for bread in the years immediately after the war or the acts of desperation to which that hunger drove him. *Im Tal der donnernden Hufe* (1957; *In the Valley of the Thundering Hoofs*) is the story of several adolescents in the Rhineland who look with distaste upon their elders wallowing in the new prosperity.

The war once again haunts a Böll novel in *Billard um halbzehn* (1959; *Billiards at Half-Past Nine*). Here is a story with complications and depths beyond any in this author's earlier work. The novel encompasses three generations, from the late nineteenth century to 1958, and is set in an unnamed city which has the atmosphere of the author's native Cologne and is distinctly identified as at least being in Germany. Although the story deals with the notable events of the period, including the two world wars, some of the famous figures of the time, such as Hitler, are not specifically mentioned. The novel focuses on the Faehmel family: father, son, and grandson are architects. The grandfather early in his career had built St. Anthony's Abbey outside the city and had then constructed hundreds of residences in his outwardly successful career. In the story Heinrich Faehmel is a mellow eighty, full of memories that help give the narrative its depth in the past.

But the great achievement of his youth, St. Anthony's, was blown up during the war. What the old man does not know is that his son, Robert, was the one who destroyed it. Robert had despised the direction his country had taken in the 1930's and, like many Germans who tried to escape the consequences but could not, he had become schizoid, outwardly going along with the regime but inwardly maintaining a psychological detachment from it. And instead of taking an affirmative part in the war, he had become an army demolition expert. As he later explained to a young American investigating officer, he had blown up the abbey knowing that its destruction, a few days before the Americans would take over, had no military advantage; besides, he was aware that his commanding general was mad.

Yet Robert Faehmel has no compunction about what he has done; his feelings concerning it are abstract and his interest professional, a matter of observing the effect of force upon the principles of stress and strain which had been involved in the construction. But, as he talks to the young officer, Robert remembers what he had forgotten: his own father had built the abbey thirty-five years earlier. Of course the young American would assume that the demolition (for which Robert received the Iron Cross) was a manifestation of the Oedipus complex. But Robert sees his motive as his unspoken anger at the churchmen who had done nothing about the politically inspired atrocities or about helping the victims of them.

Like so many current German novels, then (especially those of Günter Grass), *Billiards at Half-Past Nine* is a probing of the guilt of the Nazi years. Robert's friend Schrella, who had opposed the regime and had been forced to flee from the country (to be imprisoned elsewhere), returns after twenty-two years but cannot stay: he sees the people who piggishly went along with evil now being piggishly prosperous. Robert himself has felt this, and takes little part in the life of the community. He goes to his office for only an hour each morning, then walks to the city's grand old surviving hotel, ironically bearing the same name as his father—the Prince Heinrich. Robert observes his ritual as if it were one of the firm's blueprints: each morning at nine thirty he locks himself in a special room at the hotel and plays billiards alone until eleven.

Robert's mother is another of the complex characters in the book. In her youth she has watched the effects upon people of the growth of the state, and the deaths its wars have brought about. One of these deaths is that of her son Otto, killed in the Battle of Kiev. He had become a ferociously ardent Nazi and had once even denounced his own family to the police. His mother, always consciously or unconsciously protesting against the nullification of life, at one point in the Second World War tries to board a train taking Jews to a concentration camp. She is put into an asylum where she stays sanely, at last emerging for her husband's eightieth-birthday celebration in 1958.

But the family does not attend the consecration ceremony of the rebuilt abbey, although the work was carried out under the direction of Robert's son, Joseph, who used his grandfather's original plan. Old Heinrich tells the abbot he will go to the ceremony, though he knows he will not, for he is still not reconciled over Otto, who turned from a son into the husk of a son. And Robert, who also says politely that he will attend, is likewise unreconciled, for the same reasons that had helped induce him to blow up the abbey in the first place. His father guesses by this time that it was Robert who had accomplished the demolition; but the old man does not care.

In this book, with its many reflections and flashbacks, Heinrich Böll acutely probes the Germany of this century. The characters are believably alive, and the effect upon them of the actions of their fellow citizens— smug and self-seeking—is persuasively shown. As a panoramic novel the book has several weaknesses, notably the author's apparent inability to contrive powerfully dramatic separate scenes. The action is mostly quiet, often existing in the blurred half-world of memory; there is no sustained episode of great force.

Böll wrote two novellas about the war, "Als der Krieg ausbrach—Als der Krieg zu Ende war" (1962; "When the War Broke Out—When the War Was Over") and "Entfernung von der Truppe" (1964; "Leaving the Troop," translated as "Absent without Leave"). Each of these stories —which do not represent Böll at his most skillful, though the attitude expressed in them is typical—concerns a reluctant soldier. In the first novella, the central figure is an individualist and malcontent forced to serve in the army. The other story is about a man who tries to evade front-line service. It is plain that Heinrich Böll does not look back on the Second World War as a time of glory or pleasure.

And his disillusionment with postwar Germany appears again in *Ansichten eines Clowns* (1963; *Views of a Clown,* translated as *The*

Clown). Here Böll uses a Pagliacci figure, whom he presents in an excruciatingly sympathetic way, to attack Bürger society.

Hans Schnier is, at twenty-nine, a superior clown, one whose comedy is highly human. He has the gift of discovering moments of comic illumination in people's lives, and of projecting these in his performances, which satirize the age. But Schnier has begun to fail. At the beginning of this novel (narrated in the first person) he is returning home to Bonn after an unfortunate tour. His mistress, Marie, had left him because she wanted "to breathe Catholic air again"; she has married Schnier's boyhood acquaintance, Züpfner, a Catholic. Schnier regards their union as a profanation because she was married in spirit to Schnier. Her marriage in the Church is only, Schnier thinks, another example of the hypocrisy of the time. But Marie has had a rugged life with Schnier, living in hotel rooms, suffering miscarriages, compelled to play game after game of parchesi, and to hear her friends (not a very good lot) insulted. So she goes in for a loveless marriage.

The headaches and depression to which the clown is subject have increased since Marie left, and he has taken to drinking heavily. The quality of his performances has deteriorated and, during his Chaplin imitation the day before his return to Bonn, Schnier had fallen and injured himself. To intensify his humiliation, a critic has attacked him in the press and several managers have canceled performances they had booked.

In the lonely apartment, Schnier telephones various people and antagonizes old friends. He even rings up his preposterous mother. During the war she had hoped to preserve "our sacred German soil" from the Jewish Yankees; in peacetime she has done a fashionable about-face and become active on the Executive Committee of the Societies for the Reconciliation of Racial Differences. Schnier also telephones to his brother, Leo, who had become a Catholic convert with Züpfner as his godfather. Now Leo is studying in a theological seminary. He is able to raise some money Hans wants and needs, but Leo cannot bring it to him that night because it is a quarter to nine, too late to leave the seminary; if he is out after nine he will be "exhorted." Hans tells him this sounds like a gardening term.

In communication with a number of people, but emphatically alone in that apartment haunted by memories of Marie, Schnier's sense of desolation increases. Not even visitors can bring relief. Indeed, the clown is upset by the appearance of his wealthy father, offering subsidies for a special course in pantomiming, recommended by an expert who knows the elder Schnier. The son's misery continues to deepen. And he is embarrassed: "Perhaps embarrassment is the only means of communication between parents and children."

Later, alone again, Schnier puts on makeup, picks up his guitar and a cushion, then goes to the Bonn railway station. It is carnival time, and people are dressed like matadors and Spanish donnas and Fidel Castro: all the better, for amateurs make a good cover for a professional. Hans tosses his cushion and his hat on the third step, sits down, strums his guitar, and begins singing an anti-Catholic song. At first no one pays any attention to him, and then a coin falls into the hat.

The symbolism so evident in the novel should not impede appreciation of it as a straightforward, human story. Hans Schnier, just as a character, is a remarkable achievement, and *The Clown* keeps Böll in the front rank of newer German novelists. Perhaps as time passes he will stop reworking the old themes and find newer ones. An English translation of some of his shorter work as *18 Stories* (1966) reveals some brilliant variations that give further indication of Böll's remarkable gifts.

Uwe Johnson is another of the important newer writers. He was born in Cammin, Pomerania, in 1934. Too young to take part in the Second World War, he lived in East Germany until 1959, the year in which his first novel was published. He insists that he did not go over the border in flight, but simply moved across.

A graduate of the University of Leipzig, Johnson translated various British and American authors into German before he took up writing himself. His *Mutmassungen über Jakob* (1959; *Speculations about Jakob*) is the story of a railway switchman. Jakob's death is mysterious. He had been with the railway seven years. On the way to and from his tramcar, he always cut across the marshalling yards; but on this misty November morning a switch engine cut him down and killed him. How could such an accident happen to anyone so competent as Jakob Abs, even though the fog cut down visibility and muffled the sound of moving engines?

But this is East Germany, where much is unexplained. And Jakob had been involved with a Soviet agent and had even lived for a while in the western sector. His mother had gone over there to stay, and so had a girl Jakob knew. But those who ask how he could have died as he did can only say that his death was murder, suicide, or accident.

The style of the book is elusive, jumping from one consciousness, one point of view, one moment in time to another. If the principal mystery remains unsolved, so do a good many smaller mysteries in the story. But what Uwe Johnson marvelously conveys is the physical reality of place. This is accompanied by a projection of the fogginess of life in a police state, the ellipses, the uncertainties, the bafflement that confronts everyone trying to find an explanation. Johnson is not necessarily being critical of East Germany; rather he is merely dealing nebulously with the nebulous. As for the fate of Jakob, speculation must remain speculation.

Johnson's next novel, *Das dritte Buch über Achim* (1961; *The Third Book about Achim*), is also set in East Germany. Achim is a champion bicycle-racer there, and two officially approved books have already been written about him. Karsch, a West German newspaperman, begins (at the request of an East German publisher) to prepare a biography of Achim, "the third book" to be devoted to him. But Karsch fails to publish it because of various obstacles which confront him, frequently as baffling to Karsch as they are to the reader. In the main, Karsch's biography is too candid, asks too many questions—officials disapprove of it, often in terms of annoying vagueness.

Johnson has once again presented East German life in terms of sharp solidity, of remarkable physical density. And he writes with expertness of many matters, such as telephone communication between East and West Germany and the physical composition of bicycles used in racing.

In *Zwei Ansichten* (1965; *Two Viewpoints*), Johnson more sharply than ever contrasts East and West Germany. His principal characters are nameless, known only as B and D. The man, B, has the initial of the title of the West German state, Bundesrepublik; the woman, D, is known only by the first initial of the title of the East German state, Deutsche Demokratische Republik. The story takes place in 1961, during and after the building of the Berlin Wall.

B is a press photographer from Holstein, D a nurse from Potsdam. Their love affair becomes, for B, a mélange of shifting memories and illusions; for D, an opportunity to receive help in a time of stress. Nurse D manages to escape to West Germany, but between her and B there are still barriers as formidable as the Berlin Wall. Johnson, dealing largely in particulars (he reports only what his characters themselves experience and know), is in this book most successful in his montage-like contrasts between East and West. As the critic for the *Süddeutsche Zeitung* noted, on this occasion Johnson dispenses with "difficult formal codes" and "depends on the undisguised effect of image on counter-image." But there were some dissenting voices among the critics. Marcel Reich-Ranicki of *Die Zeit* found the East German scenes lively but the West German portions too simple, and B himself rather unreal. Although Uwe Johnson has often been called "poet of both Germanies," Reich-Ranicki said that Johnson was not "the poet of the partition": "As in *Speculations* and *Achim* he once more reveals himself in this new book as a poet of one of the two German worlds, the one between the Elbe and the Oder"— East Germany.

Like Uwe Johnson, Günter Grass came from the East, from Danzig, long a Prussian city and now once more a part of Poland. Grass's mother was Polish; his father was a German grocer. Grass (born 1927), who has been mentioned earlier as both poet and playwright, was a member of the Hitler Youth movement, was drafted into the Luftwaffe at sixteen, and was wounded and taken prisoner in the last month of the war. After his release he worked as a farm laborer and stonemason. Before he began his writing career he was a sculptor and draftsman. Grass now lives in Berlin with his Swiss wife (a professional dancer) and their children. Grass has also devised a ballet, making use of some of the scarecrow sequences from his novel *Dog Years*.

His first novel, *Die Blechtrommel* (1959; *The Tin Drum*), was an international success. And in Germany, where the book sold wildly, it caused cries of outrage, particularly from right-wing groups. For Grass had acutely satirized the history of modern Germany in terms of a dwarf and the tin drum on which he likes to beat. (Later in life Oskar is a popular drummer in a jazz band.) The story itself—partly surrealistic, partly an intensification of realism—is pounded out to the drum-beating of little Oskar Matzerath, who, as he tells his autobiographical tale, is in an asylum. He has been convicted of a murder he did not commit but for which he is willing to assume the blame, part of the all-human guilt.

Oskar is a self-willed dwarf. At the age of three he decided that he did not wish to grow any more, so he retained a child's body—and the tin drum. Yet as the years pass, Oskar develops a shrewdly adult mind. At one point he even decides to grow a bit more, but as he attempts this he develops a hump on his back.

The setting of the first part of the story is obviously Danzig and, of the later part, Cerresheim (near Düsseldorf). Oskar's father, a grocer, becomes a minor Nazi functionary whose activities as such are grotesque and hilarious. At one point, little Oskar even breaks up Nazi meetings with his compulsive drumming. At party rallies he hides under platforms and, as the bands begin to play Nazi music, Oskar drums waltzes and fox trots. The uniformed men playing marches and hymns suddenly take up the gay tunes, and the people who have come to listen to political speeches and to cry "Heil, Hitler!" break into dances.

The Tin Drum has been called among other things a picaresque novel, and it certainly is that, the comic story of a wandering rogue. Oskar's adventures, as a child on the Baltic and as an undersized adult in the Rhineland, are full of mischief and satiric humor. It is never altogether clear, however, exactly what Oskar symbolizes: Is he the infantile clownishness of Nazi Germany itself, or is he the spirit of what the Germans of the time called "innere Emigration," the secret refusal to conform to the clownishness and its accompanying brutality? The latter seems the more likely, and though a too-strict definition in these matters could hamper the imaginative force of the book, the author himself seems at times a bit lost in the material, never quite reconciling, in artistic coherence, the grimly realistic and the hilariously absurd elements of the book, its connotative and denotative aspects.

Oskar does not always remain in the realm of fantasy where he chiefly belongs because of his dwarfish state, which is itself finely realized grotesque comedy; and if he does not grow much in physical stature, he at least shows some growth as a human being. This is particularly true when, after the war, he works as a stonemason rather than becoming rich in the black market. By implication the book criticizes the smugness of the postwar prosperity; that constant theme of the newer West German writers. As for Oskar, whatever he is intended or not intended to be, his story is a delightful one, and the novel is one of the significant European inventions of its time.

In the short novel *Katz und Maus* (1961; *Cat and Mouse*) Grass again wrote of Danzig and the shores of the Baltic. This time he dealt with a group of boys who swim in the harbor, diving alongside a half-sunken wreck. One of the boys is Joachim Mahlke, a kind of hero-in-reverse, whose experiences are the central theme of the story.

He is called "the Great Mahlke," and he has a kind of greatness if only in his difference from the mob. He has a physical deformity, a huge and constantly quivering Adam's apple, known as his mouse, about which he is fiercely sensitive. One day he had been lying on the grass of an athletic field, apparently asleep, watched by his schoolmate who narrates the story. A young cat strolled over to where Mahlke was lying and saw his Adam's apple moving up and down. Thinking it a mouse, she leaped at it (Mahlke's schoolmate, who does not precisely remember, may have put the cat on his neck). Mahlke was hardly hurt physically, but spiritually badly scratched and bruised. This time the symbolism is plain: the cat is the mob, the unthinking group of the petty, always ready to pounce on the unusual. And the wreck in the harbor is also a symbol, like the overgrown cartilage in Mahlke's neck, of his apartness: under the covering water, his deformity cannot be seen.

Mahlke, driven by his sense of inferiority, becomes a leader of the group, the most adventurous and daring of them all, particularly in diving down to the hulk of the half-submerged wreck and coming up with treasures. He also becomes the best gymnast in the school and the finest student. But he continues to be sensitive about his gigantic Adam's apple; he wears a scarf over it, or a screwdriver held by a shoelace, or a medallion of the Virgin Mary—there is a religious strain in this book, as there is in *The Tin Drum*.

There are also gross episodes. On the deck of the half-sunken ship, the boys chew the droppings of sea gulls and spit them into the sea. They exhibit themselves before a girl named Tulla Pokriefke; and once Mahlke, who is also oversized sexually, drops his pants and masturbates as Tulla and the others watch. Like the rest of Grass's work, this is not a book for the squeamish.

But it tells a sympathetic story, the efforts of Mahlke, mouse and all, to come to terms with the cats of social conformity. He becomes the Great Mahlke to his schoolmates (almost in parody of the situation in Henri Alain-Fournier's novel *Le Grand Meaulnes*), and although in the Second World War he is a success as Sergeant Mahlke—receiving an important medal—he never manages to fit in, he remains always the freak. Home on furlough from the Russian front, he dives once more down to his sunken sanctuary in the harbor and drowns. The narrator tells how, at a reunion of decorated war veterans at Regensburg in 1959, he was not allowed into the hall, not having been decorated himself, but he sent in a message for Mahlke to meet him outside. Mahlke did not appear, the drowned man "did not surface."

The effectiveness of the entire story is heightened because it is told from an outside point of view, by a contemporary and close associate who reports all details with little attempt at interpretation.

In his third novel, *Hundejahre* (1963; *Dog Years*), Grass once more deals with the condition of modern Germany, again in the years before, during, and after the Third Reich. It is another of Grass's elaborately, tortuously symbolic projections of national guilt. The dog years of the title are not only what Grass regards as bad years, but he invents three generations of dogs who play emblematic roles in the action. There are also scarecrows—manufactured and mechanical scarecrows which stand for the inhuman regimentation of Nazism.

The main characters are Walter Matern and Eduard (Eddi) Amsel,

friends from childhood. Indeed, as young boys they swear a Blutbrüder-
schaft and, in the ritual of the Teutonic knights, cut one another with
a pocketknife and mingle their bloods. Eddi gives Walter the symbolic
knife to keep, but sometime later Walter throws it diffidently into the
river.

The setting of the opening section—and the book opens out later into
vast panoramas of most of Germany—is along the Vistula, near Danzig.
Walter is the son of a miller, a member of a Polish-Catholic family whose
ancestors include a medieval brigand and firebug, one Materna. Eddi,
who has a Jewish father, is clever at making scarecrows.

When the boys torment Eddi and call him names, in pre-Nazi displays
of anti-Semitism, Walter defends him. When Walter becomes old enough
to join the Communists, he does so for a while before becoming disillusioned; soon he has followed most of his schoolmates into the Nazi
Party. Of course Eddi cannot join him there, but he has encouraged
Walter to become a storm trooper. Now Eddi can ask Walter to get him
cast-off Nazi uniforms: worn-out caps, and shirts ripped apart in street
brawls. Eddi repairs these and puts them onto the lifelike scarecrows
he has continuued to make: the robot figures strut up and down, realistically goose stepping and holding out stiff right arms.

One snowy night some real Nazis, faces masked, climb over the fence
into the yard of the house where Eddi lives and beat him up. They knock
out all his thirty-two teeth and leave him unconscious.

The years pass. Grass uses letters to project a good deal of the action
in the middle part of his book. Throughout, he keeps switching styles as
spasmodically as James Joyce ever did: the language at times becomes
simultanéiste—with several events at different places narrated in a
jumble—it flashes puns, and it shows a Rabelaisian (and Joycean)
tendency to slam familiar words together to create new ones. The
subjective and the objective mingle, the sentences race and swell and roll
over and get up to skip and dance again, often sprinting away into digressions. There are catalogues of terms out of engineering, geology, and
agriculture, and there are parodies of philosophical idiom and Nazi
doctrine (some of the jests at the expense of the German existentialist
philosopher Martin Heidegger, who took up the Nazi cause with enthusiasm). Symbols explode, allegory nudges its way in, and points of view keep
shifting. Yet the novel, despite its often boring interruptions, remains
fundamentally interesting, not only as a picture of its time but also
because of its human center: the story of the relationship of Walter
Matern and Eddi Amsel.

During the war, Eddi disappears under a nom de guerre. Walter the storm trooper survives the holocaust and, afterward, becomes a radio celebrity, forgetting much of the past in his now violent hatred of the Nazis. Some young people whom he one day lets interview him give him a shock: they have a new kind of spectacles which, when put on, suddenly show the past. The parents of the young people are there, recognizable though younger themselves, yet they are not the staid Bürgers of the new prosperity; they are thugs, screaming and smashing shopwindows and indulging in sadistic anti-Semitic orgies. How can this be? And who are those nine masked hoodlums climbing over a fence to thrash a Jew? Walter, the noted defender of Jews and despiser of Nazis, will find out if the quest takes him all over both Germanies—as it does.

He finds eight of the men, discovering his first clue on the walk of the latrine of the Cologne railway station. But the identity of the ninth man consistently eludes him. As Walter goes here and there hunting out his former associates, one form of injury he does to them is to make love to their wives and daughters, infecting the women with his own gonorrhea. Then, in a powerful recognition scene, the identity of the ninth masked storm trooper is made plain to him: it is Walter Matern himself.

The story ends with a sequence on the epic scale, in a modern Dante's Inferno thousands of feet below the earth, where in a Walpurgisnacht atmosphere the manufacturer Brauxel, with a huge staff working in a former potash mine, turns out not only the spectacles of truth but also the scarecrow-automatons he has always made. For Brauxel is Amsel, with a mouthful of gold teeth.

No other postwar German novel so far (with the possible exception of Böll's *Billiards at Half-Past Nine*) has given so complicated a picture of the country in the last days of the Weimar Republic, in the time of the Third Reich, and in the present phase. Even *The Tin Drum* is not this complex, although its bitter humor often makes it more trenchant; *Dog Years* tends to stray. Yet it contains a number of powerful individual scenes.

Like Balzac, Günter Grass has constructed a world of human comedy in which some of the same figures keep appearing. Oskar Matzerath, for example, shows up several times in *Dog Years*, drum and all. And there is Tulla Pokriefke, for whom the Great Mahlke publicly masturbated in *Cat and Mouse*. Inflamed by the Nazi xenophobia, Tulla attacks Jenny Brunies, who has gypsy origins. Later, Jenny becomes a famous ballerina, providing Grass with the opportunity to include long digressions about the technique of the ballet and lists of terms applicable to dancing.

Like Grass's two earlier novels, this one projects a detailed picture of various sections of Danzig, but eventually it covers far more ground than the others. And the social probing is more thorough: whereas *The Tin Drum*, for example, viewed the Nazi Party mostly from its outer edges, and in generally symbolic terms, *Dog Years* takes the reader into the smoky beer halls and other meeting places of the storm troopers, and also inside their hearts—some purely brutal, others, like Walter Matern, divided.

As in *The Tin Drum*, the symbols of *Dog Years* are not always organically related to the action, but the author stresses them into a kind of special importance. The scarecrows, which have several meanings, importantly serve to show the consistency of Eddi Amsel, for he is making them at both the beginning and the end of the story. And the dogs have an importance beyond their merely metaphorical significance in the title. At the beginning of the book, Walter has a bitch named Senta. Senta begat Harras, and Harras begat Prinz—and Prinz became Hitler's favorite hound. In the story, Prinz escapes his master's fate in the last, fatal hideout. Prinz wanders to the bank of the Elbe on May 8, 1945, and sniffs the wind, wondering whether he should head east or west. He swims to the west—and becomes Walter Matern's dog, under the Disney name of Pluto. Ironically, Walter is unaware of Prinz's descent from Senta or of his connection with Hitler.

From this point on, the picture of West Germany is heavily satiric, often in the vein of *The Tin Drum*. Like Prinz, prosperity has come to the west, and the men who had either ridden high with the Nazis or who had silently acquiesced to wholesale murder, are now thriving in the Wirtschaftswunderkinder (economic wonderchildren). The Krupps, the Schneiders, and other munitions makers of the past rebuilt their shattered factories and once more began turning out the machinery of death. And the Walter Materns, reconciled though they might be with the Jews whom they knew as friends, have continued to feel the schizoid thing within themselves. They are still uncertain, and guilt remains stickily with them.

Grass, like various other members of Group 47, is liberal in outlook (some of them are further to the left) and he supports the Social Democratic Party. He has even written speeches for Willy Brandt, former Berlin mayor. Grass said in an interview that he does not try deliberately to embody his beliefs in his books, but admits that these beliefs "will naturally permeate anything I write." He warned American readers, however—"who tend to interpret everything in Freudian terms"—not to look too hard for symbols in such novels as *Dog Years*. That book he spoke of merely as "a report on Germany."

Perhaps—but if so it is a report loaded with symbols, and Grass in his writings deals with actual events that are wrapped in different layers of meaning, particularly when treated in a manner that can only be defined as symbolic. But maybe Grass and his fellow writers, such as Heinrich Böll and all the others who have used similar themes, will find new subject matter as time goes on. A residue of guilt lingers in West Germany, beneath all the prosperity, and various authors have found it an engrossing theme; but there is also much else in West Germany, as in East Germany. The same writers cannot continually return to the same stories, in somewhat different guises. Günter Grass and his contemporaries are between two phases of German literature. They, or writers now in the process of development, must find the new. Germany's recent history remains, and nothing can wipe out the horror of the Nazis and their corpse camps.

Grass and his contemporaries have shown themselves capable of brilliant writing. It will be interesting, in the future, to watch the way in which they apply their great gifts to fresher themes. Perhaps some of these themes will be supplied by the appalling upsurge of "neo-Nazism" that threatens West Germany in the late 1960's.

Index

Sudermann, Hermann (cont'd)
of Syracuse), 64; Bilderbuch meiner
Jugend (Picture of My Youth), 65;
Blumenboot (The Flowerboat), 64;
Die Ehre (Honor), 64; Es lebe das
Leben (The Joy of Living), 64; Die
Frau des Steffen Tromholt (The Wife
of Steffen Tromholt), 65; Frau Sorge
(tr. as Dame Care), 65; Der gute Ruf
(A Good Reputation), 64; Heimat
(Home, tr. as Magda), 64; Johannis-
feuer (St. John's Fire), 64; Litaui-
sche Geschichten (Lithuanian Tales,
tr. as The Excursion to Tilsit), 64;
Stein unter Steinen (A Stone among
Stones), 64; Der tolle Professor (The
Mad Professor), 65
Süddeutsche Zeitung, 199
Sullavan, Margaret, 82
Surrealism, 134
Swinburne, 49

Tagger, Theodor, 141; see also Bruck-
ner, Ferdinand
Krankheit der Jugend (Sickness of
Youth), 141
Tale of Jacob, The, 61
Tanden, Felix, 11; see also Spitteler,
Carl
Tandy, Jessica, 115
Taylor, Robert, 82
Tendenzstücke, 120
Terry, Ellen, 12
Theater am Schiffbauerdamm, Berlin, 39,
119
Theater of the Absurd, 145
Theatre Guild, New York, 31
Thiele, Hertha, 48
Thirty Years' War, 80, 98
Thomas, Dylan, 123
Thomas, J. Parnell, 108
Thoor, Jesse, 122–123; see also Höfler,
Peter Karl
Sonette und Lieder (Sonnets and
Songs), 123
Time and Again, 147; see also Dürren-
matt, Friedrich
Toller, Ernst, 23, 34
Feuer aus den Kesseln (tr. as Draw
the Fires), 36, 48; Hinkemann (tr. as
Brokenbrow), 35, 36, 46; Hoopla, wir
leben! (Hoopla! Such Is Life!), 36;
Die Maschinenstürmer (The Machine-
Wreckers), 35; Masse Mensch (The
Human Mass, tr. as Man and the
Masses), 34–35; Die Wandlung (Trans-
figuration), 34
Tolstoy, 85

Tone, Franchot, 82
totalitarianism, 61
Totentanz, 26
Tracy, Spencer, 115
Trakl, Georg, 8, 49, 127
Gedichte (Poems), 9; "Grodek," 9;
Sebastian im Traum (Sebastian Dream-
ing), 9
Tramin, Peter von, 187
Die Herren Söhne (Our Sons, the
Gentlemen), 187
Trojan Women, The, 30
Tumler, Franz, 187
Aufschreibung aus Trient (Writing
about Trent), 187

Uhse, Bodo, 116
Die Brücke (The Bridge), 116; Gestalten und Probleme (Forms and Problems), 116; Leutnant Bertram (Lieutenant Bertram), 116; Patrioten (The
Patriots), 116
Unruh, Fritz von, 27–28, 87
Bonaparte, 28; Ein Geschlecht (A
Family), 27; Offiziere (Officers), 27;
Phaea, 28; Platz (Town Square), 27,
28; Prinz Louis Ferdinand von Preussen (Prince Louis Ferdinand of Prussia), 27

Valéry, Paul, 124
Van Gogh, 141
Veidt, Conrad, 21
Vergil, 9
Verlaine, 9, 38
Verse-librists, 9
Viertel, Berthold, 77
Villon, François, 9
The Visit, 147; see also Dürrenmatt,
Friedrich
Volksbühne (People's Stage), 22
Volksstück, 43, 142
von Doderer, Heirnito, see Doderer, Heir-
nito von
von Golssenau, Arnold Friedrich Vieth,
see Renn, Ludwig
von Musil, Robert Edler, see Musil,
Robert
Vrba, Rudolf, 92
I Cannot Forgive, 92

Walde, Hilde, 96
Die andere Maria (The Other Mary),
96
Walden, Herwarth, 20
Walewska, Marie, 100
Walser, Martin, 160
Der Abstecher (The Detour), 156;